# Dictionary of English Colloquial Idioms

**Frederick T. Wood**

revised by Robert J. Hill

PAPERMAC

First published in 1969 by The Macmillan Press Limited
This edition first published 1979

Papermac edition published 1989 by
PAPERMAC
a division of Macmillan Publishers Limited
4 Little Essex Street London WC2R 3LF
and Basingstoke

Reprinted 1990

Associated companies in Auckland, Delhi, Dublin, Gaborone, Hamburg, Harare, Hong Kong, Johannesburg, Kuala Lumpur, Lagos, Manzini, Melbourne, Mexico City, Nairobi, New York, Singapore and Tokyo

ISBN 0-333-51739-3

A CIP catalogue record for this book is available from the British Library

Printed in Hong Kong

# Introduction

The title of the original version of this book was *English Colloquial Idioms*. It lacked a preface or introduction as F. T. Wood died before it was completed. As in his other books, its explanations were informal, avoiding abbreviations and grammatical terms where possible.

## Title
In producing this revision, I have given a slightly changed emphasis. When I compared the contents of the earlier edition with F. T. Wood's *English Verbal Idioms*, I discovered that there was some duplication in the two books. Where appropriate, the verbal idioms are marked 'colloquial' in the other book, and by omitting such duplicates in the revised book, there was space to put in many new items.

## Presentation
In deference to F. T. Wood, I have basically retained his style: explanations are of a kind which would be suitable in a lesson. As a dictionary of colloquialisms, it was in serious need of being brought up to date. Entries are written especially with the needs of the foreign student in mind. (It is interesting to see how many of the nouns are uncountable—it would seem that English tends to prefer them to countable nouns!) In a few cases, I have grouped a number of near synonyms under one heading (see *drunk*, *nervy*, *telephone*), as I felt users would find them more useful when seen together.

## Register
In working on the revision, I was repeatedly reminded of the clear distinction between what we used to call 'written and spoken English'. While still in part referring to the same things, teachers and linguists are now likely to refer to different 'registers'. This dictionary mainly deals with informal/familiar/friendly English, whereas most text books of English for foreigners present English of the formal/written, and of the standard/'safe' middle register only. This informal/colloquial English is not so often written, though it is to be found in personal letters, direct speech in fiction, advertisements, and in popular newspapers. It is the spoken English used between equals; it implies friendliness, varies very

little in different regions of Britain, and its use gives humour and zest to a conversation.

## Slang

Slang is usually considered the next register away from colloquial, and is more to be heard among people of the same age group, (especially the young) to reinforce their intimate group feeling. Slang words and phrases may have a comparatively short life and are only given here if I felt they bordered on being colloquial. There is little need for foreigners to learn slang because of its unpredictable survival, and the danger of using it in the wrong social situation. Care is needed even with colloquial English: although formal expressions are sometimes used in informal situations as a joke, informal expressions must simply not be used in formal situations, except possibly when talking about yourself. It is wise to test any new expressions with a native English speaker so as to judge its social suitability.

## Idioms

Since many of the entries are idioms, it may interest the reader to note that they may be defined firstly as phrases which allow no element to be replaced by a synonym—we look forward to a holiday, but not 'see/watch forward to a holiday'; secondly, they are phrases in which the individual parts (if taken separately) do not suggest the meaning of the whole—if your proposals are 'cut and dried', you have in fact neither cut them nor dried them; and thirdly, no part can be omitted—'we must just soldier' requires 'on' to give it meaning.

## Cross references

F. T. Wood listed some entries under their nouns, others under verbs, and quite a number under their initial prepositions and there were only a few cross references. Though I have not usually altered the position of his entries, this revision has a far more systematic cross reference system, which I hope will make the dictionary easier to use.

## Use

It is not expected that this dictionary will be much used 'productively'. I have not tried (as some larger new dictionaries do) to give explanations and notes so that the user can know exactly what changes or 'transforms' a phrase may undergo, nor with what range of collocations. I assume items will normally be looked up because the user has already heard them in a context, or merely for casual reading.

## Neologisms
New words and phrases often have single inverted commas when first used in print. If they become accepted at all they are, even so, more likely to be heard than seen in print, so they continue to have a colloquial feel about them. I have included a number of them, (e.g. *all systems go*, *catch 22*, *cliff-hanger*, *drag*, *demo*—probably none of these was known to F. T. Wood) though clearly I have not tried to make this a comprehensive dictionary of neologisms. Many would be technical and of minor importance to the majority of foreign students.

## Omissions
For the record, the following types of English are generally omitted here: slang, taboo words, vulgarisms, dialect words, drug scene words, and American English (with a few exceptions, e.g. *lame duck*, *knock up*).

## Abbreviations
These have been kept to a minimum:

| | |
|---|---|
| e.g. | for example |
| i.e. | that is |
| adj | adjective |
| adv | adverb |
| n | noun |
| prep | preposition |
| v | verb |
| cf. | compare |

Idioms or uses marked with an asterisk are those which are not recommended to be used by foreigners in ordinary speech—in some cases for reasons of register but more often because they now appear dated.

In conclusion, it must be said that the dictionary can in no way claim to be comprehensive. What is included, is a compromise between the modest size of the original edition, what I felt could be omitted, and what should be added. I hope it will be of at least as much value as the original, and only I am to blame if it is not.

Robert J. Hill   Cambridge   June 1978

# a

**A1**

(pronounced ay wun) excellent, first-class, good in every respect; originally used by Lloyd's Register of Shipping in the classification of vessels as regards general condition, seaworthiness etc.

**A to Z**

see **from A to Z**

**about**

note the colloquial construction *it is* + adjective + *about* + noun, where *about* refers to a notion implied in *it* + the noun, and understood from the context or situation

□ It's very sad about Mrs Brown, isn't it? (i.e. she has died, been injured or suffered some misfortune)

□ It's unfortunate about your holiday. (i.e. that you have had to cancel it, change the date etc.)

**absolute**

used for purposes of emphasis, with a meaning approximating to 'complete'

□ He's an absolute fool.

□ It was an absolute treat.

hence *absolutely*: completely

□ It is absolutely stupid to say that.

□ It absolutely poured with rain.

□ You can trust him to be absolutely fair.

**ace** *(n or adj)*

first-class, excellent (person)

**aches and pains**

a cliché used to denote physical pains of various kinds

□ I wish she would be a bit more cheerful; she is always complaining of her aches and pains.

**acid test**

a test that shows true worth (originally a test with acid to ensure a metal was gold)

□ You've passed your exams, but the first few months on the job will be the acid test.

**across**

see **get across someone** and **get something across to someone**

1

**across the board**

with no exceptions, through all sectors (used in pay negotiations)

□ It was the union's policy that all the workers should be treated alike, so they demanded a 5% increase across the board.

**actually**

used to suggest that the fact stated would seem incredible

□ He actually robbed his own mother.

NOTE *Actual(ly)* has an entirely different meaning from the similar words in other languages.

**Adam**

*as old as Adam*: of great antiquity; going back a long way in history (sometimes used in the literal sense of 'to the beginning of the human race', but more often as hyperbole)

□ That custom is as old as Adam.

*I shouldn't know him from Adam.* I should be quite unable to recognise him.

□ I knew him when we were at school together, but that's many years ago. If I were to meet him today I shouldn't know him from Adam.

This is sometimes used also, though illogically, of a woman. There is no equivalent idiom *I shouldn't know her from Eve.*

**admin**

short for *administration*

**advert** *or* **ad**

short for *advertisement*, mostly heard in spoken English

□ I saw your ad in the newspaper.

**affair**

piece of work, performance, sometimes even in the sense of 'object'

□ The concert was rather an amateurish affair.

□ What's that strange-looking affair over there?

usually used disparagingly, though not necessarily so

**after all**

**1** contrary to what was supposed or expected

□ I managed to get to the meeting after all.

□ We took our raincoats with us, but we did not need them after all.

**2** when everything else is taken into consideration

□ Jack may have treated you rather badly, but if he is in serious difficulties I think you should help him. After all, he is your brother.

**afters**

pudding or dessert after the main course

**age(s)**

a very long time

□ It has taken me ages to get this garden in order.

□ That happened ages ago.

□ I have not been to the cinema for ages.

*An age* is also used with a similar meaning:

□ She was away for a few minutes that seemed like an age.

for *this day and age*, see **day**

**aggro**

spoken short form of *aggression*

**agog**

(often *all agog*) in a state of excited expectancy

□ The children were all agog to hear the story.

**aid**

see **in aid of**

**ain't***

This frequently heard word is definitely substandard usage, but you need to be aware of its meanings. It provides the negative of *be* and *have*.

□ I ain't stupid; he ain't stupid.

□ I ain't got to go yet; they ain't got to go yet.

In this 'have not' meaning, it is usually used with *got* and frequently with a second negative:

□ He ain't got no car. (i.e. hasn't got a car)

You are not advised to use any of these forms yourself.

**air**

see **hot air** and **in the air**

**airy-fairy**

vague, out of touch with reality

**alec**

see **smart alec**

**alive and kicking**

very vigorous and active

□ 'I thought your grandfather was dead.' 'Far from it; he is very much alive and kicking.'

The reference may originally have been to a new-born baby. It is also suggested that this originated as the cry of a fishmonger advertising his fish.

**alive with**

filled with living creatures of various kinds

□ All my best cabbages were alive with caterpillars.

figuratively:

□ The town was alive with rumours of one sort and another.

## all along

from the very beginning of an affair, project etc.

□ I said all along that he was not a person to be trusted, but you would not listen to me.

## all and sundry

strictly, all taken collectively and individually, but in colloquial usage merely used to mean 'everyone'

□ We shall have to restrict the number of guests; we can't invite all and sundry.

## all at once

suddenly

□ I had been puzzling over the problem for over an hour without any result, when all at once the solution flashed across my mind.

All at once I saw a crowd,
A host of golden daffodils.
(Wordsworth, *The Daffodils*)

(But this idiom must not be confused with the same sequence of words in such a sentence as *We shall have to make several journeys for the goods; we cannot take them all at once.* Here *all* is the object of *take*, and *at once* is an adverb phrase meaning 'in a single operation'.)

## all at sea

completely confused

□ The guide was ready enough with his usual talk on the history of the place, but as soon as you began to question him on anything outside that, he was all at sea.

## all being well

not exclusively colloquial, but very frequently used expressing hopes that nothing will impede plans

□ 'When shall we arrive?' 'We should get there by teatime, all being well.'

see also **hopefully**

## all but

nearly, almost (used mainly before adjectives and past participles, but sometimes also before finite verbs)

□ The new building was all but complete when it was destroyed by fire.

□ She all but wept when she heard the news.

4

**all for**

entirely or completely in favour of

□ I'm all for anything that makes life easier.

□ As usual, John was all for going; taking the risk, and getting out of Germany. But Peter was cautious. (Eric Williams, *The Wooden Horse*, phase II, ch 9)

**all in**

**1** everything included

□ I reckon it costs me two hundred pounds a year to run my car, all in.

□ On top of his wages he gets tips and various other perks, so that he probably makes the equivalent of about fifty pounds a week, all in.

**2** *be all in*: be exhausted

□ I was all in after running so far.

**all in good time**

in due course; when a suitable or opportune time arrives

□ 'When are you coming to do those repairs to the roof of my house? It was over a fortnight ago that I asked you about them.' 'All in good time, madam; I haven't forgotten.'

**all my eye**

a term of contempt, used to show that one does not believe a story, a statement etc.

□ He told you he was never given the instructions? That's all my eye. Why, I gave them to him myself.

A variant is *all my eye and Betty Martin.*\*

**all of a . . .**

(followed by a verb stem) having an (uncontrollable nervous movement)

□ I was all of a tremble before the exam.

□ She is always all of a dither before giving a party.

□ He was all of a twitch.

(occasionally followed by a noun)

□ The bad news struck me all of a heap.

**all of a sudden**

suddenly

□ All of a sudden a man burst out of the hedge, and made off down the road.

**all one can do**

preceded by *it is/was* and followed by an infinitive or infinitive construction, to suggest great difficulty in doing what is stated in the infinitive

☐ It's all we can do to keep ourselves in food and clothing; holidays are out of the question.

☐ It was all I could do to refrain from laughing.

☐ The thieves drove so fast that it was all the police could do to keep up with them.

**all out**
see **go all out**

**all over**

**1** covered with

☐ His shoes were all over mud.

☐ His hands were all over grease.

**2** finished (suggesting defeat, failure or death); preceded by *it is/was/will be* and followed by *with*

☐ If the patient has another relapse, I am afraid it will be all over with him.

☐ When our opponents scored another goal only a few minutes from the end of the match, we knew it was all over with us.

**3** everywhere; over a wide area (probably a shortened form of **all over the place**)

☐ We've been looking for you all over.

**4** exactly characteristic of the person in question

☐ You say he refused to buy the goods unless he was allowed a discount? I'm not surprised. That's John all over. Always wanting things on the cheap.

**all over the place**

in many different places

☐ When you've finished playing with your toys, put them back in the toy cupboard; don't leave them lying all over the place.

☐ I've searched all over the place for that lost ring, but I've not found it.

Variants, bordering on slang, are *all over the show* and *all over the shop*.

**all over the shop/show**
see **all over the place**

**all right**

**1** satisfactory

☐ Will it be all right if I let you have the information by next Friday?

☐ If the arrangement is all right with you, it's all right with me.

**2** in a satisfactory state, condition or position

☐ I've not been very well, but I'm all right now.

☐ Are you all right for money?

☐ He doesn't care what happens to anybody else, so long as he's all right.

**3** used to suggest, in a general way, the absence of any objection, or of any need for concern or alarm

☐ Is it all right for me to see the patient for a few minutes?

☐ It's all right; don't make a fuss; there's no harm done.

Sometimes if people talk very quickly, you may hear for *It's all right* something sounding like *sore eye*.

**4** used to express approval, consent or agreement

☐ All right, I'll meet you at seven o'clock, then.

☐ 'Might I leave a quarter of an hour earlier today?' 'All right, but see that all the letters are ready for posting before you go.'

sometimes used sarcastically, or to express impatience or annoyance

☐ All right, do it your own way, but don't blame me if you fail.

**5** to link one stage of an explanation, a piece of exposition etc. to the next

☐ You have followed the explanation so far? All right, now we come to the second stage.

In speech the stress is on *right*.

**6** to introduce a threat

☐ All right, my lad, if you won't do what you're told you must take the consequences.

**7** to convey the idea of 'going the right way', 'on the right road'

☐ Am I all right for Bristol on this road?

☐ Is this train all right for Birmingham?

**8** used for purposes of emphasis: 'certainly', 'without doubt'

☐ He's dead all right.

**9** used to express the idea of 'quite capable of doing whatever is specified' (usually implying that there is a common belief of pretence to the contrary)

☐ Don't take any notice of the excuse that he could not understand the document because it was in English. He can understand English all right when it suits his purpose.

**10** used in the expression *I'm all right, Jack*, a contemptuous remark, showing total disregard for other people's troubles

NOTE This meaning is only given by including *Jack*.

## all round

**1** to every member of a group or company

☐ The organiser of the expedition stood us drinks all round.

**2** in every subject, branch or department

☐ It is difficult to say which is his best subject; he seems equally good all round.

hence (attributively) *an all-round sportsman* or *an all-rounder*

**all systems go**

all ready to go, and about to start

☐ It's all systems go—turn over your exam papers and start writing. This was popularised during the launchings of spacecraft during the late 1960s and early 1970s.

**all that**

NOTE In English *all what* do not usually come together. We say *You mustn't believe all that is written in that book* and *You mustn't believe all (that) he tells you.*

**1** *not as bad/dear/old/hot as all that*: as would seem to be suggested or implied

☐ There is no need to get alarmed; things are not really as bad as all that.

☐ Merely because I'm grey-headed, don't imagine that I'm drawing the old age pension; I'm not as old as all that.

☐ You needn't open all the windows; it's not as hot as all that.

**2** before an adjective or an adverb, with a meaning equivalent to that of the adverb of degree *so*, or the construction *so (as) ... as that* (regarded by purists as an illiteracy in written or more formal spoken English, but often used colloquially, the *that* referring to something that has been stated before)

☐ It wouldn't worry me to go without porridge for breakfast; I'm not all that fond of it.

☐ I wouldn't walk all that far, just to see an exhibition of modern art.

**3** *and all that*: and other things of that kind

☐ By cereals we mean wheat, oats, rye, barley and all that.

cf. the title of the book *1066 and All That*, by W. C. Sellar and R. J. Yeatman, a humorous treatment of various episodes from history

**all the answers to all the questions**

(generally used sarcastically) To say that a person *knows* (or *has*) *all the answers to all the questions* implies that he tries to give the impression that he can explain away all difficulties, but that his explanations are far too facile.

☐ Browning sometimes gives us the impression, especially where religious difficulties are concerned, that he has all the answers to all the questions.

**all the more**

to an even greater extent or degree

□ His mother asked him to stop teasing the cat, but he only did it all the more.

also used adjectivally:

□ I know you find the subject difficult, but that is all the more reason why you should work hard at it.

**all the rage**

very popular or fashionable; arousing great interest, excitement or enthusiasm

□ For a few years black leather jackets were all the rage among teenagers; then new fashions took their place.

**all the same**

**1** making no difference, sometimes used to express apathy or indifference

□ I think I should prefer to go on Friday morning, if it's all the same to you.

□ Well, there's my offer. You can either take it or leave it, it's all the same to me.

**2** nevertheless; although that is so

□ The fall in brewery shares this year does, of course, allow for a good deal. All the same, I feel that we shall see many shares go lower yet. (*Observer*, 26th Sept. 1965)

**all the world and his wife***

everyone (usually used hyperbolically in the sense of 'a very large number of people')

□ All the world and his wife seem to be out in the country today.

**all there**

usually used with a negative (*not all there*) in the sense of 'mentally subnormal', or positively in questions that suggest or presuppose a negative answer

□ He's not all there.

□ Do you think that man is all there?

The positive use in statements generally means 'having all one's wits about one', or 'intellectually alert'.

□ He's all there, is George, you won't take him in easily.

**all to the good**

so much the better

□ We have had six offers of help. If more people volunteer, all to the good.

**all up with**
the end of one's life, hopes, something one has been striving for etc.
(preceded by *it is/was* etc.)
□ As the enemy closed in, the faithful band of defenders realised that
it was all up with them.

**all very well**
This is used sarcastically or ironically, to express disagreement, dissent
or objection; the idea is that a suggestion, advice etc. seems
satisfactory in itself, but in the situation in question it is not
practicable.
□ It's all very well for the doctor to tell me I need a month's holiday,
but who's going to look after my business while I'm off?

**all well and good**
used to express approbation of a possible contingency or situation
□ If he offers to work on Saturday morning, all well and good, but I
shall not ask him to.
□ I am opposed to spending so much public money on higher
education. If a boy or girl can profit from it, all well and good, but so
much of what is spent nowadays is just wasted.

**all yours**
you may have it/them
□ 'May I borrow that newspaper, please, when you have finished with
it?' 'There you are; it's all yours.'

**alone**
see **go it alone**

**alright**
This is the usual American spelling of **all right**, often now used in
Britain.

**also-ran**
a person whose performance is mediocre (originally, a horse which is
not among the first three in a race)

**altogether**
*in the altogether*: without clothes on

**and**
This is used to co-ordinate two examples of the same noun, to suggest
different kinds. The *and* is usually stressed.
□ There are poets and poets.
□ There is coffee and coffee.
In most contexts the suggestion is that one is inferior to the other, and
should only be allowed the name by courtesy.

**and all**

including or together with whatever or whoever is mentioned before the phrase

□ The elephant swallowed the buns, bag and all.

□ Cromwell instructed Sir Peter Lely to paint him warts and all, otherwise he would not pay a farthing for the portrait.

In the regional usage of certain districts of the Midlands, western and northern England, *and all* is appended to a statement to give emphasis, and has something of the same meaning as 'certainly'.

□ 'It's warm today, isn't it?' 'It is, and all.'

The *d* in *and* here is not pronounced.

**and all that**

see **all that**

**and Co**.

In standard usage this is merely a commercial term, but in colloquial English it is sometimes used to mean those associated with the person named. There is often a disparaging suggestion about it.

□ I don't know who was responsible for the damage, but I shouldn't be surprised if it was Johnson and Co.

Although *Co*. is an abbreviation for *company*, it is here spoken to rhyme with *go* and *so*. *And Co*. is most often written as *& Co*.

**and that**

and other things of that kind or in that class

□ We spent over an hour clearing up all the waste paper and that which the picnickers had left behind.

**answer back**

reply impertinently to an instruction, request etc. when no reply is called for

□ He is not really a rude or ill-mannered boy, but he has an unfortunate habit of answering back.

also transitively with a personal object:

□ I'm not going to have a child of that age answering me back.

*Back* must be in the final position.

see also **dusty answer**

**anybody**

anyone of importance, distinction, social position etc.; both the ordinary and the colloquial sense of the word appearing in:

□ Anybody who is anybody would not behave in that way.

**anything but**

strictly, 'anything except', but when followed by an adjective that denotes, or a noun that implies, certain qualities or attributes, 'the very reverse or opposite of'

□ The task was anything but easy.

□ He is anything but a gentleman.

This in itself is not colloquial; it is found in formal spoken and written English. But it becomes colloquial when the descriptive word is omitted and is left to be understood from a preceding sentence.

□ 'Was the examination easy?' 'Anything but.'

A verb may similarly be omitted.

□ 'Did you enjoy your holiday?' 'Anything but.'

**apology for**

used disparagingly, to express the idea that the thing in question does not really deserve the name given it, or that it is merely a poor substitute

□ They were drinking an apology for champagne.

□ This is an apology for Yorkshire pudding.

**applecart**

see **upset the** *or* **someone's applecart**

**appro**

see **on appro**

**apron strings**

see **tied to someone's apron strings**

**argy-bargy**

(uncountable) argument, answering back

□ I don't want to hear any more of your argy-bargy; just let me get on.

**arm**

*as long as your arm*: of very great length (used of lists, questionnaires etc.)

□ I was presented with a list of complaints as long as your arm.

see also **twist someone's arm** and **up in arms**

**armed**

see **teeth**

**arty**

pretentiously, or ostentatiously, artistic

□ Prominent amongst the company were several young men and women of the arty type.

often extended to *arty-crafty*, an adjective derived from the Arts and Crafts Movement started in the late 19th century

**as broad as it is long**

see **broad**

**as deaf as a post**

  totally deaf

**as different again**

  very different (usually with the sense of a difference for the better)

  □ The weather today is as different again from what it was yesterday.

  □ You can never tell what mood he will be in. One day he will be bad-tempered, and the next day as different again.

  The expression is, of course, illogical, but it has probably developed by analogy with *as big again*, *as long again* etc.

**as ever**

  (appended to an adjective or adverb) as was formerly the case

  □ I have taken the tablets the doctor prescribed, but the pain is as bad as ever.

  □ We have reasoned with him, but it seems to be of no use, for he acts as foolishly as ever.

  After a comparative the idiom is *than ever*.

  □ I thought the weather might be cooler after that thunderstorm, but it's hotter than ever.

**as good as**

  virtually

  **1** before an adjective

  □ The patient is as good as cured.

  □ He is as good as dead.

  The last example shows that the state indicated need not be one that is considered 'good'.

  **2** before a verb

  □ She as good as said that I did not know what I was talking about.

  □ They have as good as promised to help us.

**as if**

  In the following cases, *as though* may replace *as if*.

  **1** According to the strict rules of prescriptive grammar, *as if* should take a verb in the subjunctive, since it introduces an imaginary or rejected condition. In actual fact the indicative is just as frequent in spoken and in less formal written English; and in colloquial style it is almost always used.

  □ It sounds as if it is raining.

  □ He behaved as if he was mad.

  It is quite natural to use the indicative when there is no real comparison with an imaginary state or condition.

  □ He walks as if he is drunk.

*He walks as if he were drunk* would imply 'but he is not'. But *He walks as if he is drunk* means 'He is drunk, judging by the way he walks'. Similarly, *It looks as if it is going to rain*: 'It is going to rain, judging by the look of the sky'.

**2** Note the exclamatory use of *as if* to deprecate a suggestion, assumption, supposition etc.

□ As if anyone would believe that story!

□ He warned me against associating with people of doubtful character. Just as if I ever should!

NOTE The rejoinder *Just as if!* can be used to deprecate a suggestion etc. but *Just as though!* is not said.

**3** Allied to this is the use of *as if* to express disgust or annoyance.

□ He gave me a twenty-page document to type out for him. As if I hadn't enough to do already!

**4** *It is not as if* is also used to deprecate, or express annoyance at, something.

□ He's lucky to have got off with no more than a shock. He might have been electrocuted. And it's not as if he hadn't been warned of the danger.

The sense is 'It is not as it would be if ...'.

**as it is**
as the position is at present

□ Don't do anything to make the situation worse; it's bad enough as it is.

□ I hope taxes will not be increased; they are high enough as it is.

□ We cannot accept any more work; we have more than we can cope with as it is.

**as like(ly) as not**
see **likely**

**as long as your arm**
see **arm**

**as right as rain**
completely right (usually in reference to one's health)

□ I wasn't at all well yesterday, but I feel as right as rain today.

Occasionally it may refer to one's mood or temper.

□ The moods of small children change very quickly; one minute they will be sulking or crying, and the next they'll be as right as rain.

There seems no explanation of the simile, apart from the alliteration.

**as soon (as)**
as readily (as)

□ He's a hasty-tempered man, who would knock you down as soon as look at you.

□ I shouldn't want to be bed-ridden all my life; I'd as soon be dead.

□ Venison's all right, but I'd as soon have a good piece of roast beef.

## as sure as eggs is eggs

without the least doubt

□ He'll come to grief on that motor bike one of these days, as sure as eggs is eggs.

NOTE (a) the use of *sure* as an adverb (not *surely*), and (b) the singular verb (*is*, not *are*); possibly a corruption of 'as sure as $x$ is $x$', but the explanation does not sound convincing

## as the saying is

(sometimes *as the old saying goes*) occasionally added, rather pointlessly, to a cliché or well-known metaphorical expression

□ You can't see the wood for the trees, as the saying is.

□ It will have to be a case of first come, first served, as the old saying goes.

## as they make them

added to certain derogatory adjectives when used of a person's character, intellect or capabilities, in order to suggest an extreme degree of the quality

□ That fellow's as cunning as they make them.

similarly *as lazy/idle/insolent/cheeky/thick* ('stupid') *as they make them*, probably a facetious imitation of the use of the words in reference to manufactured goods or articles: *as big/long/light as they make them*

(In this phrase, the final word *them* is nearly always shortened to *'em*.)

## as though

see **as if**, for which *as though* is often used

## as well

advisable; advisably

□ Before making a statement it is always as well to verify your facts.

□ I think the figures are added correctly, but we might as well check them.

## ask

*Ask me another!* said in reply to a question which a person is quite unable to answer—there is usually the suggestion that he is as puzzled as the questioner is

□ 'If the police know the identity and the whereabouts of the culprit, why don't they arrest him?' 'Ask me another!'

*if you ask me*: sometimes appended to, or used before, an expression of opinion, especially when it has not been asked for
□ I don't believe he is so ill as he pretends, if you ask me.
□ If you ask me, they knew all along that the goods were stolen.
*I ask you!* an exclamation of incredulity, and sometimes scorn
□ George says he's applying for the post of Principal—I ask you!

## ask for it
behave or act in such a way as to invite trouble or unpleasant consequences
□ To go out in weather like this with that bad cold is asking for it.
□ You can't complain if you get into trouble. No-one is going to put up with behaviour of that kind; you're just asking for it.

## ask time off
a colloquial shortening of *ask for time off* (from one's employment)

## ass
fool

## at a loose end
bored through having nothing particular to do
□ We had to wait just over an hour for the next train, so being at a loose end, we spent the time looking round the shops.
see also **loose-endish**

## at any price
literally, 'however much one is paid', but generally used to give emphasis to a statement, without any sense of monetary payment; sometimes approximates to 'under any circumstances'
□ I can't stick that fellow at any price.
□ She declared that she would not have a picture like that in her house at any price.

## at any rate
**1** at least
□ We are going to have a good deal of rain during the next month; at any rate, so the weather forecasters say.
**2** no matter what the position or circumstances
□ I don't know that it's of much use discussing the matter with him at this point, but I'll see him, at any rate.

## at it
**1** active; doing one thing or another
□ He's at it from morning till night; he never gives himself a rest.
□ I'm feeling tired out; I've been at it since eight o'clock this morning.
also *hard at it*:

☐ We've been hard at it for the last three hours.

**2** doing one specified thing, which is understood from the situation, context or circumstances (This use often implies annoyance or reprimand.)

☐ So you're at it again, are you, Smith? (i.e. doing something I have previously reprimanded you for, or forbidden you to do)

## at sixes and sevens

in a state of disorder or confusion

☐ It used to be a well-run business, but then disagreements arose between the partners, and now things are at sixes and sevens.

## at someone's beck and call

always ready to obey someone's summons or commands

☐ I'm tired of being at Miss Jameson's beck and call all day. I'm getting a job in a factory.

## at that

in addition to that (i.e. a fact which has just been stated); contrary to what one might expect from that fact

☐ It was quite an expensive hotel, and not particularly comfortable at that.

## at that/this rate

if things go on like this

☐ The regulations state that a person is not eligible for a pension until he is sixty-five. At that rate it will be another two years before I am able to retire.

☐ I hope the weather will improve before long. Here we are well into June, and the weather more like March. We shall get no summer at all at this rate.

## at the drop of a hat

at the merest hint or suggestion

☐ The disgruntled workers were ready to strike at the drop of a hat.

## at the moment

just now (or, in the past, just then)

☐ I know the address well enough, but I can't think of it at the moment.

☐ She said that she was busy at the moment, and that I should return on Friday.

## at the same time

nevertheless; in spite of that

☐ I have never cared for him very much. At the same time I must admit that he is a very capable workman.

## atrocious

used very loosely to express the idea of something being very bad
□ After the collapse of government, the country was in an atrocious state.
□ She had atrocious pronunciation in French.

## Aunt Sally

a person, institution, idea etc. which is a target for popular abuse or criticism; a proposition put forward merely in order that it may be demolished (from the fairground game which consists in throwing balls at the model of a woman, known as Aunt Sally, the object being to knock her down or to knock a pipe out of her mouth)
□ A number of institutions revered and respected in earlier times have become Aunt Sallys for the present generation.

## awful

like atrocious, it has come to mean simply 'very bad': *an awful headache*, *awful weather*
In such expressions as *an awful shame*, *an awful pity*, it merely emphasises the notion expressed in the noun. The adverb *awfully* is similarly used before an adjective in rather affected speech, but usually in a favourable or commendatory sense: *awfully good of you, an awfully sweet child*. This now sounds a little dated.

## awhile

see **yet awhile**

## axe *(v or n)*

**1** make cuts to save money, sometimes by dismissing staff but more often by reducing services, especially in public transport
□ It is feared that more small branch lines will be axed in the coming months.
**2** *have an axe to grind*: have an ulterior motive
□ Our chairman was quick at being able to judge when someone had an axe to grind—he soon used to stop them.

# b

## baby

one who behaves childishly, expecially one who complains about very trivial things, as a small child might (always used in a derogatory sense)
□ Don't be a baby. Susan will let you have your pencil back when she's finished with it.

*cry-baby*: a child who cries on the slightest provocation, or about the slightest thing

*holding the baby*: assuming the responsibility, or being left with a task that should be shared by others

□ I know Jack. He'll promise to help you, and then he'll forget all about the promise and leave you holding the baby.

*throw out the baby with the bath water*: reject the essential or valuable along with the non-essential or valueless

□ There may be much in the Bible that modern man cannot accept; but to reject the Bible in its entirety because of this is to throw out the baby with the bath water.

**back** *(n)*

*have one's back to the wall*: fight (either literally or figuratively) to defend oneself in a desperate situation; be cornered

□ No relaxation of the measures is possible when, economically speaking, we have our backs to the wall.

*put one's back into it*: exert the utmost effort

□ He should have no difficulty in mastering the subject, if only he would put his back into it.

□ We shall have to put our backs into it if we are to get the work done on time.

*put someone's back up*: annoy; make angry (from a cat arching its back when it is angry)

□ She is well-intentioned, but her tactless manner tends to put people's backs up.

A variant form is *get someone's back up*:

□ His tactless manner gets people's backs up.

*Get* is almost always used when the sense is 'become angry' rather than 'make angry'.

□ He's not a bad fellow, but you have to be so careful what you say to him: he soon gets his back up.

*as soon as* (or *when*) *one's back is turned*: when one is not looking, or has gone away

□ As soon as my back was turned they did the very thing I had forbidden them to do.

see also **see the back of someone**

**back** *(v)*

**1** support, help

□ On this important point all parties will back the Government to their utmost.

□ He could never have risen to power if he had not been backed by powerful financial interests in his career.

**2** believe that whoever or whatever is named will be successful (from the idea of backing a horse to win a race)

□ 'Who do you think will get the post?' 'I'm backing Tomkins.'

**back a winner**

undertake an enterprise that turns out to be successful or highly advantageous to one (from backing a horse in a race)

□ In putting this new product on the market we appear to have backed a winner, as the sales are better than our most optimistic expectations.

*Back a loser* is also occasionally heard but it is far less frequent than *back a winner*.

□ You've backed a loser there, Fred.

**back-chat**

(uncountable) an interchange of insolent or facetious remarks between two or more people, or sometimes a series of insolent replies by one person to another

□ Much of the humour of the play consists in back-chat among a group of Cockney characters in a pub.

□ Now then, do what you're told, and not so much back-chat.

**back down**

withdraw, or partially withdraw, from a position one has previously taken up in an argument or discussion; adopt a less aggressive or less obstinate attitude

□ The blustering speaker began to back down when he saw that he was unlikely to get any sympathy or support from the others present.

**back in the saddle**

back to work after a holiday, illness etc.

□ How does it feel to be back in the saddle?

*Back in harness* has the same meaning.

**back of beyond**

a spot remote from centres of human habitation (usually used with a slight sense of disparagement)

□ If you *will* live at the back of beyond, you can't complain that your friends do not come and visit you.

**back out**

withdraw (from an undertaking, a plan, scheme etc. into which one has entered)

□ Several of those who had promised to help afterwards backed out.

**back-scratching**

(derogatory) helping or supporting others who might give something in return, especially in *mutual back-scratching*, from the phrase *You scratch my back and I'll scratch yours*

□ I don't approve of our local councillors, all they're interested in is mutual back-scratching. (agreeing to help one another rather than the people they are supposed to represent)

**back-seat driver**

a passenger in a car who persists in giving instructions or advice to the driver (no longer necessarily a passenger riding in the *back seat*)

see also **take a back seat**

**back the wrong horse**

support or put one's faith in the wrong side or the wrong thing (from betting on a horse race)

□ The future of that company does not look too bright. Anyone who buys shares now, in the hope of a recovery over the next few years, may well find that he has backed the wrong horse.

**back to square one**

go back to the beginning again (taken from various board games)

**back to the drawing board**

go back to the beginning after a failure (This originated in a cartoon as the comment of an aircraft designer when his new model has just crashed.)

**back up**

support

□ It is useless to undertake a task as serious as this unless you are sure that your colleagues will back you up.

also as a noun:

□ Our bank will give you all the back-up you need.

**backfire**

go wrong (especially said of a plan that was intended to harm someone else but ends up harming its originator)

□ He thought he'd got everything arranged for his own advantage but his little plot backfired—serve him right!

**backhander**

1 a treacherous blow, given when least expected (in the literal sense, a blow given with the back, instead of the palm, of the hand; figuratively, therefore, an action aimed against someone by trickery or deception)

2 a bribe

**backwards**
 see **lean over backwards**
**bacon**
 see **bring home the bacon** and **save one's bacon**
**bad books**
 see **in someone's bad books**
**bad egg***
 a disreputable, immoral or worthless person
 (usually used of men, not often of women; now dated)
 □ At first I was inclined to trust him, but I'm afraid he's a bad egg.
**bad lot**
 same as **bad egg**, but used equally of both sexes
**bad penny**
 If you try to get rid of someone or something undesirable, it may come
 back to you or turn up again (like a counterfeit coin).
 □ You can't expect to have seen the last of him, he'll turn up again like
 a bad penny.
**badly off**
 in unfortunate circumstances; lacking (often with a negative and
 referring to money)
 □ Now he's got a better job and they aren't badly off.
 □ We're not badly off for potatoes this year.
 see also **well off**
**baffled**
 unable to understand, like *puzzled*; see **puzzle it out**
**bag** *(n)*
 *in the bag*: won; achieved; in one's possession
 □ On the eve of the election the candidate and his supporters felt that
 the seat was as good as in the bag.
 see also **let the cat out of the bag**
**bag** *(v)*
 take possession of
 □ The hall is filling up rapidly. We had better bag a seat while there
 are still some left.
 Sometimes the idea of taking possession without first asking
 permission is implied.
 □ I've bagged your newspaper. I hope you don't mind.
 *I bags**, although ungrammatical, is a set form used to stake a claim
 to something.
 □ I bags that seat.

□ I bags first go.

Even more strangely *Bags I go first* etc. is often used.

This is fairly dated except among some schoolchildren.

**bag of bones**

a very thin person or animal that appears to have nothing but bones under the skin

□ During his illness he wasted away until he was just a bag of bones.

**bag of tricks**

**1** all the accessories, appurtenances, requisites etc. (usually preceded by *the whole*); probably from the bag in which a conjuror carries everything necessary for the performance of his tricks

□ I didn't know what tools were available on the premises, so I've brought the whole bag of tricks with me.

**2** a number of articles arranged on a stall, a table etc.

□ Be careful what you're doing. If you stumble against that table you'll upset the whole bag of tricks.

**bags of***

plenty of (now a little dated)

□ We've bags of time.

□ He's had bags of opportunities.

Though *bags* is plural in form, like *plenty* it is treated as singular or plural according to the noun that follows it.

□ There *is* bags of time.

□ There *have* been bags of opportunities.

□ There *was* bags of room in the railway carriage.

**baked**

see **half-baked**

**balderdash**

(uncountable) nonsense; foolish talk

**ball**

see **court** and **on the ball**

**balloon**

*The balloon went up.* There was an angry outburst or scene.

□ He admitted that he had known the full facts all along, but had concealed most of them from his colleagues. Then the balloon went up.

□ The balloon will go up when the manager gets to know that.

**balmy**

(often so spelt, though more properly *barmy*) slightly insane, weak in the intellect (for origin, see **barmy**)

**baloney**
see **boloney**
**bamboozle**
deceive by trickery; puzzle or confuse
**band-wagon**
a term denoting any kind of organisation, but especially a political
one, the members of which have a common objective or programme;
hence, *climb on to the band-wagon*: join such an organisation (The
expression is usually used sarcastically or with a certain amount of
disparagement.)
□ They hope to gain power by climbing on to the Socialist band-
wagon.
The phrase has an American origin: a band sat on a wagon in a parade
going with a candidate at an election. Now its use is not confined to
politics, but extends to fashion, commerce etc.
**bang (up-to-date)**
The word *bang* intensifies, so this means 'including all the most recent
ideas'. Similarly you may hear *bang on target*, *bang in the middle*. It is
the same as **plumb 1**.
**banger**
**1** a sort of firework
**2** a sausage
**3** an old car (often *an old banger*)
**banging one's head against a brick wall**
usually heard in a comparison, meaning trying to do something with
no success; failing with great frustration
□ We've tried to get them to deliver our order more promptly, but it's
like banging one's head against a brick wall.
sometimes also *hitting one's head against a brick wall*
**bar** *(prep)*
except, apart from; mainly used in a few expressions like *bar none* and
*all over bar the shouting* ('the important part of some event is over, and
the only part left is the rejoicing or complaining'; taken from horse
racing)
**bargain**
*bargain for*: except (usually in negative sentences)
□ When I undertook the task I knew it would not be easy; but I didn't
bargain for all this trouble.
□ If they come on my land again they'll get more than they bargain
for. (i.e. they'll be punished)

*into the bargain*: in addition
□ If you have anything to do with such a scheme you'll endanger your good name, and probably lose your money into the bargain.

**barge into**
**1** collide with (similar to **bump into** but more violent)
□ He barged into me without looking where he was going.
**2** enter abruptly
□ He barged into the room.
□ He barged in.

**barge-pole**
*I wouldn't touch it with a barge-pole.* I wouldn't involve or concern myself in that (because it is dangerous/dishonest/unpleasant in some way).

**bark**
*His bark is worse than his bite.* He is not so severe, or fearsome, as he gives the impression of being.
□ At first I was rather afraid of my uncle, but I soon came to the conclusion that his bark was worse than his bite.
*bark up the wrong tree*: direct one's criticism to the wrong quarter, or against the wrong person; usually used in the *-ing* form
□ You're barking up the wrong tree.

**barmy**
also, though less correctly, spelt **balmy**
*Barm* was an old word for 'yeast', and is still heard in some regional dialects. Hence *barmy* means 'like the froth produced by yeast when fermenting'. So a person who is barmy is one whose intellect is frothy, i.e. 'silly', 'crazy'.

**barrel**
see **scrape the barrel**

**bash**
see **have a bash**

**bat** *(n)*
*off one's own bat*: on one's own initiative
□ No-one suggested he should do that—he did it off his own bat.
see also **blind as a bat**

**bat an eyelid**
usually *not bat an eyelid*, meaning 'not show emotion'
□ She listened to the terrible news without batting an eyelid.

**bats in the belfry***
*have (got) bats in the belfry*: be slightly crazy; the phrase is often

shortened and modified: *He's just bats*, or *his ideas are all bats, don't listen to him.*

**battle**

see **half the battle**

**battle-axe**

a middle-aged or elderly woman, of a somewhat masculine character, and rather sharp-tongued and domineering, e.g. Betsey Trotwood, in Dickens's novel *David Copperfield*; usually preceded by the word *old*

□ Our landlady's a real old battle-axe.

**batty**

crazy; derived from **bats in the belfry**

**be-all and end-all**

(always with *the*, and mostly with a negative) the one and only reason for doing something; the exclusive aim

□ English literature isn't the be-all and end-all of our course. We hope students will see something of our way of life and improve their spoken English.

**be off**

go, leave, depart

□ Half-past ten! We ought to be off if we're to catch that train.

□     Do you think I can listen all day to such stuff?
    Be off, or I'll kick you downstairs!
    (Lewis Carroll, *Alice in Wonderland*)

In an imperative, force or urgency is added by the addition of *with you*: 'Now, then, be off with you!'*

**beam**

see **on one's beam ends** and **wide in the beam**

**bean**

*full of beans*: very lively; having plenty of energy

□ A child may be listless and 'washed out' one moment, and full of beans an hour later.

□ I feel full of beans after a good night's rest.

*He hasn't a bean.* He is very poor; he hasn't a penny to his name. (often used as an overstatement)

□ Her parents objected to her marrying a chap who hadn't a bean.

*a beanfeast*: a splendid meal*

*spill the beans*: make a disclosure, let out a secret (the same as **let the cat out of the bag**, and much more common in spoken English)

*old bean**: a rather jocular (and old-fashioned) way of addressing a friend

**beano***

a variant of *beanfeast* (see under **bean**)

**bear**

see **grin and bear it**

**beastly***

This is an all-purpose word, used to express in a general way the idea of something that is unpleasant, unwelcome, objectionable etc.; usually used adjectivally, but an adverbial use is also possible. It is now slightly dated.

□ I've a beastly headache.

□ I shouldn't mind the wind and rain, if it weren't so beastly cold.

**beat**

From its use for a regular rhythm in music, it came to be used as an adjective to refer to various kinds of pop music (*beat music*, *beat group*) and in phrases like *the beat generation* for young people in the late 1950s and early 1960s who liked this music.

see also **dead beat**

**beat about the bush**

talk lengthily round a subject without ever getting to the point; usually used in negative sentences

□ I won't beat about the bush—I've come to ask you to lend me some money.

**beat someone**

puzzle; put someone at a loss for an explanation

□ These constant changes in the weather beat me; one day it's sweltering hot, and the next we're almost back to winter temperatures.

often with *it* as a subject, followed by a noun clause in apposition

□ It beats me how he did it.

usually used in the active voice, but a passive is also possible

□ Don't say you're beaten by a simple problem like that.

**beat someone hollow**

be far superior to; surpass someone by a considerable extent or amount (used mostly of achievements, accomplishments, abilities etc.)

□ He can beat me hollow at mathematics.

**beat someone to it**

be successful in attaining a destination, an objective etc. before someone else

□ It looked as if the British driver would be the first home, but then an Italian car which was close behind him put on speed and beat him to it by a few seconds.

## beauty

*the beauty of it*: the most pleasing, agreeable or (usually) amusing aspect of the matter in question

□ He offered me fifty pounds for the picture; and the beauty of it was that he never recognised it as the same one that he had sold me for half that amount last May.

note also the ironic use of *beauty* to refer to a person of disreputable character, or one who acts in a way of which the speaker strongly disapproves

□ You're a beauty, aren't you, staying out until this time of night?

## because

In conversational and colloquial English an adverbial clause introduced by *because* is often used, to give not the reason for the fact stated in the head-clause, but the reason why the statement is made, or (in the case of a question) why the question is asked.

□ 'Is Mr Jackson in the office?' 'I don't know whether he is there now, but I know that he was a few minutes ago, because I was speaking to him.'

□ Do you feel hungry? Because if you do, I've a few sandwiches here that you can have.

□ You don't want to lose your job, do you? Because that's what will happen if you go on in this way.

## beck

see **at someone's beck and call**

## become of

be the fate of (preceded by *what* or *whatever*)

□ She is a most selfish person. So long as she's all right, she doesn't mind what becomes of other people.

*What has become of* often means 'what has happened to'.

□ I can't imagine whatever became of those papers that I left on my desk.

□ What's become of your brother George? (Where is he, what is he doing etc.?)

## bed

*get out of bed on the wrong side*: be irritable or bad-tempered (used of one particular occasion only, not of someone who is usually bad-tempered or irritable)

□ What's the matter with you today? No-one seems to be able to do anything right for you. You must have got out of bed on the wrong side this morning.

**beddable**
  attractive, worthy of being taken to bed
**bedsit** *or* **bed-sitter**
  short forms of *bed-sitting room*
**bee**
  *a bee in one's bonnet*: an idea by which one is obsessed
  □ Don't get him talking on that subject—he's got a real bee in his
  bonnet about it.
  *make a bee-line for*: take the direct or nearest way to (as the bee
  with honey takes the most direct way to the hive); the expression often
  connotes a certain amount of rush or hurry
  □ Released from lectures, the students made a bee-line for the
  refectory.
**been and gone and done it**
  *You've been and gone and done it.* This is a humorous phrase used
  when someone has made a mistake or **blunder**.
**beer and skittles**
  carefree enjoyment (of a simple kind)
  □ They soon found out that the holiday was not to be all beer and
  skittles.
  □ If you think life is all beer and skittles, you'll soon find out your
  mistake.
  see also **small beer**
**beetle off** *
  move away quickly
**before one has finished**
  sooner or later (only used in this tense)
  □ Stop swinging that stick about. You'll hit somebody with it before
  you've finished.
  □ Young Brian'll have an accident with that motor bike before he's
  finished.
  generally used by way of rebuke, or to express disapproval or
  misgiving, but not necessarily so
  □ I shouldn't be surprised if he became a Cabinet Minister before he's
  finished.
**before one knows where one is**
  before one realises the position or the danger one is in
  □ Look where you're going, or before you know where you are you'll
  be over the edge of that cliff.
  □ Before she knew where she was, she had become famous.

**befuddled**

having a confused or hazy mind, as the result of drinking or of fever, influenza etc. (also *fuddled\**)

□ I felt rather befuddled when I got up this morning.

**beggar\***

Usually *lucky beggar* is used half enviously, half jokingly. Also a few other phrases (*silly beggar*, *funny beggar*) are used with no thought of the real meaning of *beggar* but as a substitute for 'person'.

see also **go begging**

**begin**

*to begin with*: **1** first

□ We had soup to begin with, followed by roast beef and Yorkshire pudding.

**2** in the first place, either in order of time, or in a series of reasons etc.

□ The new manager was very friendly to begin with.

□ There were several reasons why we did not adopt the scheme; to begin with, it would have been too expensive.

**behind someone's back**

treacherously, when someone is unaware of what is being done or said

□ You may as well let her have her own way, for if you forbid her to do a thing, she'll do it behind your back.

□ He was the kind of person who would flatter you to your face and then slander you behind your back.

**behold**

see **lo and behold**

**believe it or not**

What I say is the truth even if you don't believe me.

**bell**

see **ring**

**belly**

see **eye(s)**

**bellyful**

see **have one's bellyful**

**belt up**

stop talking (even more impatient than *shut up*)

see also **hit below the belt** and **tighten one's belt**

**bend**

see **drive someone round the bend**

**bend over backwards**

see **lean over backwards**

**bent on**
    determined (to do something)
    □ I've always been bent on visiting the west coast of Scotland.

**best**
    *the best of it*: the best, the most interesting or the most amusing aspect
    of it
    □ For nearly half an hour they were discussing how they should divide
    the money; and the best of it was that there was no money to be
    divided.
    *get the best of it*: come off victorious; prevail over one's opponent in a
    contest or argument
    □ In disputes of this kind I'm sure the woman always gets the best
    of it.

**best bib and tucker***
    one's best clothes
    □ As it's a special occasion, I suppose I had better put on my best bib
    and tucker.
    □ Kathleen was there, in her best bib and tucker.

**best foot forward**
    see **foot**

**best of both worlds**
    the advantages of two different states, positions or sets of circum-
    stances (The chief constructions are *have*, *get*, *want* and *enjoy*
    *the best of both worlds*.)
    □ Life in a large city had its advantages and disadvantages: so has life
    in the country. But if you live in a small town you can have the best of
    both worlds.

**best of it**
    see **best**

**best of times**
    when conditions or circumstances are most favourable
    □ His health was never very good, even at the best of times.
    □ At the best of times journalism is a pretty hazardous profession.

**bet**
    *I bet*: I should think; I feel so sure, that I could bet on it.
    □ Not here yet? I bet they've missed the bus again.
    □ I bet you were frightened when you saw that bull coming for you.
    *you bet*: yes, certainly
    □ Frightened? You bet I was.
    *bet one's bottom dollar/one's life*: be so sure of the fact stated that one

would be willing to wager one's last dollar or one's life on it (usually preceded by *I will* or *I would*, but *you can*)

☐ I'll bet my bottom dollar he finds some excuse not to do what he has promised.

☐ You can bet your life whoever else suffers, he won't.

*What's the betting?* What do you think is the likelihood? (The reference is probably to the odds at betting, rather than to the amount staked.)

**better**
see **had better**

**better half\***
(jocular) one's husband or wife

**between you, me and the gatepost**
in strict confidence

☐ Between you, me and the gatepost, I have been promised promotion in the New Year.

**betwixt and between**
somewhere between two things or positions that are named (*Betwixt* means the same as *between*, but is now archaic or confined to poetry, except in this colloquial expression.)

☐ 'Are you a Liberal or a Conservative?' 'Neither really; betwixt and between.'

**bicker**
quarrel, especially of people in the same family

**big deal**
a reply to someone who has offered something regarded as worthless or pointless

☐ 'If you're really good, I'll give you an apple.' 'Big deal!'

**big gun**
an important person who has much influence

☐ As the by-election is a crucial one, you may be sure that both parties will send down their big guns in support of their candidates.

**big hand**
see **give someone a big hand**

**big-headed**
conceited; hence *a big-head*: a conceited person

**big noise**
an important or prominent person in a particular sphere

☐ Mr Harris is a big noise in the banking world, so you'd better be polite to him if you want a job.

**big shot**

a similar meaning to **big gun** and **bigwig**

**bigwig**

an important person

□ All the local bigwigs were there.

□ We can't sit in the first two rows of seats; they are reserved for the bigwigs.

**bike**

This is short for *bicycle*, which is rarely spoken. You can say a person *bikes* or *cycles* to work.

**bilge**

(uncountable) nonsense, rubbish

**billy-O***

(only in the phrase *like billy-O*) used to emphasise a verb (now dated)

□ My tooth is hurting like billy-O.

**bind**

something which binds or enslaves one to it, because it needs constant attention

□ A well-kept garden can give great pleasure, but it can be a bind if you have to do it all yourself.

□ She found it a bind, having to stay in all the evening in case there were any urgent telephone calls.

**binge**

a merry-making or celebration at which there is much drinking

□ They were having a binge next door until the early hours of the morning.

*go on the binge*: go out drinking (usually with the idea of going from one pub to another)

□ There are young Lawson and his pals off out. Going on the binge again, I expect.

**bird**

**1** girl, young woman (in colloquial use for several centuries)

**2** *give someone the bird*: hiss someone to show displeasure, e.g. in the theatre

**3** *get the bird*: be hissed (in the theatre)

see also **early bird** and **kill two birds with one stone**

**bit**

**1** *a bit*: rather; slightly

(a) before an adjective or adverb of the positive degree

□ The examination was a bit difficult.

☐ It's a bit cold this morning, isn't it?

☐ It is better to arrive a bit early than to be late.

(b) before an adjective or adverb of the comparative degree

☐ My cold is a bit better today.

☐ If only we had arrived a bit earlier, we should have got a more comfortable seat.

(c) before *too*

☐ That hat is a bit too dear.

☐ We liked the house, but it was a bit too large for us.

☐ It is a bit soon for the roses to be out.

(d) before a noun (in this case the idiom is *a bit of a(n)* )

☐ He is a bit of a fool.

☐ I've a bit of a headache.

☐ There was a bit of an argument between the passenger and the conductor.

A group of phrases with similar meanings may often be heard: *It's a bit thick/rough/much/steep/off* all meaning unfair, unreasonable
see also **steep**

(e) *A bit of* can also mean 'a small amount of'.

☐ He was left a bit of money by an uncle.

☐ We had a bit of trouble to get the car started.

☐ Call round and see us, when you've got a bit of time to spare.

(f) *A bit* is sometimes used in the sense of 'a short time'. The chief phrases are *after a bit, for a bit* and *in a bit*.

☐ Let's sit on this seat and rest for a bit.

☐ After a bit my companion broke the silence by asking whether I felt hungry.

☐ I'll be with you in a bit.

**2** *every bit* (followed by *as* + adj. + *as*): just; in every respect

☐ This is every bit as good as the other.

**3** *not a bit* (*of*): not the least (or 'not at all')

☐ 'Do you mind if I sit next to you?' 'Not a bit.'

☐ She was not a bit worried.

☐ It's not a bit of use trying to help him.

☐ 'Do you think he'll follow your advice?' 'Not a bit of it!'

**bitch**

a bad-tempered, spiteful woman (literally, a female dog)

**bitchy** *(adj)*

*bitchy gossip, a bitchy thing to say*: based on the truth but likely to cause trouble hence, *a bitchy employer/woman/person*: one who makes bitchy remarks

## bite off more than one can chew

undertake more than one is able to perform; begin a task that proves to be too difficult for one

□ If he thinks he's going to do all that on his own, he'll find out that he's bitten off more than he can chew.

## bite someone's head off

reprimand someone very sharply for a trivial fault

□ If I am at fault I don't mind being corrected, but you needn't bite my head off.

## bits and pieces

oddments of various shapes and/or sizes

□ We have used up most of the cloth; all we have left is a few bits and pieces.

sometimes used also of a miscellaneous collection of small parts or articles

□ Put all your bits and pieces in that box; don't leave them lying about.

## bitter end

*to the bitter end*: to the absolute end, especially in a situation where you have almost lost patience

## black and white

see **in black and white**

## black books

see **in someone's black books**

## black list

a list of undesirable, untrustworthy or suspicious people; to *black-list*: put on such a list

□ We shall have to put him on our black list.

□ We shall have to black-list him.

## black mark

This is an indication or expression of disapproval or of dissatisfaction; the chief phrases are *get a black mark* and *give someone a black mark*.

□ I'm afraid I shall get a black mark this week; this is the second time I've arrived late.

□ She is most efficient and conscientious at her job, but I'd give her a black mark where punctuality is concerned.

## blank

see **draw a blank**

**blanket**

see **wet blanket**

**blazes\***

a euphemism for *hell*, found in such expressions as *like blazes* (They ran *like blazes*), *what the blazes* and *go to blazes*

**bleeding**

This is a substitute for **bloody** but less acceptable socially than **blessed**; *bloody* is the least acceptable of these.

**blessed**

a euphemism for some profane word (probably **bloody**), or substituted for its opposite, *cursed* (The final *-ed* is pronounced as a separate syllable.)

□ This blessed fire keeps going out.

□ There's that blessed cat scratching up my seeds again.

**blighter\***

This is used to designate a person who irritates or annoys one, or whom one dislikes.

□ I'm thankful to be rid of that blighter.

sometimes used jokingly to someone whom the speaker knows well

**blind-alley job**

a job that leads nowhere, or in which there is no promotion

**blind as a bat**

quite unable to see (usually used of temporary blindness due to some external cause, not of permanent blindness)

□ Stepping from the bright sunlight into the darkness of that cellar, I was as blind as a bat until my eyes became used to it.

**blind bit of notice**

*He didn't take/pay a blind bit of notice*. He paid no attention at all.

**blind drunk**

completely drunk (perhaps from the idea of one who is completely drunk staggering about and colliding with things as a blind person might)

**blind spot**

To *have a blind spot for* something is to be quite unable to remember about it or understand it.

**blinking\***

a euphemism for **bloody**, as acceptable as **blessed**

□ I can't get this blinking door open; the lock seems to have jammed.

**blithering**

This is used to express contempt or annoyance; it has the meaning of

**bloody** but also of *jabbering*: talking nonsensically. The chief
combinations are *a blithering fool*, *a blithering idiot* and *a blithering
nuisance*.

**blitz**

During World War II, this meant an air-raid, from the German
*Blitzkrieg*. There is now another meaning: *have a blitz on* (a cupboard,
an office, a garden etc.): to clean up, make it tidy, clear it out.

**block**

see **chip off the old block**

**bloke**

man (somewhere between a colloquialism and slang)

☐ Who's that bloke in the brown suit over there?

**blood**

see **cold blood**, **make someone's blood boil** and **turn
someone's blood cold**

**bloody**

Probably the most commonly heard swear word, it still gives offence in
some circles and foreigners are recommended not to use it. It is
believed to be a corruption of *by our Lady*.

**bloomer***

a mistake; a blunder

☐ As soon as the remark had passed my lips I realised I had made a
bloomer.

**blooming**

an adjective of condemnation, usually pronounced *bloomin'*, and
probably one of several euphemisms for **bloody**

**blow**

a mild oath used to express

**1** surprise

☐ Blow me if it isn't snowing!

☐ Well I'm blowed! Here are George and Vera.

**2** annoyance

☐ My watch has stopped, blow it!

☐ Blow! I've come out without any money.

☐ I'll be blowed if I do it!

The last often amounts to a form of asseveration.

NOTE When the verb is used in this sense, the past participle is *blowed*,
not *blown*.

**3** An important phrase is *blow one's own trumpet*, meaning to boast.

☐ Just stop blowing your own trumpet and get on with the job.

## blow one's top
lose one's temper

## blow up
rebuke or reprimand very strongly or severely

☐ My father will probably blow me up when he gets to know of this.

hence *a blowing-up*

☐ I shall probably get a good blowing-up when I get home.

## blower
*I've just been on the blower to Chris*: on the telephone to Chris

## blue
*feel blue*: feel unhappy, depressed

*a blue film*: a pornographic film

see also **out of the blue**

## blue fit*
a mental shock caused by unwelcome news or an unexpected occurrence

☐ Your mother would have a blue fit if she knew of this.

☐ I had a blue fit when he walked into the room; I thought he was dead!

There does not seem to be much point in the adjective, unless it means 'a fit that causes one to go blue in the face'.

## blue moon
*once in a blue moon*: only on very rare occasions

☐ You get a chance like this once in a blue moon.

## blue murder
found in expressions such as *scream/shout blue murder*: scream in great alarm

☐ Two women came running from the house, screaming blue murder.

## blunder
a bad mistake (also used as a verb)

☐ I've blundered again.

## board
used in many expressions, among which you should notice:

**1** The *Board* is short for the *Board of Directors* or *Executives*. This, being a collective noun, is sometimes followed by a plural verb.

☐ The Board are (*or* is) meeting again tomorrow.

**2** *above board*: frank, honest, nothing hidden

**3** You need a *boarding card* to *board* or enter an airliner; *everyone on board* means everyone in the aircraft and may be used as a question.

☐ Is everyone on board?

see also **across the board** and **go by the board**

**boat**

*in the same boat*: in the same situation or circumstances

□ I should be only too pleased to help you out of your difficulties if I could, but I am in the same boat as you are.

*rock the boat*: imperil an organisation, body, project etc. by one's behaviour

□ Now that we are on the way to economic recovery we cannot allow any section of the community to rock the boat by unreasonable demands or irresponsible action.

**bobby**

a policeman, derived from the name of Sir Robert Peel, who as Home Secretary in 1829 established the Metropolitan Police Force (For the same reason policemen were at one time called Peelers, but this is no longer used.)

**body**

see **keep body and soul together**

**bogged down**

oppressed, feeling troubled

□ I'm quite bogged down with all this homework.

**boggle**

*The mind boggles* (*at the idea*). The mind can scarcely conceive the idea, as it is so costly, fantastic, wild, dangerous etc.

**bogus**

dishonest, not genuine, fictitious

□ His story sounded a bit bogus to me.

□ Those are bogus antiques—don't waste your money on them.

**boiled shirt***

an evening-dress shirt, with starched front and cuffs

**boiling**

very hot (colloquial only when used of things other than liquids)

□ I'm boiling, after climbing that steep hill.

□ It's boiling in this room. Can't we have a few windows open?

also *boiling hot*

□ Aren't you uncomfortable in that thick suit, on a boiling hot day like this?

**boloney**

(uncountable) rubbish, nonsense; also spelt *baloney*

**bolshy**

troublesome, argumentative; derived from *Bolshevik*

□ The children are very bolshy with their aunt.

## bomb

*It went like a bomb*. It was very successful.

*It cost a bomb*. It cost a lot of money.

## bone

*bone-dry*: as dry as a bone, perfectly dry

□ The house is bone-dry, not a trace of damp anywhere.

*bone-idle*: very lazy, disinclined to exert oneself to the least degree (literally 'idle to the bone')

□ It isn't that the work is difficult, or that he hasn't the ability to do it, he's just bone-idle.

*have a bone to pick with someone*: have something to complain about with someone

*near the bone*: bordering on the indecent or indelicate (of stories, jokes etc.)

□ His speech in reply to the toast was quite witty and entertaining, but parts of it were a bit near the bone.

## bones

*a feeling in the bones*: a feeling or notion for which one has no rational grounds

□ I wouldn't trust that fellow. If you ask me why, I can't give you any definite reason; it's just a feeling in the bones.

This can also be expressed as *I feel it in my bones*.

*in one's bones*: part of one's essential nature

□ You'll never cure him of his meanness; it's in his bones.

*make no bones about something*: be quite frank and outspoken about it

□ I shall say what I think of him, and make no bones about it.

see also **bag of bones**

## bonkers

(near slang) crazy

□ He went bonkers.

## boo

see **say 'boo' to a goose**

## boob

like a blunder but perhaps not so serious

## booby prize

In a large competition, after the first three prizes, there are often a set number of *consolation prizes* for entrants who did very well. In a small competition or race, the entrant who comes last or who has done worst is sometimes given a *booby prize* as a joke. In America a *booby* is a silly person, but this is not very common in Britain.

## book of words

printed instructions (not necessarily in a book)

□ I can't quite see how to put this thing together. Where's the book of words?

see also **go by the book** and **in someone's bad books**

## book *(v)*

**1** enter one's name in a book, on a list etc. for the fulfilment of an engagement

□ Can I book you to lecture to the society on 25 September?

Hence *booked up* is having all the engagements one can undertake.

□ I'm booked up for September, but I could come in October.

**2** used more specifically of a policeman entering in his notebook the name, address, alleged offence etc. of a motorist who has infringed the traffic regulations

□ You're lucky to have got off with a caution; most policemen would have booked you for that.

## boost

used both as a verb 'stimulate' and as a noun, especially in *give a boost to*

□ The Government's latest measures should give a much needed boost to the industry.

## boot

*Now the boot is on the other foot*. Now the situation is reversed.

□ He said I was wrong and now the boot is on the other foot (i.e. it is evident that he was wrong).

*get the boot*: be dismissed/sacked; similarly *give someone the boot*: dismiss/sack someone

## boots

*too big for one's boots*: conceited, imagining that one is more important than one really is

□ It's about time someone put that fellow in his place; he's getting too big for his boots.

see also **heart** and **lick someone's boots**

## booze

This is probably the commonest conversation word for alcoholic drinks. Notice the noun for the drink is uncountable, but the word exists as a verb too.

□ He's gone boozing with his mates.

By extension, *they've gone for a booze-up/on the booze* is used to mean 'they've gone to have not just one drink, but a lot'.

## born

*born with a silver spoon in one's mouth*: born into a moneyed family, or with every social advantage

*not born yesterday*: experienced in the ways of the world; not easily deceived, taken in or imposed upon (usually used with a suggestion of sarcasm)

□ You don't think I'm going to believe that story, do you? I wasn't born yesterday.

## bosh

(uncountable) rubbish, nonsense

## boss

the person in charge of a business, institution or organisation; the immediate superior to whom an employee is responsible

□ I am having to run the office while my boss is on holiday.

*Chief* is also sometimes used, but notice that a *chef* is the boss of a kitchen!

## boss someone about

order someone about; act like the boss towards someone (always used in a derogatory sense)

□ He's never so happy as when he's bossing others about.

□ I'm not going to be bossed about by someone nearly twenty years my junior.

## boss the show

take charge of or assume authority in a project, undertaking etc.

□ No matter what she is concerned in, she always wants to boss the show.

## bossy

inclined to be dictatorial

□ Some secretaries become more bossy than their own bosses.

## bother

Whether used as verb or noun, *bother*, in the sense of 'trouble', is normal spoken English in such sentences as *Don't bother about it, He always makes such a bother about a simple matter*. The following are some colloquial uses.

**1** *Bother!* a mild exclamation to express annoyance or irritation that may be used either independently (*Bother! This door is jammed*), or with an object (*Bother this door! It's jammed again*)

**2** *I can't be bothered.* I am disinclined to take the trouble.

□ I'll do that later, I can't be bothered now.

**3** *I'm not bothered*: used as an expression of indifference, with a meaning roughly equivalent to that of 'I don't mind', though possibly expressing a greater degree of apathy (more characteristic of the Midlands and the northern parts of England than of the south)

☐ 'Would you like lunch now, or later?' 'I'm not bothered.'

**4** *hot and bothered*: confused, flustered

☐ Take the situation calmly, there's no need to get so hot and bothered about it.

**5** *a spot of bother*: trouble, though not too serious

☐ If you're not careful you'll find yourself in a spot of bother about this.

## bounce

*I hope his cheque won't bounce*. I hope his cheque will not be returned by his bank with a refusal to pay because his account is in debt.

## bound

**1** *I'll be bound*: I am certain (I am so sure of it that I should be willing to be bound by an oath to that effect)

☐ He didn't get the money by honest means, I'll be bound.

**2** *bound* (+infinitive) expresses certainty or inevitability

☐ You are bound to feel weak after that long illness.

## bounds

see **by leaps and bounds**

## bowl someone over

take all the spirit out of someone (usually as the result of a shock, a surprise, bad news etc. but also of good events)

☐ The news of his son's death quite bowled him over.

## box

*the box*: television

☐ What's on the box this evening?

see also **gogglebox**

## boy friend

a girl's or woman's sweetheart, though not one to whom she is engaged

see also **girl friend**

## boys

see **jobs for the boys**

## brain(s)

*have something on the brain*: see **on the brain**

*have brains*: be intelligent

☐ He has brains but he won't use them.

☐ She hasn't the brains to see what I am driving at.

NOTE Although *brains* is a plural, the idiom is 'he hasn't *much* brains', not '*many* brains'.

**brain drain**

the flow of young academics, scientists etc. from a poorer country to a richer one (in Britain, usually referring to those moving from Britain to the U.S.A.)

**brain-wave**

a sudden inspiration or bright idea

☐ We had almost given up the problem as insoluble, when John had a brain-wave.

**brainy**

clever, intelligent, bright intellectually

☐ His mother was brainy.

☐ That's a brainy idea.

**brass farthing***

the smallest conceivable amount of money; found chiefly in the expressions *don't care a brass farthing* and *wouldn't give a brass farthing for it* (The idea is probably that a brass farthing was of even less value than a copper one.) Now that farthings are no longer used, this phrase is becoming rare.

**brass-hat***

originally an important or high-ranking officer in one of the armed forces; from there applied to an important official in any organisation

☐ The rank and file, I am convinced, do not want this strike. It is only the brass-hats who are interested in keeping it going.

**brass tacks**

Cockney rhyming slang for 'hard facts'; it is now used colloquially in all parts of the country in the expressions *get down to brass tacks* and *come down to brass tacks*, meaning 'deal with the essentials'

see notes on Cockney under **use your loaf** and **not on your nelly**

**bread**

see **know which side one's bread is buttered (on)**

**break-through**

a big unexpected advance in research

☐ They still really don't know why some people get migraines, but they're hoping for a break-through soon.

**breath**

see **save one's breath**

**breathe down someone's neck**

☐ I don't feel I can work properly when the boss *is breathing down my neck*: I am unable to work at my best when the boss is supervising me too closely, perhaps watching for my mistakes and making me tense.

**brick***

a staunch person; one who can be relied upon; one who has remained loyal and rendered inestimable service in a crisis or in difficult circumstances (now a little dated)

□ George has been a brick during my illness, when things were so difficult for the family. I don't know what we should have done without him.

see also **banging one's head against a brick wall**, **cat**, **come down on someone like a ton of bricks** and **drop a brick**

**bright spark**

an intelligent person

**bring home the bacon**

be successful; achieve the desired result

□ His methods may be unorthodox, but they bring home the bacon.

**broad**

*as broad as it is long*: amounting to the same; making no difference one way or the other

□ If you leave by the 10.30 train you will go straight through to your destination, and if you go by the 10.05 you will have to change at Derby and wait for the 10.30 there, so it is as broad as it is long.

**broke**

having no money; penniless

NOTE *Broken* would not have this sense.

□ It's no good relying on me to pay the fares. I'm broke.

sometimes *stony-broke*

**brolly**

umbrella

**browned off**

fed up, depressed

**brush**

see **tarred with the same brush**

**brush-off**

*get the brush-off*: be shown you are not wanted

similarly, *give someone the brush-off*: show someone this; dismiss impolitely

**bubbly**

(uncountable) champagne or spumante

**buck**
see **pass the buck**
**bucket**
see **kick the bucket**
**buckle to**
set to work in earnest
□ It shouldn't take us so long, if everyone buckles to.
**budding**
used to describe a person who is in the early stages of development
into whatever is specified
□ She is a budding architect.
**budge**
move, shift
□ I couldn't get it to budge.
**bug**
**1** (noun) a germ
□ I don't know where I picked up this bug. (i.e. caught this infection)
**2** (verb) (a) fix secret microphones in a room for spying
□ Do you think these rooms are bugged?
(b) (slang) irritate, annoy
□ Don't bug me.
**bull**
*take the bull by the horns*: meet or face a difficulty boldly/bravely;
when used of talking about problems to someone, often the opposite
of **beat about the bush**
for *red rag to a bull*, see **red**
**bump into**
literally, collide with; colloquially, used of meeting someone by
chance
□ I bumped into John in the market.
**bumper**
excellent, very profitable, successful
□ It was a bumper year for oranges.
□ The eastern area had a bumper crop.
**bumph**
(uncountable) used pejoratively of masses of printed material, files etc.
such as occur in publicity materials or in government offices
**bung***
**1** throw (rather vigorously)
□ Bung it over here!

**2** put

□ Bung it in the fridge.

**bunged up**

filled, blocked (used of one's head or nose when one is suffering from a cold and can't breathe properly)

**bunk**

**1** *do a bunk* : escape, run away without warning

**2** (uncountable) rubbish, nonsense; contrast with **3**

**3** (countable; not a colloquialism) one of two or three beds arranged above one another, as on trains or ships

**burble (on)**

talk indistinctly

□ What are you burbling (on) about now?

**burn a hole in someone's pocket**

see **hole**

**burn one's boats**

act on an irrecoverable decision; after which you might say you 'can't go back on it'

**burn one's fingers**

run into trouble through dealing in things that one does not understand, or through meddling in the affairs of others (often a financial loss is implied)

□ I've burned my fingers once through dabbling in stocks and shares; I'm not taking the risk a second time.

**burton**

see **go for a burton**

**bury one's head in the sand**

refuse to consider unpleasant facts or dangers; persistently associated with ostriches though this is ornithologically quite incorrect!

**bury the hatchet**

stop quarrelling

**business**

see **sticky business**

**bust** *(v)*

**1** (slang) break

□ 'Don't bust it.' 'It just bust(ed) in my hands.'

**2** (used after *go*) like **broke** but more used of a business than an individual (*Bankrupt* is the formal word.)

□ That new clothes shop has already gone bust. Modern fashions just don't sell here.

**butch**

(of a person, clothes etc.) appearing very masculine

**butt in**

interrupt in an unmannerly fashion

□ I wish you wouldn't butt in when your father and I are having a serious conversation.

butt *into* a conversation or discussion: butt *in with* a remark or a suggestion

□ We had just got to the most interesting part of the discussion when someone butted in with a frivolous remark.

**butter**

She looks as if *butter wouldn't melt in her mouth*. She looks quite innocent and we can hardly believe she has done any wrong.

see also **know which side one's bread is buttered** (on)

**butter-fingers**

one who frequently drops things

The word may be used with an indefinite article (*I've never come across such a butter-fingers before*), or vocatively, without the article (*Now then, butter-fingers, be careful with those plates*).

adjective: *butter-fingered*

**butterflies**

a nervous palpitation, or fluttering feeling in the stomach, caused by misgivings or stage fright just before one undertakes a task one is worried about

□ She was the last of the three candidates to be interviewed, and as the time drew near she got butterflies in her stomach.

**button up***

be quiet, say no more

**buttonhole**

After the meeting, I shall try *to buttonhole him*. I shall try to catch him and talk to him before he leaves.

**buy a pig in a poke***

buy an article with no opportunity to examine it and without a guarantee (*Poke* is an old word for 'sack'.)

**buzz off**

(usually only imperative) go away

**by a long chalk**

**by a long way**

by a large extent; by any means (used only in negative sentences, to suggest that more could be said)

□ That's not the whole of the story, by a long chalk. Wait till Helen tells you how he treated her!

□ Your work isn't finished yet, by a long way.

**by all means**

used to express ready consent

□ 'Could I keep that book you lent me a few days longer?' 'By all means.'

□ If you think the use of my name in connexion with your application will be of any help to you, by all means use it.

**by and by\***

presently, soon

□ Leave that task for the moment; we can attend to it by and by.

**by and large**

on the whole; generally speaking

□ By and large, the new measures announced by the Government are welcomed.

**by any manner of means**

colloquial variant of *by any means*: at all, in any way

□ That's not the last word on the subject, by any manner of means.

**by half**

*too clever by half*: much too clever (used sarcastically to imply that the person so described imagines himself to be smarter or cleverer than he is, and that his self-styled cleverness will one day lead him into trouble)

□ I've seen some of these bright ideas of Smith's before. He's too clever by half, is that young man; one of these days he'll come a cropper.

**by hook or by crook**

by one means or another (used to express determination)

□ I'll get the work finished this week by hook or by crook.

**by jove\***

a euphemism for *by God*, though now considered quite a mild exclamation

**by leaps and bounds**

very rapidly (The idiom is confined to contexts where the idea of making progress is expressed.)

□ He has progressed in his studies by leaps and bounds this term.

□ The economy of the country is improving by leaps and bounds.

**by the book**

see **go by the book**

**by the look of it**
> judging by appearances
> □ We are going to have some rain, by the look of it.
> □ By the look of it we shall not get that pay increase for another year at least.

**by the skin of one's teeth**
> see **skin**

**by your leave**
> *without so much as* (*a*) *'by your leave'*: without asking permission
> □ Without so much as 'by your leave' he helped himself to one of my cigarettes.

**bye-bye**
> a familiar form of *good-bye*

**bygones**
> see **let bygones be bygones**

# C

**caboodle**
> usually, *the whole caboodle*: all the equipment needed for a particular job (no plural use)

**cackle**
> see **cut the cackle**

**cadge**
> beg
> □ If you're going my way, could I cadge a lift in your car?
> often used in a depreciatory sense:
> □ That fellow's always cadging from other people.
> see also **scrounge**

**cadger**
> one who has the habit of cadging

**caff**
> a vulgarisation of *café*; often used humorously for a rather scruffy café

**caffuffle**
> a lot of talk or excitement (no plural use but used with *a*; also spelt *kerfuffle*)

**cagey**
> secretive; very reluctant to give information
> □ The Chairman was very cagey about what took place at the meeting.

**cake**

see **have one's cake and eat it**, **piece of cake** and **sell like hot cakes**

**call**

*call a spade a spade*: say precisely what one means; speak plainly
□ Mr Robinson prided himself on the fact that he always called a spade a spade, but Mrs Higgs thought he was too outspoken.
*have no call to* (*do something*): have no reason or justification for
□ He may not see eye to eye with me, but he's no call to insult me in that way.
*call it a day*: consider that one has done enough of whatever one is engaged on, and therefore decide to stop for the day
□ There's only another ten minutes to teatime, and this seems a convenient point to break off, so we might as well call it a day.
*call someone names*: call someone by rude, uncomplimentary or abusive names (really the same idiom as *call someone a fool, a rogue, a liar* etc. but without any particular name being specified)
It can be used (a) in a general sense, without any grammatical object being expressed (*It is rude to call names*), and (b) with a personal object (*Stop calling your brother names, You shouldn't call people names*).
In the passive voice it is the personal object of the active that becomes the subject (*I object to being called names*, not *to names being called me*).
*call off*: cancel (an appointment, or an event that has previously been arranged)
□ The meeting fixed for Monday next has now been called off.
see also **telephone**

**camp**

an adjective covering two meanings:
**1** Originally only heard in homosexual contexts, it is the opposite of **butch** and means very effeminate.
**2** It has subsequently developed a second use in theatre and film criticism to describe a performance (often deliberately exaggerated and mannered in style) which is so lacking in any subtlety that it is considered amusing.
There is rather an amusing phrase punning on the usual meaning of *camp*: *He's as camp as a row of tents.*

**can**

see **carry the can**

## cap

**1** (*cap* a story or anecdote) tell a better one

**2** complete or surpass (a series of events or occurrences) chiefly in the phrase *to cap it all*: to bring the situation to a climax

□ First the lights fused, next a water pipe burst, and then, to cap it all, part of the ceiling fell down.

## card

There are many idioms derived from playing cards.

Here are some very common ones.

**1** *it's on the cards that* . . .: it seems very probably that . . . (taken from fortune-telling with cards)

**2** *lay one's cards on the table*: don't conceal anything (especially in negotiations)

**3** *play one's cards carefully/well*: act cautiously/skilfully in a situation

**4** *hold one's cards near one's chest*: conceal one's plans/intentions

**5** *be given one's cards*: be dismissed from work (referring to the National Insurance card, union membership card etc. that are given to an employee on leaving; not playing cards, although they might be more fun if you were out of work)

## care

*I don't care what you say*: whatever you may say to the contrary (often used to express strong affirmation of the statement that follows)

□ I don't care what you say, you won't find a pleasanter spot than this.

*couldn't care less*: an expression that came into vogue about 1950 to express complete indifference

□ 'Do you realise the serious consequences that such conduct may have?' 'I couldn't care less.'

## carpet

see **on the carpet**

## carry-on *(n)*

a way of conducting one's affairs or business (generally used disparagingly or to indicate disapproval)

□ No check was ever made of the stock, no proper accounts were kept, and no-one seemed to know what his duties were; I never saw such a carry-on.

## carry on *(v)*

**1** conduct oneself or one's affairs

□ Any self-respecting person would not associate with people who carry on as they do.

□ If he carries on in that way for much longer he will find himself in the bankruptcy court.

When we speak of a man or a woman carrying on with one of the opposite sex, it implies unlawful sexual relations between them.

□ The defendant declared that during his six months' absence from home his wife had been carrying on with another man.

**2** speak angrily and at length

□ It was clear that something had upset him, from the way he was carrying on.

One can *carry on at* a person who has annoyed one; *carry on about* something or someone that is the subject of the angry outburst.

□ She carried on at me for being late.

□ They are always carrying on about the cost of living, but they go away for expensive holidays every year.

## carry the can

place oneself, or be placed, in a position where one may incur blame, censure or a penalty; act as a scapegoat for others

□ When the danger of the enterprise became obvious, one by one his confederates backed out, and left him to carry the can.

The can referred to is a tin containing explosives, used in blasting and quarrying.

## carryings-on

conduct (used only in the plural, and always in a derogatory sense)

□ I am not going to put up with his carryings-on much longer.

## cart

see **in the cart** and **put the cart before the horse**

## case

see **in case**

## cash in on

seize an opportunity presented by a situation or occurrence, and turn it to one's own advantage

□ Manufacturers of rainwear were not slow to cash in on the prediction of a wet summer.

□ South Vietnam Cashes in on Gold-Hoarding Craze. (headline in *The Times*, 2 Sept. 1966)

see also **spot** *(adj)*

## cat

*like a cat on hot bricks*: in a fidgety, nervous state; unable to keep still

□ He was up and down, here, there and everywhere, like a cat on hot bricks.

*Look what the cat's brought in!* a heavily sarcastic greeting to someone entering a room

*not room to swing a cat (in)*: very little room (used of rooms and apartments of various kinds, and always implying that the size is insufficient; here the *cat* may be the sort of whip, not the animal)

□ You are very lucky to have a spacious study like this; there's not room to swing a cat (in) in mine.

see also **curiosity killed the cat** and **let the cat out of the bag**

## cat-and-dog life

a life in which people are constantly bickering and quarrelling

□ They have led a cat-and-dog life almost since the day they were married.

## cat's whiskers

a thing or person that is particularly attractive, smart, pleasing etc.

□ She thinks Michael is the cat's whiskers.

## catch (n)

*a catch in it*: a concealed trick in an apparently generous or advantageous offer

□ If the goods are really what they are said to be, no firm could possibly afford to sell them at that price; there's a catch in it somewhere.

## catch (v)

*catch it*: be punished or severely reprimanded

□ You'll catch if it your father finds you trampling about on his flower beds.

*catch me doing that!* an emphatic form of denial, meaning, 'I don't intend doing that'; sometimes expanded to *You don't catch me doing that*, sometimes shortened to *catch me!*

see also **hop**

## catch on

become popular; be generally taken up and adopted

□ The new style in men's suits failed to catch on.

## catch someone out

force someone to admit the error in a story (usually by a question or statement which cannot be denied); taken from the game of cricket

□ He had almost convinced us that his tale was true, when a chance question from one of the company caught him out.

## catch 22

a dilemma, whereby you are the loser, whatever course you choose to take (originally American)

**ceiling**
　　see **hit the roof/ceiling**
**cert**
　　short for *certificate* (In slang, *cert* sometimes means certainty.)
　　see also **dead cert**
**chalk**
　　*as different as chalk from cheese*: entirely different
　　see also **by a long chalk**
**champion**
　　(especially North country) used colloquially as adjective or adverb to
　　express high commendation, satisfaction or approval
　　□ 'Is this all right? I've done the best I can.' 'That's champion. I
　　couldn't have done better myself.'
　　□ We're getting on champion.
**chance of a lifetime**
　　a chance such as is not likely to occur again during one's lifetime
　　□ It would be foolish to let such an opportunity slip; it's the chance of
　　a lifetime.
　　see also **dog's chance**, **give someone a chance**, **give someone
　　the chance** and **half a chance**
**change one's tune**
　　adopt a different attitude
　　□ At first he was very contemptuous of our offer, but when he realised
　　that he was not likely to get very far by this method he began to
　　change his tune.
　　This is very similar to **sing another tune**.
　　see also **get no change out of someone**
**chap**
　　man
　　□ Jim is a strange sort of chap.
　　□ Look at that poor old chap over there.
**char**
　　abbreviation of *charwoman*
**charge**
　　There are two similar sounding expressions with different meanings:
　　**1** *I'm in charge of Mark*. I'm looking after Mark.
　　**2** *I'm in the charge of Mark*. Mark is looking after me.
　　Of the two, the second is much less common.
**Charley***
　　(in the expression *a proper Charley*) a fool

□ He contradicted everything I said before the assembled company, and made me look a proper Charley.

originally applied to an incompetent, bungling soldier; perhaps an allusion to Brandon Thomas's popular farce *Charley's Aunt*

**chase**

in colloquial style used intransitively, with a phrase introduced by a preposition following it

□ The two youths went chasing down the road.

□ He came chasing after me as fast as his legs would carry him.

To speak of a man chasing after a woman, or vice versa, often implies pursuing (metaphorically) with amorous intention.

□ Bob's been chasing after Jenny for months.

**chat up**

talk to a person you don't know, hoping to get something from him/her (in particular, to get to know someone you are interested in sexually)

□ He's spent the whole evening chatting up that bird.

□ We've been chatting up a prospective buyer.

**cheap**

see **dirt cheap**; for *on the cheap*, see **on the** ( + adjective)

**check**

for *spot check*, see **spot** *(adj)*

**cheek** *(n)*

impudence

□ I'm not going to stand any more of your cheek.

*have a cheek*: be impudent; show impudence in one's behaviour or remarks

□ He has a cheek to expect you to help him, after all the unpleasant things he has said about you.

*I like your (his) cheek*: used ironically as a comment on a person's conduct, attitude or remarks, to express the idea that the speaker considers them impudent

hence the adjective *cheeky* (impudent), applied to a person (*a cheeky little boy*), his conduct (*a cheeky smile, a cheeky wink of the eye*), or a remark

see also **tongue**

**cheek** *(v)*

use impudent language to (someone)

□ You mustn't cheek your elders in that way.

□ If you're going to cheek me, I'll cheek you back.

**cheeky**
see **cheek** *(n)*

**cheer**
see **wotcher**

**cheesed off**
tired of (something) through having it repeatedly and to excess
□ We're all cheesed off with his jokes.
□ We've had rice pudding for dinner day in and day out, till I'm cheesed off with it.
for *as different as chalk from cheese*, see **chalk**

**chest**
see **get something off one's chest**

**chestnut**
an oft-told and well-worn joke; usually *an old chestnut*

**chew over**
discuss over and over again, at great length
□ They spent the best part of an hour chewing the matter over.

**chicken**
*She's no chicken.* She is far from being a young woman.
□ Mrs Baker may not be sixty yet, but she's no chicken.

**chicken-feed**
something (usually a sum of money) that is worth very little to one
□ Some people would be pleased to receive a hundred pounds, but to a person of his wealth it's mere chicken-feed.

**chief**
see **boss**

**child's play**
*That will be child's play.* That will be very easy to do.

**chinwag**
a conversation, especially a friendly chat
□ Drop in and have a chinwag sometime, Anne.

**chip in**
**1** interrupt a speech or conversation in an impolite or unmannerly fashion
□ I wish you wouldn't keep chipping in with frivolous remarks.
*chip into* a conversation
**2** contribute (money), as in a **whip-round**
□ Everyone chipped in 50p, and Steve went and bought some wine.

**chip off the old block**
a child who resembles its father in character or some particular

attribute of character (used only after the verb *to be*: *he is/was a chip off the old block*)

**chip on one's shoulder**

a grievance or grudge that one cannot forget

☐ His experiences of those years of hardship left him with a chip on his shoulder.

see also **have had one's chips**

**chock-a-block**

packed full

☐ These drawers are all chock-a-block. We must get a new filing cabinet.

**choice**

see **Hobson's choice**

**choosy**

inclined to be very selective and particular (There is usually a slight sense of deprecation about the word.)

☐ He is very choosy about the wines he drinks.

☐ They are very choosy about whom they admit to that club.

**chop and change**

change repeatedly (with an object either expressed or implied)

☐ He never stays in one job for very long; he is always chopping and changing.

☐ If you chop and change jobs like this, you'll never get experience in any of them.

**chortle**

laugh triumphantly; a word invented by Lewis Carroll (who wrote the 'Alice' books) made up of *snort* and *chuckle*

**christen**

in standard usage, to give a child a name in a Christian baptism; colloquially, merely to bestow a name or nickname on a person or thing

☐ His friends christened him the Demon, because of the daring things he did.

☐ They christened the speedboat Lightning.

**chronic**

used of anything or anyone who is hopelessly bad (it is not colloquial when it is used of medical cases)

☐ He's always late. He's a chronic timekeeper.

**chrysanth**

short for *chrysanthemum*

**chuck**
 throw
 □ If that cigarette packet is empty, chuck it in the fire.
 *chuck it* : cease whatever one is doing
 □ If you don't chuck it, I'll call the police.
 □ I'm fed up with this job; I think I shall chuck it.
 *chuck out* : throw out; expel
 □ Two youths were chucked out of the hall for rowdyism.
 Hence *a chucker-out* is one engaged to chuck out rowdy or ill-behaved
 people from a meeting, a building etc.
 *chuck up* : throw up; give up (a job)
 *chuck one's hand in* : a slangier version of **throw one's hand in**
**chuffed**
 very pleased or satisfied
 □ My word, you look chuffed—what's happened?
**chum***
 **1** a very close friend (mainly used by older people)
 □ They have been chums since they were only a few years old.
 **2** a familiar mode of address, used by the less educated, by one man to
 another (even to a stranger)
 □ Can you tell us the time, chum?
**chump**
 a stupid or foolish person (less offensive than *fool*)
 □ That's not the way to do it, you chump.
 *off one's chump* : slang for 'off one's head', i.e. crazy
**churn out**
 produce a lot of (work) seemingly without much effort
 □ They churn these toys out at a great rate and sell them all over the
 world.
 □ He has churned out lots of articles on Medieval English.
**cissy***
 an effeminate man or youth
**clamp down**
 try to restrict something or prevent it; put pressure on it to put an
 end to it
 □ The Government should clamp down on tax evasion.
**clanger**
 see **drop a clanger**
**clap-trap**
 (uncountable) empty or nonsensical talk

☐ I'm not going to waste my time listening to such clap-trap.

**clean sweep**

see **make a clean sweep** and **come clean**

**clear as mud**

not at all easily understood

☐ His explanation was as clear as mud.

**clear off**

go away

☐ The unruly youths soon cleared off when they saw the policeman coming.

☐ Now then, clear off, before I set the dog on you.

The imperative can be strengthened by the addition of *with you*\*.

☐ Now then, clear off with you.

**cleft stick**

*in a cleft stick*: in a situation where you can move neither forward nor back

**clever dick**\*

the same as **smart alec**

for *too clever by half*, see **by half**

**cliff-hanger**

a prolonged tense situation

☐ Will they go on strike or not? It's becoming a real cliff-hanger.

**clink**

prison

see also **quod**

**clobber**

**1** (uncountable) a person's belongings, clothes etc.

☐ You can dump your clobber in this corner for the time being.

**2** (verb) hit

☐ Who just clobbered me on the head?

**clock-watcher**

an employee who will not work a minute over time, and is always watching the clock and waiting impatiently for the moment when work finishes; hence also *clock-watching*

see also **put the clock back**

**clog up**

*be/get clogged up* has nothing to do with Dutch clogs but means 'be(come) blocked or congested'

☐ I can hardly breathe with this wretched cold—my nose is all clogged up.

☐ The streets were clogged up with traffic.

**close shave**

a narrow escape

☐ I just managed to jump out of the way of the car, but it was a pretty close shave.

**clot**

a fool; a stupid fellow (*Clot* usually suggests 'thick-headedness' or lack of intelligence, whereas **chump** more often refers to one who acts foolishly on a particular occasion.)

**clouds**

*be in the clouds*: not pay attention to people or events round you
for *have one's head in the clouds*, see **head**

**clout**

beat or strike with the hand, usually by way of chastisement; also as a noun *give one a clout*

☐ Joe clouted Frank, so Frank gave me a clout too.

**clover**

see **in clover**

**clue**

*not have a clue*: be completely ignorant; not have the faintest idea

☐ I spent about half an hour showing him how to do it, but at the end of it all he still hadn't a clue.

☐ I must soon think of something to say in my speech after tomorrow's dinner. So far I haven't a clue.

**clueless**

silly, stupid

**clutter**

**1** (uncountable) things in disorder

☐ Whose is all this clutter in the passage?

**2** (countable) disordered state

☐ All the files were in a clutter on the desk.

**3** (verb) cause a blockage with disordered things

☐ Whose are these papers cluttering the desk?

**coach**

see **slowcoach**

**cock and bull story**

a long, complicated but ridiculous story

**cock-eyed**

(literally, squinting) colloquially

(a) crooked or askew (*You've hung the pictures all cock-eyed*),

(b) stupidly irregular (*a cock-eyed way of doing things*),

(c) inaccurate ( *You've got your statistics all cock-eyed.*)

## cock-sure

convinced that one is right; unwilling to admit that one can be in the wrong

□ He's so cock-sure that it's no good arguing with him; you'll never convince him of anything he doesn't wish to believe.

## cocked hat

see **knock into a cocked hat**

## cocky

conceited; boastful

□ You needn't be so cocky about your achievements.

## codger

see **old codger**

## codswallop

*a load/lot of codswallop*: a lot of nonsense

## co-ed

short for *co-education(al)*: both sexes together

## cold

*out in the cold*: socially isolated from, or ignored by, others (often used with *left*)

□ Come and join the rest of us, and be sociable; don't sit out in the cold.

□ With none of the company paying much attention to her, she felt left out in the cold.

## cold blood

*do something in cold blood*: do something cruel or harsh without pity or emotion

□ He sacked Jenny in a fit of temper; he'd never have done it in cold blood.

## cold feet

*have/get cold feet*: be/become afraid, and so be deterred from taking action

□ The politician was ready enough with threats, but when it came to the point of carrying them out he got cold feet.

## cold shoulder

*give someone the cold shoulder*: become unfriendly and even ignore someone

## collar *(n)*

see **hot under the collar**

**collar** *(v)*

    lay hold of; grab; seize

    ☐ The thief was collared by the police as he was leaving the building.

    usually used of people, but can also be applied to inanimate things,
    when it may mean merely 'take' rather than 'seize' or 'grab'

    ☐ Do you realise you've collared my umbrella?

**colour**

    see **off colour**

**come**

    **1** used as a term of deprecation

    ☐ Come now. You surely know whether you spoke to her or not.

    **2** used as a term of persuasion or encouragement

    ☐ Come, dry your tears.

    **3** used as the equivalent of a clause of time relating to the future

    ☐ I shall have been with the firm thirty years, come Christmas. (i.e.
    when next Christmas comes)

    see also **come (someone)** and **come (something)**

**come a cropper***

    **1** sustain a fall (originally from a horse; later from anything on which
    one is mounted or perched some height from the ground)

    ☐ Be careful; if that bough breaks you'll come a cropper.

    **2** (metaphorically) suffer a reverse or setback which has serious
    consequences for one

    ☐ So far he has been lucky in all his speculative ventures, but one of
    these days he will go too far and come a cropper.

**come again**

    a colloquial way of asking someone to repeat what has been said

**come along**

    used as an imperative to express encouragement or persuasion

    ☐ Come along, now, cheer up; things are not as bad as they seem.

**come clean**

    reveal all the facts or information, withholding nothing

    ☐ All the time he refuses to come clean over that deal, there is little we
    can do to help him.

    often used of a suspected person revealing (or refusing to reveal) the
    full facts about his part in the crime with which he is charged

**come-down**

    a humiliation, a fall from a better position

**come down on someone like a ton of bricks**

    attack verbally, suddenly and harshly

## come home with the milk

come home in the early hours of the morning, after a late night out

□ What's the matter with Paul this morning? He looks as though he came home with the milk.

## come in (for)

**1** receive

□ She will probably come in for a considerable fortune when her uncle dies.

**2** be subjected to

□ The manager came in for criticism at the last meeting.

**3** prove to be of use for whatever or whoever is stated

□ Those old dusters may come in for polishing the car.

□ She always saved any garments that the elder child had outgrown, in the hope that they might come in for the younger one.

We also often say . . . *might come in handy/useful for* . . .

## come off

**1** (of plans etc.) be successful

□ If this method doesn't come off, we shall have to think of another way.

□ The trick they had planned to play on their parents didn't come off.

**2** take place

□ When does the Old Students' dinner come off?

## come off it

**1** stop boasting, pretending, or trying to deceive people

□ Now, come off it, Harry; we've heard that tale before.

**2** stop whatever one is doing (a mild form of reprimand)

□ Now, you boys, come off it; haven't I told you you're not to tease the dog?

## come off with

emerge from an accident, ordeal, test, competition etc. with

□ Luckily I came off with just a few bruises; others were not so fortunate.

## come on

used colloquially in the imperative for the following two purposes:

**1** to persuade, cajole or encourage a person

□ Come on, lend me a fiver till Wednesday.

□ Come on, you can do it if you try.

**2** to call a person to attention

□ Come on, don't sit there dreaming.

## come out in the wash
see **wash** *(n)*

## come over
take possession of (used of impulses, desires etc. which cause a person to act or behave in a particular way)

□ Your father seems to be pretty generous with his money these days. What's come over him?

sometimes also used of inanimate things that seem to behave in an unusual way

□ A burst of spring in late October, and now snow in May. I don't know what's come over the English weather.

The question *What's come over you?* when someone does or says something surprising, is commonly used.

## come (someone)
act as though one were, or in a manner characteristic of

□ He came the heavy father with me when I told him I wanted to get married.

□ Don't come the schoolmaster with me!

## come (something)
indulge in whatever is specified (always with disapproval)

□ Don't come those tricks with me!

□ I know better than to come high and mighty with Ed.

## come to a sticky end
## come to grief
meet disaster; end in ruin

## come to that
an ellipsis of *if it comes to that*, used as an addition to, and a modification of, a previous statement

□ I was not very well off at that time. Come to that, not many of us were.

## come to think of it
see **think**

## come unstuck
(of a scheme, plan etc.) go wrong; fail to work out as expected

□ The conspirators never realised their aim of seizing power, for their carefully prepared plans came unstuck.

## comfortably off
having plenty of money (usually used after the verb *to be*)

## comfy
frequently used in conversation for *comfortable*

## coming

*not know whether one is coming or going*: be in a state of mental confusion
□ For the last hour I have been so badgered with inquiries on one thing and another that I don't know whether I'm coming or going.
see also **up and coming**

## coming to

heading for, as in *I don't know what things are coming to*, said to show disapproval of a situation or of current developments; similarly
□ There used not to be all this violence and juvenile delinquency. I don't know what the country's coming to.
□ It makes you wonder what we're coming to, when people can indulge in all sorts of dishonest practices and get away with them.

## commie

communist, used as noun or adjective

## common or garden*

a facetious variant of the simple word *common* (meaning 'no more than usual, normal, not special') made up on the analogy of *the common or garden butterfly*; not much used nowadays, but something of a vogue expression about forty years ago
□ I'm only a common or garden salesman, I haven't got a fancy title.

## con someone

trick someone, possibly from a *confidence trick*
□ You'll be conned if you don't watch out.
also as a noun:
□ Don't you think it's all a con?

## conchie

an abbreviated form of *conscientious objector*, usually used contemptuously; sometimes spelt *conchy* (Obviously, this is not often heard in spoken English now.)

## confab

(stress on the first syllable) an abbreviation of *confabulation*
□ Mrs Brown and her neighbour are having a confab over the garden wall.
There is usually a suggestion of sarcasm.

## confound*

a euphemism for *damn* (verb only) now not often heard
□ Stop that confounded noise!

## conk out

go wrong, stop working

□ That photocopier has conked out again.

also used of people when they faint or die, but this is closer to slang

**conker**

a horse chestnut

There is a schoolboy game of *conkers*, in which each of two contestants has a horse chestnut with a hole bored through the middle and a piece of string threaded through it. Each in turn holds up his conker suspended by the string, while the other strikes it with his, with the object of smashing it. Thus the winner has a *conqueror*—which seems to have been shortened to *conker*.

**cons**

see **mod cons**

**considering**

sometimes used in colloquial English with the grammatical object omitted, and left to be understood from the context or situation

□ You've done pretty well, considering. (i.e. considering your age, your inexperience, your lack of practice, as the case may be)

**content**

see **heart**

**contraption**

a humorous word for a machine or gadget

**contre-temps**

see **word(s) 2**

**cook**

falsify (*cook statistics, cook the evidence, cook the accounts*)

**cook up**

make up; concoct (*cook up a story, an excuse*)

**cooking**

*What's cooking?* What is happening (next)? (not just used of food)

**cool**

**1** used (usually by young people) as a term of approval

**2** (of people) confident; impressive

*He'll leave you to cool your heels* and *he'll let you cool your heels* both mean 'he'll make you wait'.

**co-op**

short for *co-operative stores/society*

**cop**

catch, in the sense of 'find one doing something that one shouldn't'

□ If I cop you stealing my apples again, I'll give you a good hiding.

□ The thief was copped with the goods as he left the shop.

hence the slang word *copper*, for a policeman, which in its turn becomes abbreviated to *cop* (*a speed-cop*: a policeman whose duty it is to check excessive speeding by motorists)

**cop it**

catch it, in the sense of 'be punished or severely reprimanded'

□ You'll cop it if the farmer finds you trespassing on his land.

**cope**

In standard usage the idiom is *cope with* (a situation, a difficulty etc.); in colloquial English a new idiom has appeared with the use of *cope* as an intransitive verb without the *with*-adjunct.

□ The task looks a formidable one, but I think we can cope.

□ In whatever situation he found himself, he always feared he wouldn't be able to cope.

A commonly heard reply to *How are you getting on?* is *Coping!*

**copper**

slang for *policeman*

see **cop**

**corner**

see **tight corner**

**corny**

(of a joke, story etc.) hackneyed; well known, and therefore falling rather flat

**corporation**

often used for a large belly on a man

**cotton on to**

follow, understand

□ I just can't cotton on to what he's saying.

**cough up**

**1** (intransitive) pay up

□ The young man spent quite recklessly, for he knew that rather than let him get into debt his father would cough up.

**2** (transitive) give up (goods, property etc.)

□ We know the stolen watch is in your possession, so you may as well cough it up.

**couldn't care less**

see **care**

**country**

see **line of country**

**couple**

in normal usage applied to two people or two things thought of in association with each other (*a married couple, a couple of card-sharpers*); colloquially used as synonymous with *two*, without the idea of very close association: *a couple of minutes, a couple of days' time, a couple of schoolgirls, a couple of envelopes*

**court**

*The ball is in your court now.* It's for you to take the initiative now, it's up to you (see **up to 3**). This expression is taken from tennis.

**cover up**

As a verb, this means 'hide'. As a noun (*cover-up*) it is used of criminals covering up their activities, and also of any deception.
☐ His smile was a cover-up; he was really very angry.

**cows**

see **till the cows come home**

**crack** *(adj)*

top quality
☐ We sent a crack team to India.

**crack** *(n)*

for *have a crack at*, see **shot**

**crack up**

**1** (intransitive) break down in health
☐ If you go on working at that rate, you'll crack up before long.
☐ Old Mr Simpson does not look at all well these days; I'm afraid he's cracking up.
**2** (transitive) praise very highly
☐ I didn't think much of the novel, though at the time of its publication it was cracked up by several reviewers.
☐ Skiing holidays aren't all they're cracked up to be.

**cracked***

stupid, crazy

**crackers**

(adjective) mad, crazy
☐ Don't take any notice of what he says; he's crackers.
☐ If I have to put up with those mischievous children much longer, they'll drive me crackers.

**cracking**

see **get cracking**

**crackpot***

a foolish person
☐ I've never come across such a crackpot as that fellow is.
☐ That's not the way to do it, you crackpot.

**crank**
  **1** an eccentric, an individualist
  **2** someone obsessively keen on the thing specified, especially *a health crank*
  also, an adjective: *cranky*

**crap**
  (uncountable) Although this strictly means 'excreta', it is used very commonly for 'rubbish, nonsense'.

**crashing***
  usually in the phrase *a crashing bore*: something or someone intensely boring

**create**
  make a fuss, get agitated and bothered
  □ Now, don't create before I've had a chance to explain.

**creek**
  see **up the creek**

**creep**
  an obsequious person; one who flatters those from whom he hopes to gain something

**creeps**
  *give someone the creeps*: cause someone to feel a nervous nausea or horror
  □ Don't keep making those horrible noises; it gives me the creeps to hear you.
  similarly *get the creeps*
  □ I stayed listening to all the strange noises in that deserted house until I began to get the creeps.

**creepy**
  frightening, especially used of the supernatural

**creepy-crawly**
  This is a compound adjective applied to those things which creep and crawl; a feeling of repugnance is usually implied. *Creepy-crawly* insects are sometimes called *creepy-crawlies*.

**crest-fallen**
  depressed, disappointed
  □ You look a bit crest-fallen, what's up?

**crib**
  copy, and pass off as one's own work
  □ When questioned, the schoolboy admitted that he had cribbed his homework.

*From* may be added to indicate the source: *from another boy in the form, from an old exercise book he had found lying about*. Though, as a verb, *crib* is colloquial, the noun *crib* (a translation, usually of a classical text, to assist students to understand the original) is accepted standard English.

### cricket
*It isn't cricket*. It is not a fair way of doing things; it is against the accepted rules or code. (This is now rarely used except humorously or facetiously by those laughing at the old-fashioned equation of cricket with rules for living.)

□ You shouldn't take advantage of another's ignorance or simplicity; it isn't cricket.

### crikey!
an exclamation to express surprise (perhaps a euphemism to avoid using the name of Christ profanely)

□ Crikey! That's a big fish you've caught.

### crock
see **old crock**

### crocodile
a long line of schoolchildren walking in pairs, one pair behind another

### crocodile tears
grief that is not sincere (According to an old belief, the crocodile makes a sound like weeping while it is eating its victims.)

### crony
a very close friend, of long standing

□ Every year, on his birthday, Dr Easton gave a dinner party for a few of his cronies.

### crop up
appear or arise unexpectedly

□ No sooner had we overcome one difficulty than another cropped up.

□ The committee may be recalled before the appointed date if any urgent business crops up.

### cropper
see **come a cropper**

### cross purposes
(of two people or groups) *be/talk at cross purposes*: misunderstanding the aims of the other, or having different ideas or plans for something

### cross words
*have cross words (with someone)*: argue (with someone)

This is usually in the plural and both words are stressed. In a
*crossword* (*puzzle*) only *cross* is stressed.

## crotchety

bad tempered; taking offence, or becoming annoyed, at the slightest
thing

□ My uncle became very crotchety in his old age.

## crude

often used to mean 'vulgar' because of sexual implications

□ They're fond of telling crude jokes.

Remember uncooked food in English is called 'raw food'.

## crummy

of poor quality

□ What a crummy meal!

## crunch

the final moment of decision/crisis

□ When the crunch comes, it'll be the unemployed who'll suffer.

## crush

a tightly packed crowd of people

□ I don't know how we're going to make our way through this crush.

*have a crush on someone*: be infatuated with whoever is mentioned

□ Your friend Jack Turner seems to have a crush on Susan Tomkins.

used especially of a schoolgirl who becomes infatuated with one of her
teachers, and usually when there is no reciprocation of the feeling

## crust

see **upper crust**

## cry-baby

see **baby**

## cry off

withdraw from an undertaking or arrangement

□ Three of those who promised us their support have since cried off.

## cry one's eyes out

weep bitterly

□ A small girl came running down the street, crying her eyes out
because she had lost her mother.

NOTE 'cry one's *eyes* out', but 'weep, or sob, one's *heart* out'

## cuckoo*

(adjective; only used after verbs) crazy

□ His grandma's a bit cuckoo.

## cuff

see **off the cuff**

## cup of tea

*one's cup of tea*: the kind of thing one likes, or is interested in

□ Sitting in a deck chair on a crowded beach hour after hour is all right for those who care for it, but it's not my cup of tea.

□ See what you can make of this problem, John; it's just your cup of tea.

## cupboard

see **skeleton in the cupboard**

## cuppa

a cup of tea

□ Care for a cuppa?

## curate's egg*

This is an oblique reference to an old joke about a curate (who helps a priest in the parish) who was offered a boiled egg to eat. On opening it, he found it was bad but decided he must eat it. Anxious not to offend his host when he was asked if it was all right, he answered, 'Parts of it are excellent!' Thus in reply to an enquiry such as 'What was the play like?' 'How was your holiday?' you may hear *Like the curate's egg, (good in parts)*.

## curiosity killed the cat

said by way of deprecation to someone who is very inquisitive

## cushy job

an easy job, which is well paid but does not require much exertion

□ He's got a cushy job; I wouldn't mind having it myself.

The word *cushy* comes from Hindi and originally meant 'happy'.

## cuss*

**1** curse; found chiefly in the expression *a tinker's cuss* (*I don't give a tinker's cuss*: I don't care) It is probably felt to be something of a euphemism.

**2** person (*an awkward cuss*, *an odd old cuss*) used more often of men than of women

This is probably an abbreviation of **customer** used in the same sense (see below), though it may be a euphemistic substitution of *cuss* in the sense of *curse* (see **1** above) for some profane word, in order to avoid using the curse-word itself, and *customer* may then, in its turn, be a further substitution for that.

## cussedness*

perversity; a desire to be 'awkward'

□ Whatever proposal you make, he will always object to it, just from sheer cussedness.

**customer\***

person: *a sly customer*, *an awkward customer*, *a strange customer*
see **cuss** and **slippery customer**

**cut** *(n)*

a share in the profits, especially of something illegal
□ After they had paid the night watchman his cut for 'forgetting' to lock the factory, there wasn't that much money to go round.
*a cut above others*: socially superior to others
□ She always considered herself a cut above her neighbours.
*a short cut*: a short way, which cuts out some of the distance of the recognised or normal way
□ If you take the short cut across the fields, you can get there in ten minutes or a little more.
□ There is no short cut to learning.
also a verb: *to short-cut a problem*

**cut** *(v)*

**1** absent oneself from some function or event that one ought to attend
□ She cut the lecture on the Second World War as she'd read three books on the subject.
**2** deliberately ignore or refuse to recognise a person on meeting him (a stronger form is *cut one dead*)
□ His old-fashioned politeness had none of the ease of the present day, which permits you, if you have a mind, to cut the person you have associated with for a week. (Scott, *The Antiquary*)
for *cut to the quick*, see **quick**

**cut across**

**1** take a short cut across
□ We cut across the fields.
**2** go contrary to and so interfere with
□ I do not wish to press my suggestion if it would cut across anything you have in mind.
□ He'll oppose anything that cuts across his own interests.

**cut and dried**

ready prepared, leaving no room for question or modification
□ He had got the proposals all cut and dried, and was most annoyed when we wanted to discuss them.
□ Everything in the office had to be done according to a cut-and-dried system.

**cut and run**

cease abruptly whatever one is doing, and run away precipitately

☐ For several minutes those boys stood there teasing the old gentleman, but as soon as they saw the policeman approaching, they cut and ran.

## cut both ways

produce two effects, one opposed to the other

☐ That argument cuts both ways: if it justifies your breaking promises given to other people, it also justifies their breaking promises given to you.

## cut it fine

leave a very narrow margin of time

☐ We've got seven minutes to get to the station. We might just manage it, but we're cutting it rather fine.

## cut no ice

be ineffective

☐ That argument will cut no ice; you'd better think of a better one.

*With* is used to indicate the person or the body on whom the thing in question will have no effect:

☐ That argument will cut no ice (*or* won't cut any ice) with me.

## cut off

**1** *be/feel cut off*: be isolated, not in touch with friends etc.

☐ Their house in Spain is completely cut off—there isn't even a road!

**2** *I was cut off* (while on the telephone). Our conversation was interrupted and stopped.

## cut off one's nose to spite one's face

This means to bring harm upon, or create difficulties for, oneself by attempting to harm others. A typical example might be that of a person who discharges an employee for some petty fault, even though he knows he will not be able to get anyone else who does the work so efficiently.

## cut out

**1** omit

☐ If time is running short we shall have to cut out the last item on the programme.

☐ Just call me by my surname; cut out the Mr.

**2** *have one's work cut out*: have difficulty in performing a task

☐ We shall have our work cut out to get the job finished by the week-end.

similarly, in the passive:

☐ Our work will be cut out if we are going to finish this job today.

**3** *cut it out*: stop doing that (usually only imperative)

## cut out (for)

suited for, by ability, inclination, temperament etc.

□ It is hardly surprising that after a few years he resigned his living in the Church of England to take up a lay occupation. He was not cut out to be a clergyman.

## cut someone down to size

make a person who has an exaggerated idea of his own importance realise his real position

□ Jackson seems to be adopting a high and mighty attitude these days. It's time someone cut him down to size.

## cut the cackle

stop all the irrelevant or superfluous talk, and get to the point you want to make

## cut the ground from under someone's feet

act in such a way (often unwittingly) as to prevent a person from doing what he had intended

□ I think I could have put in a word that would have got you that post, but now, by your talk of emigrating in the near future, you have cut the ground from under my feet.

## cut up

grieved (only used in the passive)

□ He was very cut up by the death of his son.

## cut up rough

become angry or threatening

□ I hope he'll be amenable to reason, but if he cuts up rough I'll threaten him with legal action, and let's see what effect that will have.

# d

## dab hand

one who is skilful in some particular direction or at some kind of work (followed by *at*, to indicate the direction or work)

□ He is a dab hand at repairing furniture.

## dabble in

have some (small-scale) dealings in

*Do you dabble in shares?* Do you buy and sell shares a little? Are you at all interested in the stock market?

**dad(dy)**
father
*Daddy* is usually used by young children, *dad* is used by people of any age in talking direct to their father, while *father* is more used when talking about him to other people, especially outside the family.

**daft**
stupid, silly
□ She must be daft to act in that way.
□ I never heard of such a daft idea before.
also used adverbially:
□ Don't talk so daft.

**damn**
a mild swear word
*He doesn't give/care a damn.* He is indifferent to what people say or think of him.

**damned***
*I'll be damned if*: followed by a positive statement, to express a strong negative asseveration or vice versa
□ I'll be damned if I'll do it.
□ I'll be damned if it isn't snowing.
*Well, I'll be damned!* an exclamation expressive of surprise, annoyance or indignation
□ Well, I'll be damned, my watch has stopped again.
*Well, I'm damned* is also used in the same sense.
All these expressions are a bit dated.

**damp squib***
an anecdote, a joke etc. that fails to evoke much response; a scheme that peters out without achieving anything
□ The story which he thought would rouse the company to laughter or applause proved a damp squib.

**dark horse**
see **horse**

**darn**
a euphemism for **damn**
□ We've missed the bus, darn it.
similarly *darned* for *damned*:
□ The darned thing won't start.

**dart/dash**
both used as verbs with words like *into/out/up/down* for rapid movement

☐ She darted across the road.

☐ He dashed into the garden.

**dash\***

This is one of the many euphemisms for **damn**. The adjective *dashed* for *damned* is heard. This use originated in the days when it was considered indelicate to print swear words. In place of *damn it*, the reader saw — *it*. Such a line is called a *dash* and so this word was read for the mark.

**date**

see **have a date**

**day**

*day in, day out*: continuously, one day after another (cf. *year in, year out*)

☐ It rained the whole of last week, day in, day out.

*have one's day*: enjoy a period of popularity and then fall into neglect or oblivion (Hence *it has had its day* often means 'it is out of date' or 'people are no longer interested in it'.)

☐ Some people would have us believe that religion has had its day.

*late in the day*: at a late stage in the development of events, schemes, arrangements etc.

☐ It is rather late in the day to raise objections, now that the plans are all drawn up.

☐ I wish we had never committed ourselves to the proposals, but it's too late in the day to withdraw now.

*off day*: a day when one feels 'off' (not very well)

☐ She has her on days and her off days, and today is one of her off days.

*a day off*: a day free, off duty; similarly a *morning*, *week*, *evening* etc. *off*

*one of these days*: some day (unspecified) in the future

☐ One of these days you'll be sorry for what you have done.

*the other day*: a few days ago

☐ It was only the other day that I saw him.

*these days*: the present time

☐ Not many men wear top hats these days.

*in those days*: at that time (Notice the use of the preposition here, but that none is used with *these days*.)

*in this day and age* (cliché): at the present time (Usually the reference is to characteristics associated with the time.)

☐ It is incredible that some people should still believe in witchcraft in this day and age.

*That'll be the day!* used when something very desirable is suggested, but which is likely never to happen
□ 'I'll clean the car soon.' 'That'll be the day!'
for *call it a day*, see **call**

**daylight robbery**
literally, in standard usage, a robbery committed in daylight; figuratively and colloquially, an exorbitant price asked or charged for something
□ Fancy their asking £15,000 for a small house like that! It's daylight robbery.
see also **knock the daylights out of**

**dead beat**
completely exhausted (NOTE *beat*, not *beaten*)
□ I can't go any farther. I'm dead beat.

**dead cert**
abbreviation of *dead certainty*, something about which there can be no doubt
□ You can't fail to make money if you use this method; it's a dead cert.

**dead duck**
see **duck**

**dead easy**
very easy
□ 'What was your examination paper like?' 'It was dead easy.'

**dead from the neck up**
having no intelligence
□ Try as you like, you'll never teach that boy anything; he's dead from the neck up.

**dead heat**
The phrase *it's a dead heat* is used when two competitors in a race both qualify for first place. Do not confuse this with the use, also in athletics, of *heat* to mean an elimination or trial race.

**dead loss**
*It's a dead loss* suggests it is no good trying any more, we must give up. *He's a dead loss* similarly means he is no good, we can't rely on him.

**dead-pan face/expression**
a face showing no feelings

**dead set**
**1** *dead set on something*: having a strong desire for whatever is specified

□ He is dead set on becoming a chemist.

**2** *make a dead set at* : (a) make a persistent and resolute attempt to attract

□ Jill's husband made a dead set at that blonde girl.

(b) make a resolute attack on

□ Throughout the debate the Opposition parties made a dead set at the Government.

## dead to the world

fast asleep

□ I found him stretched out on the bed, dead to the world.

## deaf as a post

see **as deaf as a post**

## dear life

see **for dear life**

## dear me

see **oh dear (me)!**

## death

*you/they/he* etc. *will be the death of me* : an overstatement used to express disapproval of, or annoyance at, someone's conduct or behaviour

□ You really must show more sense of responsibility. If you go on in this way, you'll be the death of me.

NOTE *the death of me* not *my death*

see **feel like 4**

## debunk

lower in esteem ; expose the hollow pretensions of (persons, organisations, institutions etc.)

□ In the few years immediately following the First World War, a number of biographies were published which tried to debunk some of the famous figures of the past.

## decent

**1** a vague term of praise or approval

□ She's a decent sort.

□ At last Pat's found a decent job.

**2** fairly large (for size, quantity or amount), or fairly long (for distance or length of time)

□ Steve gets a decent salary.

□ They have a decent-sized house.

**3** pleasant, considerate, generous (usually when used predicatively)*

□ When the headmaster realised that the whole affair had been due to a misunderstanding, he was quite decent about it.

□ It is very decent of your aunt to offer us the use of her tennis court.

**deep end**

see **go off the deep end** and **throw someone in at the deep end**

**dekko***

a look (from a Hindi word)

□ Let's have a dekko at your photos.

**deliver the goods**

fulfil one's promises; perform whatever one undertakes to do

**demo**

a demonstration by students, protestors etc.

NOTE This is not called a *manifestation* in English.

**demon***

**1** a person inordinately addicted to whatever is specified

□ Mr Willis is a demon for work.

**2** a mischievous child (often with the adjective *young* in front)

□ That child has been a demon ever since I have known him.

□ What are you up to now, you young demon?

**dense**

thick-headed, stupid

□ He's so dense that you'll never teach him anything.

**depend**

*it (all) depends*: in standard usage normally followed by *on*, but in colloquial idiom, when a clause follows, the *on* is often omitted (*It all depends what you mean, It depends whether the weather is fine or not*), but it is not correct to say *It depends the weather*

**depth**

see **out of one's depth**

**deuce***

a euphemism for *devil* (not usually used where *devil* would be a subject)

**devastating**

often used colloquially to mean 'extremely effective'

**devil***

**1** used as an intensive or emphatic expression after interrogative words like *what?*, *where?*, *how?*, *when?*, *why?* always preceded by the definite article

□ How the devil did that cat get into the house?

□ I don't know when the devil we're going to get this work done.

Nowadays *the hell* is much commoner.

**2** one who treats others harshly or makes excessive demands upon them
☐ He's pleasant enough socially, but he's a devil to those that work for him.

**3** one who is inordinately addicted to whatever is specified (followed by *for*)
☐ I have never known such a devil for work as you are.

**4** Preceded by an adjective, it is used to express a strong feeling about a person. The feeling may be, and usually is, one of annoyance or dislike (*old devil, little devil, young devil*) or it may be pity or sympathy (*poor devil*). *A little devil* and *a young devil* usually mean 'a mischievous child'.
☐ The old devil refused to pay me.
☐ When I told him off, the little devil merely grinned.
*Poor devil* can be appended to a sentence as a kind of comment on it.
☐ He's had more than his share of troubles, poor devil.

**5** *A devil of a* + noun is used to express a strong feeling of annoyance, dislike, disapproval etc. Sometimes *the devil of* is used instead of *a devil of*.
☐ That electric drill makes a devil of a noise.
☐ We had the devil of a job to get the car going.
*A hell of a* is commoner nowadays (see **hell**)

**6** *between the devil and the deep blue sea*: in a dilemma
see also **talk of the devil and he's sure to appear**

**dicey**
rather uncertain, unpredictable, unstable
☐ Look out, that ladder's a bit dicey.

**dickens***
a euphemism for *devil*, expressing surprise or anger quite unobjectionably
☐ What the dickens are you doing here?

**dicky**
mostly heard in the phrase *have a dicky heart*: weak, not healthy

**diddle**
cheat (The expressions are *diddle a person* and *diddle him out of something*.)
☐ You want to keep an eye on that fellow; he'll diddle you if he gets the chance.
☐ The bus conductor tried to diddle me out of tenpence.

**difference**
see **split the difference**

## dig*

(an American import, used especially by young people in the 1960s)
enjoy
NOTE An archaeological excavation may simply be called a *dig*, and you may also talk of *giving the garden a dig* or *having a dig in the flower beds*.

## dig at

make sarcastic remarks or insinuations about
□ I don't know exactly what he meant by that remark. He was obviously digging at somebody, but I don't know who it was.
hence *have a dig* or *get in a dig* at someone
□ She never fails to get in a dig at me if she has the chance.

## dig oneself in

establish oneself securely in a post or position, or with a firm or organisation (taken from trench warfare)
□ If anyone is to be dismissed when the company falls on hard times, it won't be Jack; he's dug himself in too well.

## digs

lodgings
□ Owing to a shortage of hostel accommodation, many university students have to live in digs.
□ Are your digs comfortable?

## dilly-dally

waste time by working half-heartedly; vacillate and hesitate in coming to a decision or in carrying out a project
□ Put your back into the work, man; you'll never get it done if you dilly-dally in this way.

## dim

slow of understanding or at grasping a point: not very intelligent
□ He's so dim that it is useless trying to explain anything to him.
see also **take a dim view**

## din

**1** (verb) *To din something into someone's head* is to force someone to remember something by insistent repetition.
□ The new teacher is dinning phrasal verbs into our heads every day.
**2** (noun) a terrible noise

## dinner

for *got up like a dog's dinner*, see **dog**

## dip *(n)*

bathe: *go for a dip*, *have a dip*, *take a dip*

☐ Until he was well over seventy my grandfather always had his morning dip.

**dirt cheap**

very cheap (literally, 'as cheap as dirt')

☐ You would be foolish to turn down the offer. At that price, it's dirt cheap.

**dirty**

see **do the dirty on someone** and **wash one's dirty linen in public**

**dirty dog***

see **dog**

**dirty look**

a look of contempt, disapproval, anger etc.

☐ As he passed, he gave me a dirty look.

**dirty old man**

a man of loose sexual habits, or one whose behaviour towards women is suggestive of sexual desire (There is not necessarily any implication that he is old.)

**dirty trick**

an unfair, dishonest or treacherous act

☐ He's not above playing a dirty trick on anyone, if it suits his purpose.

☐ That was a dirty trick, to invite your confidence and then betray it. The usual idiom is *play a dirty trick on someone*, but *play someone a dirty trick* is also used.

**dirty word**

a word or expression that has come to be regarded as objectionable, not on ground of morals or good taste, but from some kind of social or political prejudice

☐ In certain educational circles *streaming* had become a dirty word.

**disc**

a gramophone record, though strictly it means anything flat and round, and could be made of any material

**dish out**

hand out, distribute

☐ Who dished out these tickets to you? *or* Who dished these tickets out to you?

**dither (about)**

hesitate

☐ Don't just stand there dithering (about).

**do** *(n)*

**1** a social function

□ The Youth Club have a do in the church hall this evening.

But *a to-do* means 'a fuss', 'a commotion', or 'a state of confusion'.

□ You may have hurt yourself, but you needn't make all that to-do about it.

**2** affair*

□ 'Do you remember the burglary at the Manor House a few years ago?' Yes, I've always thought that there must have been several people involved in that do.'

The most frequent expressions are *a queer do*, *a rum do* and *a strange do*.

**do** *(v)*

**1** cheat

□ An unscrupulous agent did me over the sale of that house.

hence *do someone out of something*

□ 'They're trying to do me out of my little bit of money, Bill.'

(W. W. Jacobs, *A Spirit of Avarice*)

**2** be satisfactory

□ Will it do if I pay you at the end of the week?

In the negative it often means 'be inadvisable':

□ It doesn't do to trust strangers.

**3** *That will do* is literally *that is enough* but covers a wide range of use from politeness to extreme anger and frustration, in this case being the same as *shut up*.

**4** *Do London*, *do Scotland* etc., used mainly by Americans and other English-speaking tourists, means to visit London etc. and see all the important sights.

**5** Remember *do* is frequently used to give emphasis to imperatives.

□ Do come and see us.

□ Do stop making that row.

**do away with**

abolish; get rid of

**do down**

**1** perform some operation such as dusting or painting on a surface where a downward motion is used

**2** cheat, swindle

□ He'll do you down if he gets the chance.

**do-gooder**

one who is anxious to do good for others whether they want it or not

(The word always carries a sense of disapproval, suggesting egotism, importunity or a desire to interfere in the affairs of others.)

□ We've had enough of the attention of church workers, public welfare officers, and other do-gooders; what we need is a little more human sympathy and understanding.

## do in
1 (slang) kill, murder
2 exhaust; take all the strength from (used only of human beings or living creatures such as horses or dogs)

□ The long, toilsome climb up that hill almost did me in.

Also *done in* used predicatively as an adjective, is quite common.

□ I can't go any farther: I'm done in.

## do one's homework
see **homework**

## do one's stint
do one's allotted or fair share of work

□ I'm willing to do my stint, but I object to being exploited or imposed upon.

The metaphor is from coal-mining, where a stint is the amount of work, or the area of coal-face, allotted to an individual miner.

## do one's sums
think clearly; draw logical conclusions from given facts; put two and two together

□ If that is what you think, it's about time you learned to do your sums.

□ You won't deceive me with that kind of talk; I'm quite capable of doing my sums.

## do one's whack
do one's fair share—or possibly a little more

□ Someone else can take on the digging now; I think I've done my whack.

## do someone out of something
see **do** *(v)*

## do someone proud
1 entertain lavishly; treat someone splendidly, or on the grand scale

□ During our week's visit to the city the authorities certainly did us proud.

also used reflexively: *He does himself proud these days*. He gives himself a very comfortable life.

2 give someone cause to be proud

□ By attaining such distinction at so early an age, the young man did his parents proud.

**do the dirty on someone**

play a mean, or dirty, trick on him

□ His life-long friend, whom he had always trusted, did the dirty on him.

**do the trick**

be effective in achieving the desired result

□ If you can't loosen the screw, put a little oil on it; that may do the trick.

□ All attempts to persuade the child to stop howling were in vain, until someone thought of offering it a piece of chocolate, and that did the trick.

**dock**

cut short; in standard usage applied to cutting short the tail of an animal, especially that of a horse, in colloquial English used also of deducting a certain amount from a sum of money, a period of free time etc. which is due to one, or which one is normally allowed

□ His holiday was docked.

□ They threatened to dock his pay.

It is sometimes used with a personal object, followed by *of* to indicate the amount of that which has been docked.

□ They have docked us of two days of our annual leave.

**doctor**

see **just what the doctor ordered**

**dodge** *(n)*

trick; a clever ruse

□ He's up to all kinds of dodges.

□ One of his favourite dodges for getting money from people was to pretend that he had had his pocket picked.

**dodge** *(v)*

cleverly or cunningly avoid doing what one ought to do

□ Dodging tax is stealing from the community.

**dodge the column\***

avoid taking one's fair share of duty

□ Wherever you go you'll find some people trying to dodge the column.

This was originally used of soldiers attempting to evade military duty. The modern equivalent for avoidance of military duty is *draft-dodging*, which came in from America during the Vietnam war.

## dodgy

A *dodgy* situation or object is dangerous or uncertain—not very different from dicey.

A *dodgy* chap is a man not to be trusted.

## dog*

a man who leads a dissolute life

□ He was a bit of a dog in his younger days.

*a dirty dog*: a person (usually a man) who acts meanly towards others

*got up like a dog's dinner*: dressed smartly, or ostentatiously

□ She arrived for the party, got up like a dog's dinner.

(It is often *the dog's dinner*. The origin is not known.)

All these uses are rather dated.

see also **go to the dogs**, **tail** and **top dog**

## dog in the manger

a person who prevents another from using or enjoying something though he has no use for it himself

□ He's a dog in the manger about those books; he doesn't want to read them himself but he won't lend them to me.

## dog-collar

colloquial word for the 'Roman' collar worn by clergymen

## dog-tired

exhausted, tired out

## dog's chance

the least chance (used only in the negative)

□ We haven't a dog's chance of reaching Wales tonight. We'd better find a hotel.

## dog's dinner

see **dog**

## dog's life

a miserable life; a life of ill-treatment and vexation

□ Poor woman! She's had a dog's life of it since she married that man.

## dogsbody

one who performs menial or unpleasant tasks for another (sometimes written *dog's-body*)

## doing

**1** happening

□ In a small town such as this there is very little doing in the evening.

**2** *Anything doing?* a way of inquiring as to the likelihood of compliance with one's request or desires

□ I'd like a lift home in someone's car tonight. Anything doing?

□ I don't know of anyone who has a house for sale, but I'll make inquiries, and let you know if anything's doing.

**3** *Nothing doing*: a way of refusing a request

□ 'Could you lend me five pounds for a week or so?' 'Sorry, Pete, nothing doing.'

□ I asked about a job, but there's nothing doing.

## dole

used colloquially for the state unemployment benefit

*on the dole*: drawing the dole

□ In the early 1930s nearly every employable person in some of the South Yorkshire villages was on the dole.

## doll up

dress smartly and rather showily (used only of women and girls)

□ She arrived at six o'clock, all dolled up for the occasion.

also transitively:

□ She dolled her children up in scarlet silk dresses.

## dollar

for *bet one's bottom dollar*, see **bet**

## done

tricked, cheated, caught

□ You paid £35? You've been done!

## done for

**1** so ill or so badly injured as to be beyond hope of recovery

□ I'm afraid the poor fellow's done for.

**2** so badly worn or damaged as to be beyond further use or service

□ This old suit is just about done for; I shall have to get a new one soon.

## done thing

*That's not the done thing.* That is not the accepted way to behave.

## donkey work

hard, monotonous, uninteresting work

□ Mr Stryver employed Sidney Carton to do all the donkey work on the cases which he himself presented with such brilliance in the Courts.

## donkeys' years

many years (Donkeys are reputed to live to a great age.)

□ I've not seen a real, old-fashioned pantomime for donkeys' years.

□ It's donkeys' years since I was last in Paris.

□ You could once get a glass of beer for twopence; but that was donkeys' years ago.

see also **talk the hind leg off a donkey**

**doodle**

draw meaningless pictures, patterns and designs (*doodles*) on paper, especially while listening to something

**door**

see **foot** and **next door to**

**dope**

a colloquial term for drugs or medicines of any kind

□ I've taken all kinds of dope to try and get rid of this cold.

also as a verb:

□ He's always doping himself for this, that or the other.

Nowadays this is particularly used for narcotic drugs though the medical meaning survives. The noun *drug* has similarly developed both meanings.

**dopey**

drowsy, half-asleep; slow-witted

□ This stuffy atmosphere makes me feel dopey.

□ He doesn't understand half you say to him: he seems to be dopey.

**dot**

*dot the* (or *someone's*) *i's*: correct someone on small details (The full expression is *dot the i's and cross the t's*.)

□ The last speaker has given a more or less accurate statement of the facts, though I hope he will not mind if I dot his i's for him.

*on the dot*: punctually

□ We asked him to come at 2.30, and he was there on the dot.

*the year dot*: a very long time ago

□ If people ever dressed like that, it must have been in the year dot.

see also **sign on the dotted line**

**dot and carry one**

limping in one's gait; dragging one foot behind one as one walks

□ He came slowly up the road, dot and carry one.

**dotty**

silly; crazy

□ She must be dotty, to think that we shall believe that.

□ What a dotty idea!

**double dutch**

see **dutch**

**down** *(adj)*

depressed

□ She's feeling very down today.

□ Don't let him get you down.

**down** *(n)*

a grudge; a spiteful desire to harm someone (found chiefly in the expression *have a down on someone*)

□ He suspected that the fire had been started by someone who had a down on him.

□ If once she gets a down on anyone she will see an ulterior motive behind everything he does.

see also **ups and downs**

**down and out**

fallen on evil times, and almost penniless

□ When I last saw him he looked as though he was down and out.

also as a noun meaning 'one who is down and out'

□ A place of doubtful character, frequented mainly by down-and-outs.

**down at heel**

see **heel**

**down in the dumps**

miserable; depressed

□ He's feeling very down in the dumps about his failure to get that job.

**down in the mouth**

more or less the same as *down in the dumps*, except that *down in the mouth* is more often used of *looking* miserable or depressed

□ What are you looking so down in the mouth about?

**down on one's luck**

experiencing a run of misfortune or bad luck

□ I seem to be down on my luck these days; every investment I make turns out to be ill-advised.

**down the drain**

**1** (of money) thrown away; lost irretrievably

□ Several of his friends have tried to help him by lending him money, but he's none the better for it; it all goes down the drain.

□ I shouldn't invest in a doubtful concern like that; it's money down the drain.

**2** (of a person) deteriorating in character

□ He used to be a reliable, hard-working person, but he seems to have gone down the drain recently.

**down to the ground**

entirely; in every respect (used chiefly in the expression *suit someone down to the ground*)

□ A job like that would suit me down to the ground.

□ That hat suits you down to the ground.

**down under**

a colloquialism for Australia and New Zealand, because from the point of view of a dweller in Britain they are down under his feet

□ We are very pleased indeed to welcome our visitors from Down Under.

□ Customs down under differ somewhat from those in our own country.

**dozen**

see **nineteen to the dozen**

**draft-dodging**

see **dodge the column**

**drag**

**1** (verb) *drag on/out*: last far too long

□ The recital dragged on (and on)—I could scarcely keep awake.
*Drag out* is also similar to *spin out*

**2** (uncountable noun or adjective) transvestite clothes; originally slang, phrases like *acted in drag*, *drag club* are now usual in the context of entertainment

**3** *a drag*: a bore

□ It's a real drag having to be back at six.

□ What a drag!

**drain**

see **down the drain**

**draught**

see **feel the draught**

**draw a blank**

achieve no result from one's search, investigation or inquiries (from the idea of drawing a blank ticket in a raffle)

□ We have followed up all the clues we have received, but so far we have drawn a blank.

**draw in one's horns**

**1** live less extravagantly; spend less freely

□ He has been entertaining lavishly for the past few years, but now he is less secure financially he is having to draw in his horns.

**2** make less excessive demands; adopt a more conciliatory tone or attitude

□ The landlord began threatening the poor woman with legal action if she did not comply with his demands, but when it was pointed out to him that he was placing himself in a vulnerable position, he began to draw in his horns.

perhaps from a snail drawing in its horns and shrinking into its shell when it feels in danger

**dream**

have the remotest idea or thought (of)

□ I should never dream of such a thing.

□ In his younger days, when he was a poverty-stricken clerk, he never dreamed that one day he would be a millionaire.

□ I never dreamed of meeting you here.

**dream up**

invent, imagine, think of

□ She spends half her time dreaming up new schemes of decoration for the various rooms in the house.

□ I wonder who dreamed that idea up; it's pretty absurd, anyhow.

**dress down***

reprimand severely

□ If he behaves in that nasty fashion again, send him to me and I'll dress him down.

hence the compound noun *a dressing-down*, and the expression *give someone a dressing-down*

**tear someone off a strip** means the same as this, and both phrases come from the armed forces, when a man suffers demotion.

**dressed up to the nines**

smartly, though somewhat ostentatiously, dressed

□ There's Mrs Barton, dressed up to the nines as usual.

see also **mutton dressed as lamb**

**dribs and drabs**

*in dribs and drabs*: not all together but in small groups

**dried**

see **cut and dried**

**drive at**

attempt to express or explain in words

□ Although I listened carefully to what he was saying, I couldn't understand what he was driving at.

□ Don't beat about the bush so much; tell us plainly what you're driving at.

**drive someone round the bend**

**drive someone up the wall**

Both phrases are used to express exasperation.

☐ This delay is driving me up the wall.

☐ All that noise will drive me round the bend.

**drop**

give up

☐ I dropped smoking about six months ago.

*drop names*: bring names of well-known or influential people into conversation to impress your hearer(s) (noun: *name-dropping*)

*a drop in the ocean*: a very small amount which makes no difference to the great quantity in question

☐ I'm afraid her kind contribution is only a drop in the ocean compared with what we need.

see also **at the drop of a hat**

**drop a brick**

**drop a clanger**

say something unintentionally hurtful or embarrassing; be tactless

☐ You *did* drop a brick (*or* a clanger) when you offered Mr Hayes a whisky. Didn't you know he's a strict teetotaller?

**drop a line**

send a short letter

☐ Drop me a line before you come, just to make sure that I shall be at home.

Perhaps the idea is that of dropping the letter in a post box.

**drop in**

call on a short visit

☐ Drop in any time you are passing.

☐ Who do you think dropped in at the office this afternoon?

**drop it**

stop whatever one is doing

☐ I won't have you behaving in that unruly manner, so you'd better drop it.

**drop off**

fall asleep (usually unintentionally)

**drop too much**

rather more drink than is good for one (found chiefly in the expression *have a drop too much*: become rather intoxicated)

☐ By the way he walks, he looks as though he has had a drop too much.

☐ If he gets a drop too much, he is apt to become quarrelsome.

**drug**

see **dope**

**drunk**

There are many colloquial and slang expressions round the state of being drunk (intoxicated). You should be ready for these:

**1** *He drinks like a fish.* He drinks a lot of alcohol.

**2** *He is the worse for drink.* He is drunk.

**3** These expressions, which are unobjectionable, show increasing degrees of being drunk:

*be merry, tiddly, tipsy, tight, sozzled, sloshed, smashed, plastered, blind drunk*

see also **drop too much** and **one over the eight**

**dry up**

find oneself quite unable to say any more; also used of conversation itself, and of artistic inspiration

see also **high and dry**

**duck** *(n)*

a term of endearment, used especially by adults when addressing children

□ Would you like a sweet, duck?

often *my duck, duckie,* or *my duckie*

*a dead duck*: an issue, question or subject which is no longer of any interest

*sell a dead duck*: attempt to arouse interest in, or enthusiasm for, such a subject

□ You had better get someone else to put that idea over to them; I'm not much good at selling dead ducks.

*a lame duck*: someone who can't cope with life and is probably being cared for by someone else; nowadays extended to business concerns that can't survive without government money

□ Mary always seems to collect a few lame ducks, no matter where she lives—she's too generous.

(In America, the phrase has an entirely different meaning: it refers to an elderly employee who is waiting to complete his necessary years of work to retire, and now no longer works well.)

see also **sitting duck** and **dying duck in a thunderstorm**

**duck** *(v)*

ignore: seek to avoid (as *duck an issue*)

□ One could argue that Hemingway was escaping from the mid-West just as much as Isherwood may have been ducking the industrial north of England, where he was born. (*The Times Literary Supplement*, 4 July 1966)

## dud
counterfeit, and therefore worthless
□ He showed me a dud five pound note.
also used as a noun
□ The jewels proved to be duds.
Furthermore, *dud* is used of anything which doesn't work:
□ The dud firework just fizzled out.

## dumb
primarily means unable to speak, but colloquially used for 'stupid', 'silly'

## dummy
see **stuffed dummy**

## dump
**1** (noun) a place that appears unpleasant, gloomy, boring etc.
**2** (verb) leave (a thing or person) somewhere unceremoniously
□ Just dump my bag on the table.
□ The taxi driver dumped me on the corner.
see also **down in the dumps**

## dust-up
a quarrel
□ They were quite good friends until they had a dust-up over a gambling debt.

## dusty answer
a curt, unfriendly or unwelcome answer
□ I got a dusty answer from the bank manager when I asked him for a loan.

## Dutch
*double Dutch*: incomprehensible talk
□ What he said was all double Dutch to me.
*Going Dutch* is used of a social gathering or outing where each person pays for himself instead of one treating the other or others; especially when a woman goes out with a man, and, according to traditional etiquette, the man would pay. A group where each pays for himself is called a *Dutch treat*.

## Dutch uncle
*talk like a Dutch uncle*: talk very gravely and seriously to one; lecture one severely
□ There was old Sid Thomson, talking to the children like a Dutch uncle.
There is no equivalent expression *a Dutch aunt* for a woman.

**Dutchman\***

*or I'm a Dutchman* is appended to the end of a statement to imply that the speaker is certain he is right. The meaning is probably 'or I don't know what I am talking about'.

☐ It won't be long before they are falling out over that money their father left them, or I'm a Dutchman.

**duty**

see **off 4**

**dyed-in-the-wool**

(not used after a verb) complete, through and through

☐ He's a dyed-in-the-wool academic.

**dying**

longing very much (followed by *for* or an infinitive)

☐ I'm dying for a cup of tea.

☐ She was dying to know what was in the letter.

**dying duck in a thunderstorm**

used of someone looking very sad or hopeless, spoken lightheartedly to try to cheer the person up

☐ What's the matter? You look like a dying duck in a thunderstorm!

# e

**ear**

*a flea in someone's ear*: a rebuke or reprimand

☐ If he comes pestering me for money again, I shall send him off with a flea in his ear.

*I should think his ears are burning*. This is said of someone who, unknown to himself, is the subject of much discussion. (a reference to an old saying that if a person's ears burn, it is a sign that someone is talking about him)

see also **in (at) one ear and out at the other**

*all ears (and eyes)*: keen to hear (and see) everything

*keep your ear to the ground*: listen for any hints of what may happen

*ears flapping*: trying to listen to what is said

*have no ear*: be unable to distinguish various notes of music, sounds in different languages etc.

☐ He has no ear for Arabic.

see also **keep one's ears open** and **prick one's ears up**

**early bird**

a person who is up and about early, sometimes applied to one who arrives at work earlier than he needs to (from the proverb *It's the early bird that catches the worm*)

□ The early birds went for a long walk along the sea shore before breakfast.

**earth**

see **on earth**

**earthly**

used adjectivally in negative sentences, or sentences with a negative import, as an emphasising word, with the meaning 'none at all'

□ There is no earthly reason why you should do that.

□ It is no earthly use relying on him to help you.

□ He hasn't an earthly chance of succeeding.

The last is often shortened to *He hasn't an earthly*. It is sometimes found after an interrogative *what?*

□ What earthly reason prompted you to do that?

**ease up**

**1** relax one's efforts

□ If you go on working like this, you'll endanger your health; you ought to ease up a bit.

**2** become less severe (used especially of storms, gales, rain etc.)

□ After about twenty minutes the rain began to ease up.

**easier said than done**

a common answer to an impractical suggestion

**easy**

**1** (adjective) contented; having no objection

□ 'Would you prefer to go to the theatre or stay at home and watch television?' 'I'm easy either way.'

**2** (adverb) Normally, of course, the adverb is *easily*, but in colloquial English *easy* is sometimes used instead:

□ You can do it easy.

**3** *easy come, easy go*: almost a cliché, expressing the idea that people who get money, friends etc. easily are content to lose them just as easily

**4** *easy as pie*: very easy (This probably doesn't refer to pies to eat but ironically to $\pi$ used in mathematics.)

**5** *easy as winking*: very easy indeed; also adverbially: *I did it as easy as winking*; not *as easily as winking*

see also **dead easy** and **go easy**

**easy does it**

We shall achieve our object by easy, or gentle, means.

□ Don't tug at that bolt: easy does it.

**eat one's hat**

This is added to a statement to express the idea that the speaker is sure that what he says is right. It may be attached to a clause beginning with *if* (*If that isn't the man who accosted us outside the railway station, I'll eat my hat*) or co-ordinated with a previous statement by *or* (*That's the fellow who accosted us just outside the railway station, or I'll eat my hat*).

The construction with *if* uses a negative verb to express a positive idea in the mind of the speaker; that with *or* uses in the first clause a positive verb for a positive idea, and a negative verb for a negative one.

**eat one's head off**

eat voraciously or greedily; eat a large amount of food (used mainly of animals, but sometimes also of human beings)

□ For several months of the year the horses are just eating their heads off and doing no work.

□ When boys get to the age of fifteen or sixteen they eat their heads off.

**eat someone out of house and home**

generally used of one's children or one's family, with the meaning 'eat so much that it is difficult to provide for them'

□ Those three boys of mine have such large appetites that they eat me out of house and home.

**edge**

(*all*) *on edge*: in a state of nervous tension or restlessness

□ Throughout the evening he was (all) on edge to get away.

see **teeth**

*have the edge on*: be slightly superior to or better than

□ This make is the dearer of the two so far as initial outlay is concerned, but it has the edge on the other for economy of running-costs.

□ As a violinist, Margery has the edge on Judith.

**edgeways**

see **get a word in edgeways**

**edgy**

having the nerves on edge: irritable because of this

□ What's the matter with Harry this morning? He seems very edgy.

see **nervy**

**egg**

see **curate's egg**, **nest-egg** and **as sure as eggs is eggs**

**egg-head***

a derogatory or depreciatory term for an intellectual

□ What do these egg-heads know about practical things? They've had no experience of them.

presumably a reference to the fact that a high forehead, giving the head something of an egg shape, is supposed to denote a larger brain and more intelligence than the average

**eight**

see **one over the eight**

**elbow-grease**

(uncountable) continuous hard rubbing with the hand and arm

□ The secret of getting a brilliant polish on furniture is to use plenty of elbow-grease.

**elbow one's way**

literally, use one's elbows to push one's way through a crowd etc., but also used figuratively

□ Bloggs will soon be elbowing his way on to the committee, you mark my words.

**elbow room**

room in which to move one's elbows freely when engaged in some work or activity for which such freedom of movement is necessary

□ It's awkward working in such a confined space; there isn't much elbow room.

**elevenses**

a drink and light refreshments taken about eleven o'clock in the morning

□ It's about time we had a break for our elevenses now.

□ 'Some Suggestions for Your Elevenses.' (from the menu card of a café)

**eleventh**

*at the eleventh hour*: at the last moment, when it is almost too late.

**end**

*there's an end of it*: that is all there is to be said; it is no use discussing the subject any further

□ I am aware of all the advantages of the scheme you propose, but we haven't the money to put down in the first place, and there's an end of it.

*It's not the end of the world.* It isn't as bad as it seems.

see also **in the end, keep one's end up, make both ends meet, make someone's hair stand on end, no end, on one's beam ends, sticky end, tail end, tether, wedge** and **wit**

**enough**

added to certain adjectives and adverbs for purposes of emphasis

□ I said that he would fail his examination, and sure enough he did.

□ Don't believe that story of his deafness; he can hear well enough when he wants to.

Sometimes it has the meaning of 'certainly':

□ It is true enough that he had quarrelled with his uncle, but that does not prove that he had anything to do with the murder.

□ Strangely enough, you are the first one to have noticed the mistake.

This is a very common idiom which can be easily learnt with other adverbs, all giving a similar meaning: *oddly/funnily/strangely/curiously/surprisingly/amazingly enough*.

**enough to wake the dead**

used to describe a very loud noise

□ The noise coming from the room was enough to wake the dead.

also adverbially:

□ They were bellowing and shouting enough to wake the dead.

**equal to**

see **up to 1**

**etceteras**

the other things that go with whatever is mentioned

□ He cooked roast turkey and all the etceteras.

The word always has the -*s* termination when used in this sense, though actually there is no justification for it, since *etcetera* is already plural.

**ever**

appended to superlative adjectives as a substitute for an adjective clause such as *that has ever happened, that has ever been heard of, that has ever been known*

□ This year's motor show in the biggest ever.

□ These Mediterranean cruises are the cheapest ever.

*did you ever?* short for *did you ever see/hear/know/of such a thing?* used to express surprise, amazement, disgust etc.

□ 'After insulting me to my face, he coolly asked me if I would lend him five pounds.' 'Well, did you ever!'

**ever so**

very (before adjectives and adverbs): *ever so cold, ever so good, ever so fast*, *ever so quickly* regarded by some speakers as rather uneducated, as is the following entry

**ever such**

used before an adjective and the noun it qualifies, to suggest something rather stronger than *very*

□ It's ever such a pretty cottage.

□ They're ever such nice neighbours.

*Ever such* may also be used before certain nouns which are not preceded by an adjective, if something of an adjectival notion is suggested in the noun itself: *ever such a noise, ever such a storm, ever such a wind, ever such a struggle, ever such a job*.

**every bit as**

(+ adjective) see **bit**

**every man jack**

all; every one

□ Every man jack of our workers was at the football match.

**every now and then**

occasionally; at recurrent but irregular intervals

□ Every now and then, the engine would stutter.

**everything in the garden is lovely**

Everything is just as one would wish, and could not be improved. (often used with a suggestion of sarcasm)

□ 'How does Jennifer like her new job?' 'At the moment everything in the garden's lovely. But that's only her first impression: she may alter her mind when she's been in it for a few months.'

**exam**

short for *examination*

**expecting**

pregnant (i.e. expecting a baby)

□ I hear Mrs Brown is expecting again.

**eye(s)**

*eyes bigger than one's belly*: said of a person who takes or asks for more food than he can eat (rather vulgar)

□ I thought he'd leave half of that great helping of pudding; his eyes are bigger than his belly.

*give someone the glad eye*\*: (try to) catch the eye of someone sexually attractive; similar to *make a dead set at* someone (see **dead set 2**(a))

*give one's eyes for*: be very glad to have whatever is specified; be willing to give a lot for (The idea is that the sacrifice of one's eyesight would be the greatest sacrifice one could make.)

□ Many people would give their eyes for an opportunity like that.
*Haven't you any eyes in your head?* said to one who fails to see
something that is plain or obvious
*keep an eye on someone or something*: keep a watch on
□ Just keep an eye on the children while I am out, will you, please?
□ We asked the police to keep an eye on the house while we were
·away.
*My eye!* an exclamation of surprise or astonishment
see also **all my eye, cry one's eyes out, have an eye for, keep
one's eyes open, keep one's eyes skinned, keep one's
weather eye open, make eyes at, sight for sore eyes, smack
in the eye** and **up to the eyes in work**
NOTE In these and the many other idioms using *eye(s)*, the use of the
singular or plural seems fixed and cannot be changed, nor is this usage
determined by meaning.

**eye-opener**
a surprise; something that (metaphorically) opens one's eyes
□ Those pictures of his were an eye-opener to me: I never dreamed he
could do such work.

**eyelid**
see **bat an eyelid**

**eyesore**
anything visually offensive in its environment
□ Those new office blocks are a real eyesore.

**eyewash**
(uncountable) pretence; something that is intended to deceive or
mislead one
□ Don't take any notice of his story; it is just a lot of eyewash.

# f

## face

impudence; boldness (mainly in the expression *have the face to do something*)

□ She had the face to deny all knowledge of the matter, when she knew I had proof that she was concerned in it.

see also **laugh on the other side of one's face**, **lose face**, **save one's face**, **two-faced** and **wipe that smile off your face**

## fad

an interest or enthusiasm which is unlikely to last

□ Peter's latest fad is collecting car brochures.

## fag

**1** cigarette (back-formation from *fag-end*: the small remaining end of anything)

□ Could you lend me a fag, Susie?

**2** exertion; tiring effort

□ I'm not going to climb all those steps; it's too much fag.

hence the verb *to fag* (exert great physical effort that tires one) and the predicative compound adjective *fagged out* (tired out)

□ I fagged all the way up that hill, only to find that I had been misdirected.

□ I'm feeling fagged out; I can't go a step farther.

**3** perform menial tasks (from the *fag* at a public school, a junior boy who performs menial tasks for a senior one)

□ I'm going to give up this job; I'm tired of fagging for the foreman.

In American usage, *fag* is short for *faggot*: a homosexual. Maybe because of this use, the British uses **2** and **3** are obsolescent.

## faintest

used colloquially for *the faintest idea* or *the faintest notion*

□ 'How much is the work likely to cost?' 'I haven't the faintest.'

To express the same idea *remotest*, *foggiest* and *slightest* can also be used.

## fair enough

used to express assent, agreement or approval, and more or less equivalent in meaning to *all right*

□ 'If you'll attend to the visitors when they arrive, I'll see that everything is in order in the hall.' 'Fair enough.'

## fair to middling

not too bad and not too good (a rather grudging admission that the thing in question is satisfactory rather than otherwise)

□ 'How are you feeling today?' 'Fair to middling.'

□ 'What kind of weather did you have on your holiday?' 'Fair to middling.'

NOTE *Fair*, used to comment on work done, means it is just a little less good than satisfactory.

## fake

counterfeit, forge; make an imitation of something with the intention of passing it off as genuine or authentic

□ Expert examination showed that someone had faked the signature at the foot of the letter.

□ The so-called antique bureau has been cleverly faked.

hence *a fake*: something that has been faked

## fall between two stools

be in an awkward situation because you don't come into either of the two usual categories with the result that you can take advantage of neither possibility

□ They live quite a long way from London and yet the rates they pay are not as cheap as they would be in the country—they fall between two stools.

## fall on one's feet

be lucky and successful, as with a new job or useful opportunities

□ I hear Mark has just landed a most fantastic job in Iran; he always falls on his feet!

sometimes *land on one's feet*

## famous last words

a comment made when someone cheerfully says something is easy to do

□ 'I'll get that lid off for you in a jiffy!' 'Famous last words.'

## famously

excellently

□ We're getting on famously.

## fan

an enthusiastic admirer of a person of talent (or of supposed talent in the eyes of the admirer); one who is inordinately devoted to some sport, pastime or pursuit (abbreviation of *fanatic*)

□ As the singer left the hall he was surrounded by a crowd of fans clamouring for his autograph.

(hence such combinations as *football-fan*, *film-fan* etc.)

*fan-mail*: letters received by a person from his fans

**fancy**

**1** be attracted sexually by

□ All the girls fancied David.

**2** used in exclamatory sentences to express surprise or astonishment at the fact stated

□ Fancy meeting you here!

□ Fancy him doing that; I should never have believed it.

also *Just fancy!*\*, more often used as a comment, by way of reply, on a previous statement

□ 'We had not met for over ten years, and then one day I found myself sitting opposite him in a restaurant.' 'Just fancy!'

**fancy piece**\*

a woman other than his wife to whom a man is devoted, or with whom he is on very friendly terms for the time being

□ I've just seen Roger with his fancy piece.

**fancy price**

a price far in excess of what a thing is worth

□ I'll certainly consider buying the house, but I'm not paying any fancy price for it.

**fantastic**

wonderful, marvellous

**far-fetched**

exaggerated, incredible: *a far-fetched story/excuse/explanation*

**fat** *(n)*

*The fat is/was/will be in the fire*. There is/was/will be trouble.

□ If you are not careful the manager will get to know of this, and then the fat will be in the fire.

**fat** *(adj)*

large, in such expressions as *fat profits*, *a fat salary*

*get (very) fat on*: live comfortably or prosperously on (nearly always used in negative sentences, as an understatement)

□ He boasts a great deal about the good job he's got, but if the firm does not pay him a better salary than they pay most of their employees, he won't get very fat on it.

**fat-head**\*

a fool

□ What did you do that for, you fat-head?

□ I should never have believed that he could be such a fat-head.

**fat lot***

much (always preceded by *a*, and used ironically, implying 'very little' or even 'none at all')

□ A fat lot of good that is to us!

□ 'Jim told me that . . .' 'A fat lot Jim knows about it!'

□ He offered us his sympathy? That's a fat lot of help.

**fate**

*a fate worse than death*: something unpleasant (usually used humorously)

□ I've got to see the boss. That's a fate worse than death!

see also **sure**

**fathom**

understand

**fear**

see **no fear**

**feather**

see **knock someone down with a feather**

**fed up**

This expression interestingly combines the two meanings of being 'bored' and being 'irritated'. Many phrases in other languages combine these ideas into one expression. *Fed up with* may be followed by a gerund.

□ I'm fed up with listening to his complaints.

□ I got fed up, so I went home.

Even stronger than *fed up* is *fed up to the teeth*.

□ I'm fed up to the teeth with this wretched weather.

Even stronger than this is *fed up to the back teeth*.

**feel like**

**1** feel as if one could, or would like to do something (followed by a gerund)

□ When I saw the extent of the damage, I felt like weeping.

□ At that insolent and unfeeling remark, she felt like slapping his face.

**2** have an inclination for

□ Do you feel like a cup of tea?

□ I didn't feel like climbing all those steps.

□ I feel like a rest, after that long walk.

**3** feel oneself to be

□ When I realised what a stupid mistake I had made, I felt (like) a fool.

(*like* is usually omitted here)

**4** *feel like death warmed up*: feel terrible, very ill
**feel oneself**
feel well, in good health
□ I wasn't really feeling myself yesterday, but I'm much better today.
NOTE *Feel* followed by an adjective must not be reflexive. (*she feels happy* and never *she feels herself happy*)
**feel the draught**
suffer inconvenience or misfortune; be affected adversely
□ With the falling off of orders and the introduction of short-time working, a number of us who thought we had safe positions are feeling the draught.
**feeling**
see **bones**
**fellow**
frequently used for a man or boy of any age, like **chap**
**fellow-traveller**
This curious expression is used for a sympathiser with a political party who is not formally a subscribing member. In fact, it is usually only used about the Communist Party. The phrase can of course still be used to mean 'another passenger' on a train/plane.
**fetch and carry**
perform menial tasks such as running errands, transporting small articles and packages etc.
□ I am expected to fetch and carry for everyone in the office.
□ Her whole morning was spent in fetching and carrying.
The verbal parts most frequently used are the infinitive and those ending in *-ing* (i.e. the present participle and the gerund), but others are not impossible: *I have fetched and carried for other people long enough.*
**few and far between**
uncommon, infrequently found; used (unlike *few* alone) after a verb and not before a noun
□ In Northern England, some butterflies are few and far between nowadays.
see also **good few**
**fib**
a euphemism for a lie
□ You shouldn't tell fibs.
hence the verb *to fib*, and the noun *fibber* (one who tells fibs); mostly used by children, and by adults speaking to children

**fiddle** *(n)*

dishonest business (not as strong as **racket 2**)

see also **second fiddle**

**fiddle** *(v)*

**1** play rather aimlessly; occupy one's time on trivial things or in a trivial way (also *fiddle about*); followed by *with* to denote that to which one's attention is given

☐ Don't fiddle with your tie.

☐ He's been fiddling about with his motor bike for the last two hours.

**2** falsify (accounts etc.), used transitively

☐ It was quite obvious that someone had fiddled the accounts.

**fiddle-faddle**

(uncountable) unimportant action or talk

**fiddling** *(n)*

a verbal noun from **fiddle 2**

☐ They suspected that some fiddling had been going on.

**fiddling/fiddly** *(adj)*

**1** very small (often followed by *little*)

☐ We don't bother about fiddling sums of money like threepence or fourpence.

☐ It's tedious work, counting these fiddly little things.

**2** (of a task or a piece of work) requiring very close attention on account of the smallness of the object on which one is working

☐ Cleaning or repairing a wrist watch is fiddly work.

**fifty-fifty**

equal

☐ Our chances of success are fifty-fifty.

hence the attributive use: *a fifty-fifty chance*

*go fifty-fifty*: share equally

☐ We'll go fifty-fifty in the profits.

**fight tooth and nail**

fight with all available resources

**fill the bill**

serve the required purpose

☐ 'We need something to entertain the spectators until the display begins.' 'What about some recorded music? Will that fill the bill?'

**fillip**

*give a fillip*: stimulate, give stimulus

**find one's feet**

feel at ease in a (new) job or surroundings

**fine**

**1** often used with heavy sarcasm

□ That's a fine thing to say about your friend after all he's done for you.

**2** *It's turned out fine again.* The weather is dry and clear again, like yesterday.

**3** *one of these fine days*: a jocular way of saying one day, some day in the future (Remember *once* does not give this meaning.)

see also **cut it fine**

**finger**

*have a finger in the pie*: have a share in a task or project

□ If we allow him to have a finger in the pie he will want to take charge of the whole business, and there won't be room for the rest of us.

*his/my fingers are all thumbs*: clumsy or awkward in the performance of a task or a piece of work which involves the use of the fingers

□ Could you help me tie up this parcel, please? My fingers are all thumbs.

*not lift a finger* (*to help*): see **lift a finger, green 4**, **keep one's fingers crossed**, **light-fingered** and **slip 1**

**fire**

dismiss from employment on account of incompetence, or misconduct, or at the whim of the employer

□ He was fired at a moment's notice.

see also **fat** *(n)*, **sack**, **irons in the fire** and **out of the frying pan into the fire**

**first of all**

a phrase frequently used at the beginning of a conversation or lesson, which may sound like 'festival' (You will also hear *to start with* and *to begin with*, and in neither case can *with* be omitted.)

see also **in the first place**

**first refusal**

the chance to buy something before it is offered to anyone else

□ When you're thinking of selling your house will you give me first refusal?

**first thing**

(used adverbially, and usually followed by *in the morning* or *this morning*) at the beginning of the morning

□ We'll leave that task over for today, and do it first thing in the morning.

□ It was very foggy first thing.

similarly, *last thing (at night)*:

□ Take one of these tablets last thing. (i.e. immediately before going to bed)

## fish

see **kettle of fish**

## fish out of water

a person who clearly doesn't fit in the present situation or environment

□ She felt quite like a fish out of water when she first went home after two years abroad.

## fishy

arousing suspicions of dishonesty, falsehood, untrustworthiness etc.

□ His story sounds pretty fishy to me.

□ I've never liked that fellow: there's something fishy about him.

also attributively: *a fishy business*

## fist

see **hand over fist** and **ham-fisted**

## fit

(followed by an infinitive) **1** (adjectival) in a condition or state in which one could do whatever is specified in the infinitive

□ After hearing his pitiful story, she felt fit to cry.

□ I must sit down and rest for a moment; I feel fit to collapse.

**2** (adverbial) to the extent or point where the result specified in the infinitive might have followed

□ He shouted fit to burst himself.

□ She sobbed fit to break her heart.

## fiver

a five-pound note; *a tenner* is a ten-pound note

## fix *(n)*

*in a fix*: in a difficult situation

□ We're in a fix now; it's going to cost us over eighty pence to get home, and we haven't a penny between us.

also followed by *for* to indicate that in respect of which the difficulty exists: *in a fix for money, in a fix for a speaker to address the meeting*

*Fix* is also the usual word for a dose of narcotic drugs, especially when given by injection.

## fix *(v)*

**1** put right (not necessarily by fixing anything in the normal sense of the verb)

□ There's nothing much wrong with the machine. A small screw has come out, and we can soon fix that for you.

**2** persuade a person to withdraw opposition or an objection by threats or by the offer of a bribe

□ There is only one person who is likely to oppose the proposed scheme, and we can soon fix him.

**fizzle out**
come to nothing
□ Owing to lack of support, the scheme fizzled out.

**flabbergasted**
amazed; astonished
□ I was flabbergasted at the suggestion.

**flaked out**
exhausted
□ I was flaked out by the time we'd finished.

**flame**
a person with whom one is in love, or fancies oneself to be in love (applied to either sex)
□ Joan Heathcote, did you say? She's an old flame of mine.

**flaming**
terrible, frightful (usually applied to an argument/row)

**flap**
(countable in these contexts) a panic, especially in the phrases *be in a flap*, *get in(to) a flap*
□ Something nasty has happened but don't get in a flap.
see also **ear**

**flare-up**
a sudden quarrel

**flash** *(adj)*
smart; deceptively gaudy; clever at deceiving people (used also before the names of confidence tricksters, like *Flash Harry*)

**flash in the pan**
an effort which quickly comes to nothing
□ His latest proposal was another flash in the pan.

**flashy**
impressive in a vulgar way, ostentatious

**flat**
**1** definitely, so as to leave no doubt
□ I told him flat that I refused to have anything to do with such a scheme.

also as a predicative adjective, in the expression *that's flat*:

□ You needn't look to me for any assistance, because I shall not give it; and that's flat.

**2** He did it in 10 minutes *flat*: in exactly 10 minutes; implying 'more quickly than expected'

**3** (noun) a puncture

□ We had a flat on the M3 and were late for the appointment.

see also **fall flat**

**flat out**

**1** (adjective) exhausted, sometimes even unconscious

□ We had to leave him flat out by the roadside.

**2** (adverb) using all power to give greatest results

□ He always drives his car flat out.

□ We worked flat out to get the job done in time.

**flea in one's ear**

see **ear**

**flicks***

still sometimes used for the *cinema*

**fling**

see **have one's fling**

**flit**

see **moonlight flit**

**flog**

**1** (a topic, subject, idea etc.) press it upon people repeatedly; spend great effort in trying to get people interested in it

□ He alienated a number of potential supporters by flogging the idea in season and out.

Especially common is to *flog a dead horse*: to waste one's efforts trying to revive something (e.g. a plan) which is out of date/no longer practicable.

**2** Sell, or try to sell, by persistent effort.

□ He travels the country flogging religious tracts.

**3** Sell dishonestly or illicitly.

□ Even if the thief is discovered there is not much hope of recovering the goods; he's probably flogged them by now.

**floor**

defeat (a person), usually by a question, an argument etc.

□ The question floored everyone in the room.

□ To think I should be floored by such a simple question as that!

see also **hog the floor**

**flop** *(n)*

a failure or a fiasco

□ Despite all the care that had gone into its production, the play was a flop.

**flu**

the usual spoken form of *influenza*, also written *'flu*.

**fluke**

a mere chance happening

□ It was only by a fluke that the culprit was discovered. No-one suspected him at all.

**flummox**

confuse; cause one to become muddled

□ So much conflicting advice, and so many different explanations were given me, that I was completely flummoxed (*or* they completely flummoxed me).

also *get one flummoxed*: get one into a flummoxed state

**flutter**

a small bet, or a gamble on the Stock Exchange

□ I don't go in for betting as a general rule, but I have a flutter now and again.

□ A flutter in tin shares came off lucky, but he was not so fortunate in some of his later speculations.

**fly/flies**

*I must fly.* This is spoken when you suddenly see how late it is, and must leave in a hurry.

*There are no flies on you/them/her.* You are/they are/she is very alert, not easily tricked.

**fly high**

have high ambitions

□ Those who fly too high may come to grief.

hence the noun a *high flyer* (or *flier*) a brilliant person who hopes, or perhaps even more is expected by others, to be promoted quickly or do well in his career

**fly in the ointment**

something small which spoils an otherwise pleasant experience

**fly into a passion/rage**

lose one's temper violently

**fly off the handle**

lose one's temper; give vent to a sudden outburst of anger (not *fly the handle off*)

□ Just listen to what I have to say; there's no need to fly off the handle in that way.

**flying start**

*get off to a flying start*: make a good start (early, successful etc.)

**fogey**

usually an *old fogey*: a person with old-fashioned ideas

**foggiest**

see **faintest**

**fold up**

(used of a business, club etc.) close down, cease to operate

**fool about/around**

use one's time aimlessly

□ Don't you children fool around/about in here. Go and do your homework.

**fool-proof**

so simple that even a fool could use or handle (whatever is in question) without making a mistake

□ I cannot understand how the accident occurred, for the machine was supposed to be fool-proof.

**foot**

*get/have/put a foot in the door*: make sure you get involved in an activity

□ Alf has just been talking about the new plans. Trust him to get his foot in the door.

*my foot!* a scornful exclamation added at the end of a comment— usually repeating what another person has just said, to show disbelief or disgust

□ Mother: 'John says he wants to buy a motor-bike.' Father: 'Motor-bike, my foot!'

*get cold feet*: see **cold feet**

*put a foot wrong*: make the smallest mistake

□ He complained that if he put a foot wrong, the manager was down on him at once.

But the negative *can't put a foot wrong* usually means 'cannot do anything wrong: is never criticised or found fault with'.

□ The manager is down on the rest of us for the slightest fault, but Jackson can't put a foot wrong.

*put one's best foot forward*: hasten; walk as quickly as one can

□ You will have to put your best foot forward if you are going to get there in time.

NOTE The singular is always used, even when the reference is to more than one person. We should never say *we put our best feet forward*.

*put one's foot in it*: make a bad mistake or blunder (usually through tactlessness or lack of forethought)

☐ No sooner had he made the remark than he realised, by the stony silence with which it was received, that he had put his foot in it.

It is sometimes jokingly said of a person who has a reputation for being rather tactless in what he says, that *every time he opens his mouth he puts his foot in it*.

*set off on the wrong foot*: make a mistake at the very beginning; start off in the wrong way

☐ I am afraid we set off on the wrong foot by openly showing our hostility to the proposals; we might have achieved our purpose, and got them modified, if we had adopted a different approach.

see also **one foot in the grave**, **itchy feet**, **stand on one's own feet**, **start off on the wrong foot**, **two left feet** and **walk someone off his feet**

## footling

trifling, insignificant (used disparagingly or contemptuously)

☐ I'm tired of all these footling complaints.

## for a song

for a very small sum of money; for a price that is very much less than what a thing is actually worth (The usual expression is *go for a song*.)

☐ At the furniture auction quite a valuable carved oak chest went for a song.

## for all

so far as whatever is mentioned is concerned

☐ Her mother may be starving, for all she cares.

☐ He may be dead, for all I know.

☐ I might as well never have taken the medicine, for all the good it's done me.

## for all one is worth

to the extent of one's greatest effort

☐ He ran/shouted for all he was worth.

## for all the world

**1** in exchange for, *or* if I were given, all the world (used in this sense only in negative sentences)

☐ I wouldn't part with that picture for all the world.

**2** as an emphatic expression, conveying the idea that there seems no reasonable doubt about whatever is mentioned

☐ The person sitting next to me in the bus looked for all the world like your uncle Jack.

☐ I thought for all the world that the car would leave the road and land us all in a ditch.

## for dear life

as if one's life depended on it (used mainly in the expressions *run for dear life* and *shout for dear life*)

☐ As soon as they saw the farmer coming the boys dropped the apples they had stolen, and ran for dear life.

## for it

**1** destined for punishment or a severe reprimand (the stress is on *for*)

☐ If anyone in authority gets to know of what you have been doing, you'll be for it.

**2** in order to escape (in such combinations as *jump for it*, *run for it*, *dash for it*, *swim for it*)

☐ The boat overturned, and the occupants had to swim for it.

## for keeps

found in the colloquial expression *have (something) for keeps*: keep it

☐ There's no need to return it when you have finished with it; if it will be of any use to you, you can have it for keeps.

## for now

for the time being

☐ We've about twenty pounds between us. That will be enough for now, though we may need some more later.

☐ That will do for now. We will have a rest, and finish the job after lunch.

## for one

so far as one is concerned; to name only one

☐ I, for one, shall vote against the proposal.

☐ 'Who's against us?' 'Alan, for one.'

NOTE *One* here is not a substitute for a pronoun. The phrase always requires *one* and is only used in the singular.

## for sure

see **sure**

## for that matter

so far as the matter is concerned

☐ I could call and see you at eight o'clock this evening if it would be convenient to you; or I could come now, for that matter.

## for the record

see **record**

**for two pins**
> used colloquially to express the idea that it would take very little to make one act as is suggested (impatience or annoyance is usually implied)
> □ I was so disgusted at his impudence that for two pins I could have told him off there and then.

**for you**
> a formula added to a statement to emphasise it and to attract one's attention to the thing referred to
> □ There's a fine rose for you! You wouldn't see better in the Chelsea Flower Show.
> □ That's a big apple for you.

**fork out**
> pay
> □ My companion had no money to pay his bus fare, so I had to fork out (forty pence) for both of us.

**form**
> usually *in good form* but sometimes just *in* or *on form*: in good health, fit
> □ Are you in (good) form this morning? We have a lot to do.

**forty winks**
> a very short sleep (mainly in the expression *to have forty winks*)
> □ I was just having forty winks after my lunch when that confounded dog set up a yapping and disturbed me.

**foul-mouthed**
> using indecent language
> □ A foul-mouthed hooligan yelled at me as I passed the school.

**four-letter word**
> an obscene word (originally one of four letters, but in colloquial usage no longer restricted to that number)

**fours**
> see **on all fours with**

**fox**
> confuse or fool
> □ He foxed me with that lie about his money.

**frame**
> incriminate (a person) or make him appear guilty, by concocting evidence against him
> □ The accused declared that he was quite innocent of the crime, and alleged that he had been framed by some of his enemies.

**frame-up**

a false charge brought against someone who has been framed (see previous entry)

□ Many of those who knew him felt sure he would never be guilty of espionage, and thought the whole business was a frame-up, with political motives behind it.

**freak**

as an adjective meaning unusual, *freak* is not very colloquial (*a freak snow storm*) but as a noun it is more colloquial. It can mean either a strange, perhaps crazy person, or, in more modern usage, someone keen on the thing specified (*a health freak*, *a music freak*)

**freak someone out**

excite or amaze someone (this word came into fashion in the late 1960s and may not last till the 1980s)

□ The view over the mountains really freaked him out.

**free and easy**

**1** requiring, or characterised by, little effort or exertion

□ She leads a free and easy kind of life.

**2** informal

□ I found him reclining on the sofa in a free and easy manner.

*a free-and-easy* (noun): an informal social gathering

**free-for-all**

a fight in which everyone joins, whether he was originally involved in the quarrel or not

□ What started as a quarrel between two drunken fellows soon became a free-for-all.

**free hand**

permission to spend money freely and/or do as you think best; the same meaning as the French *carte blanche*, which is also used

□ I was given a free hand to decorate the room for the party.

**freeze**

allow no increase in (payments, grants etc.; also a noun)

□ In hard economic times the Government decides to freeze prices.

**French leave**

used only in the expression *to take French leave*: to absent oneself without permission

see also **pardon my French**

**fresher**

abbreviation of *freshman*: a student in his first year at university (used of women students as well as men)

## fridge

colloquial abbreviation of *refrigerator* (sometimes written *'fridge*, *frig* or *'frig*)

☐ If you need any more milk, you will find some in the fridge.

## frightened to death

very frightened

☐ She was frightened to death by the howling of the wolves.

☐ I should be frightened to death of travelling in an old plane like that.

## frills

inessentials

☐ We cannot afford so elaborate a scheme of decoration. We shall have to restrict ourselves to what is really necessary, and cut out all the frills.

## fritter away

waste (usually time or money)

☐ He just frittered away the family fortune.

## frog in one's throat

a huskiness, or a temporary inability to speak clearly, owing to a small piece of mucus becoming lodged in one's throat

☐ I must apologise for this frog in my throat. (a B.B.C. newsreader who had several times been afflicted by this embarrassment within the space of a few minutes)

## from A to Z

in great detail, thoroughly (the usual idiom is *know something from A to Z*)

☐ He knows his Shakespeare from A to Z.

☐ At one time a shop assistant served a long apprenticeship, so that he knew his business from A to Z.

## from pillar to post

from one place to another (There is normally a sense of unwillingness, compulsion or harassment implied; the usual idiom is *drive from pillar to post*.)

☐ The small community of settlers was driven from pillar to post by the invaders.

## frying-pan

see **out of the frying-pan into the fire**

## fuddy-duddy

a person with old ideas, and quite out of touch with modern thought and ways (often preceded by *old*)

□ We shall never make any progress all the time we are governed and controlled by old fuddy-duddies who have been asleep for the last forty years.

**full of beans**
see **bean**

**full steam ahead**
originally used of steam engines and railways, now used of any situation involving starting; often an imperative, simply meaning 'Let's start'.

**fun and games**
what you might expect at a children's party, but also used euphemistically for adults enjoying doing something they should not
□ There were some fun and games down at the pub last night. (i.e. there was a fight)
similar to the feeling given in **up to no good**
see also **have fun**

**funeral**
*that's/it's your funeral*: no-one will suffer by that but yourself: you have no-one but yourself to blame for any misfortune that results from that
□ If you choose to waste your time and so risk failing your examination, that's your funeral.

**funny**
strange
□ What's that funny noise I can hear?
□ It's funny that we haven't heard from them for so long. They used to write regularly once a week.
□ It is funny that you should say that, for the very same thought was passing through my mind.
Because *funny* has two such different meanings it is quite common to say: *Do you mean funny peculiar or funny ha-ha?* (i.e. amusing)

**fuss-pot**
a person who gets anxious about small unimportant matters; also called a *fussy* person
NOTE A *particular person* and a *fastidious person* are near synonyms with a *fussy person* and a *fuss-pot*.
□ Don't be such a fuss-pot; we'll see that nothing is forgotten.
often qualified by the adjective *old*, used in a derogatory sense, not to indicate age
□ Don't take any notice of Jim; he's just an old fuss-pot.

*make a fuss*: get agitated or excited about a small matter; complain
noisily (e.g. in a restaurant or a shop)

**fuzz**

(slang; usually used with *the*) the police

☐ My bike lights aren't working—hope the fuzz don't notice.

# g

**gab**

see **gift of the gab**

**gad** (about)

go about, especially to several entertainments; travel frequently
for pleasure (A *gad-about* is someone who does this.)

☐ She's been gadding about in London all week.

☐ He wants to gad off to Spain in the summer.

**gaffer**

an old man, especially a countryman, generally used rather
contemptuously or disparagingly

☐ Ask that old gaffer over there the way to the farm.

also, the master or foreman of a number of workmen

☐ Keep out of the way of the gaffer; he's not in a very pleasant temper
this morning.

When used by non-manual workers, it usually has a touch of humour
about it.

**galore**

(an emotive word ultimately from Gaelic, used after the noun) a large
amount of; in abundance

☐ There were tourists galore wandering round the town.

**gambit**

(sometimes an *opening gambit*; taken from chess) any initial move
which may be rather cunningly planned

☐ It was his conversational gambit to ask people whether they had
ever seen a ghost.

**game\*** *(adj)*

willing

☐ 'What about a walk across the moors?' 'I'm game.'

sometimes followed by *for*:

☐ I'm game for anything with a bit of adventure in it.

**game** *(n)*

used rather loosely to refer to conduct, behaviour, a particular line of activity etc.

*I've had enough of that game*: that way of going on; that business or activity

□ I shan't indulge in speculation again; I've had enough of that game.

*I'll soon stop his (little) game.* I'll stop something he is doing that I object to.

*a mug's game*: something that only a mug (i.e. a fool) would do

□ Gambling is a mug's game.

*What's the game?* What are you doing? (Usually there is a suggestion of suspicion; very similar to *What are you up to?*)

□ Now then, what's the game? (a policeman to someone who is acting suspiciously)

*come that game*: act in that way

□ In his last post he had the reputation of taking odd days off on frivolous excuses. If he comes that game here, he'll soon lose his job.

see also **come (something)**

*play the game**: act fairly

□ You can't expect anyone to trust you if you don't play the game.

see also **fun and games**

**garbled**

confused, unclear recitation of messages, stories etc.

□ My son gave me rather a garbled message about school finishing early tomorrow.

**garden**

see **common or garden** and **everything in the garden is lovely**

**gas**

(1970s slang) a joke; an amusing event, person etc.

□ What a gas!

**gas-bag**

a person who talks at great length about trivialities

□ I'm tired of listening to that gas-bag.

□ Never before have I met such as old gas-bag as he is.

You may sometimes hear *to gas*, meaning to talk at great length.

**gash**

(an adjective originally coined in the Forces, but still occasionally heard) free, available, not wanted by anyone else

**gate-crash**

intrude into a gathering or party to which one has not been invited

(from the idea of non-ticket holders storming the gates at a sporting event or some mass-gathering, and crashing their way in)

□ At the Lord Mayor's reception there were fifty more people than was expected. Some of them had probably gate-crashed.

hence *gate-crasher*: one who gate-crashes

**gay** *(adj)*

homosexual (the word used to show tolerance, in contrast to **queer**)

□ They went to a gay club.

**gear**

(uncountable) equipment and clothing for a particular activity, or more as slang, to describe very fashionable clothes (*rig-out* is also used for this)

**geezer**

see **old geezer**

**gen**

(uncountable) correct information; full details or particulars (sometimes written with a full-stop)

□ I couldn't get to the meeting. Could anybody give me the gen?

□ You'll find all the gen. in that pamphlet.

**get**

**1** understand

□ I don't get you. Could you say it again?

□ Do you get me?

□ That's the third time I've explained the matter to you. If you haven't got it now, you never will have.

**2** bring oneself to the point where one is or does whatever is specified (followed by a participle: *get started*, *get going*, *get moving*)

**3** in very frequent use for the passive, to show a change

□ When the programme started, I didn't think I would want to watch, but after a few minutes I soon got interested in it.

see **landed with** and **lumbered with** for further examples

**get a load of this**

look at this or listen to this

**get a move on**

see **move**

**get a word in edgeways**

chiefly in the negative sentence *can't/couldn't get a word in edgeways*: have/had difficulty in finding an opportunity to say anything

□ Two of the party monopolised the conversation; the rest of us couldn't get a word in edgeways.

**get across someone**

incur someone's displeasure

□ He left his situation with the firm in a hurry, having got across the manager.

**get along with you**

see **go along with you**

**get along without**

be able to go on tolerably well without the person or thing specified

□ I can get along without the car for a few days, but I need it on Saturday.

**get-at-able**

accessible; similarly *unget-at-able*

□ They live in a most unget-at-able place.

**get-away** *(n)*

escape

□ He made a quick get-away.

**get away!**

used as an exclamation to express incredulity

**get away with**

**1** escape challenge regarding the truth of a story, excuse, report etc.

□ Half the excuses she gives are not true, but she always seems to get away with them.

**2** do something with impunity or without reprimand

□ He hardly ever arrives at work on time: I don't know how he gets away with it.

**get away with murder**

commit even the gravest fault with impunity (used hyperbolically)

□ The rest of us are reprimanded for even the smallest transgression, while he can get away with murder.

**get away with you**

see **go along with you**

**get cracking**

begin on a task; start work

□ We'll just have a cigarette, and then we'll get cracking.

**get into a flap**

see **flap**

**get into hot water**

see **hot water**

**get it ?**

short for *Do you get it?* Do you understand?

**get it in the neck**
be severely punished or reprimanded
□ If his dubious transactions come to the notice of the authorities, he'll get it in the neck.

**get no change out of someone**
get no sympathy or information from
□ She can complain as much as she likes about her misfortunes: she'll get no change out of me.
□ For over half an hour we asked the stranger questions, but we got no change out of him.

**get off**
**1** be acquitted; escape punishment
□ We were astonished when we heard that the accused person had got off.
**2** be excused or freed from (followed by a gerund)
□ No-one should get off paying his taxes.
**3** *get off with*: begin a flirtation or affair with
**4** *get a letter off*: send a letter
**5** *get off the ground*: literally used of flying (at take-off), but also used of a newly established business or organisation when it begins to make progress

**get off to a good start**
start well; make a good, or promising, beginning
□ By leaving at five o'clock in the morning, when the roads were fairly free of traffic, we got off to a good start.
□ In contrast with last year, the cricket season has got off to a good start.

**get on the right/wrong side of**
earn approval or favour (or disapproval or disfavour) of
□ You'll find him a very kind-hearted person, if you get on the right side of him.
also *keep on the right side of*

**get on to**
**1** communicate with (more particularly by telephone)
□ If we don't receive a reply by tomorrow morning, I shall have to get on to him.
**2** pester by continually finding fault or expressing dissatisfaction
□ Don't keep getting on to the boy in this way; it will not do any good.
followed by *about*, to indicate the matter complained of

☐ The headmaster got on to him about his clothes.

**get out of bed on the wrong side**
see **bed**

**get out of hand**
see **out of hand**

**get round someone**
persuade by cajolery
☐ I must see if I can get round my father to lend me the money to buy a new car.
☐ You can easily get round him, if you use a little tact.

**get round to**
come to (the performance of some task) in order of rotation
☐ I still have to write up the minutes of the Annual General Meeting, but I've not got round to doing it yet.
NOTE *To* in this expression is a preposition, and a verb following must be an *-ing* form.

**get someone's back up**
see **back** *(n)*

**get someone's goat**
annoy (somewhere between colloquial and slang)
☐ That fellow gets my goat, with his constant boasting of his own achievements.

**get something across to someone**
cause someone to understand something; explain adequately (*Put something across (to someone)* is also heard.)

**get something off one's chest**
confess; express pent-up, repressed feelings
☐ Don't beat about the bush; if you've anything to say, get it off your chest.

**get the hang of**
see **hang**

**get the wind up**
become frightened

**get to**
the perfect tense is used in direct or indirect questions to inquire concerning the whereabouts of something or someone
☐ Where has that letter got to? I left it on my desk, but it's not there now.
☐ Jack should have been here over an hour ago, and there's no sign of him yet. I wonder where he's got to.

**get tough**
>take up a determined attitude, showing one is not to be trifled with
>□ He'll never pay up unless you get tough with him.

**get-up** *(n)*
>dress; one's manner of dressing

**get up** *(v)*
>**1** organise; arrange
>□ John's going to get up a party for the theatre.
>**2** dress, with a reflexive object (usually with some disapproval)
>□ She gets herself up like a girl of eighteen.

**get used to**
>see **used to**

**get (very) fat on**
>see **fat**

**get weaving**
>begin, start

**get wind of**
>hear indirectly about

**getting on for**
>see **going on for**

**ghost**
>see **give up the ghost**

**gibberish**
>(pronounced and sometimes spelt with a *j*; uncountable) meaningless jargon

**gift horse**
>see **horse**

**gift of the gab**
>facility in public speaking (often used in a derogatory sense, implying a fluency of speech that conceals a poverty of material or ideas)
>□ In persuading a crowd, well-reasoned arguments count for little; all you need is the gift of the gab.

**gild the pill**
>make something unpleasant appear to be attractive, especially when presenting plans

**gills**
>see **green**

**gimmick**
>(adjective *gimmicky*) a trick to catch the public's attention (and make the thing popular)

**ginger up**

   put new energy into; invigorate

   □ Sam has become very lethargic recently; he needs something to
   ginger him up.

**girl friend**

   often used to describe a man's sweetheart, but sometimes suggestive of
   a less serious attachment

   see also **old girl**

**give a damn**

   see **damn**

**give and take**

   (uncountable) mutual concessions; mutual forbearance

   □ Relations between them would be much more harmonious if only
   there were a little more give and take.

**give me . . .**

   I prefer (whatever is specified)

   □ Some people like town life, but give me the country.

**give one's eyes**

   see **eyes**

**give someone a big hand**

   greet someone with a loud and prolonged round of clapping; applaud
   (somewhere between colloquial and slang)

   □ As the candidate appeared on the platform, his supporters gave him
   a big hand (*or* he was given a big hand).

**give someone a chance**

   The imperative or the plain verb stem is used colloquially to suggest
   that what is expected of someone is, in the circumstances,
   unreasonable.

   □ 'Have you replied to his letter yet?' 'Give me a chance. It was only
   about a quarter of an hour ago that I received it.'

   □ 'Charlie isn't home yet, is he?' 'Give him a chance; he doesn't leave
   work until five o'clock.'

**give someone a hand**

   help someone

   □ After the party several of the young people offered to give a hand
   with the washing-up.

   □ Could you give me a hand with these books? (help me to carry
   them, dust them, put them on the shelves etc.)

   The activity referred to is usually one in which the hand is employed;
   but it need not be.

☐ I've got all these figures to check. Could someone give me a hand? The passive form is *I was given a hand*, not *a hand was given me*. *Lend someone a hand* has the same meaning and is equally common.

## give someone (or something) a miss

miss out the person or thing in question

☐ For the past few years we had visited Canterbury in the course of our tour, so we thought we would give it a miss this year.

☐ We will give Mr Baker a miss this time; he has responded to our appeal very generously on previous occasions, and we don't want to take advantage of his generosity.

## give someone a piece of one's mind

tell someone firmly or angrily all the unpleasant things one is thinking about him

☐ I'm going to ask for the manager and give him a piece of my mind.

## give someone a turn

give someone a shock; cause to feel faint

☐ The sudden swerving of the bus gave her such a turn that she felt she would collapse.

## give someone something to think about

surprise someone; cause someone to consider one's ideas or opinions

NOTE This expression always has *something* in it.

☐ The sight of so much poverty amongst a part of the community that we had always considered to be fortunate compared with ourselves gave us something to think about.

## give someone the chance

The plain verb stem is used with a conditional sense.

☐ I would emigrate tomorrow, given the chance.

## give someone the slip

evade; escape from, by a clever dodge or trick

☐ The police followed the suspect as far as the crossroads, where he gave them the slip.

## give someone what for

chastise or reprimand someone severely (on the border between colloquial and slang)

☐ If he tries any of his insolence on me, I'll give him what for.

## give up the ghost

Literally, to die, but it is now used jocularly when someone stops trying, as in a race; you cannot use *up* at the end here.

☐ Edward seemed quite good at French, but after his bad exam result, he gave up the ghost, and has since done very badly.

**glad eye**
see **eye(s)**

**glad to see the back of someone**
see **see the back of someone**

**glory-hole**
a cupboard or room where articles are kept (or just left!) probably in disorder

**glossies**
the more expensive magazines, printed on glossy (shiny) paper

**glove**
see **hand**

**glutton**
*A glutton for punishment* is someone always ready to do some unpleasant job.
□ Our neighbours have started the job of redecorating their whole house: they are gluttons for punishment.

**go** *(n)*
  **1** turn
  □ It's my go next.
  □ I want a go on the swing.
  **2** attempt
  □ He hit the target first go.
  □ I don't know whether I can do it, but I don't mind having a go.
  **3** *no go*: not profitable; not such as one desires
  □ I found myself working long hours for little money. It did not take me long to decide that that job was no go.
  see also **make a go of something** and **on the** (+verb stem)

**go** *(v)*
  *from the word 'go'*: from the very beginning
  □ Generally a man can view his mother-in-law objectively . . . but daughters-in-law seem to vary between open suspicion and bitter hostility from the word 'go'. (*Observer*, 24 July 1966)
  *What you say goes.* What you say is accepted and acted upon. (Any other personal pronoun, or a noun, may be substituted for *you*.)
  □ If that's what he wants, that's what we'll do. What he says goes.
  *Where do we go from here/there?* What do we do next? What is the next step?
  see also **how goes it?**

**go ahead**
  (verb) start, hurry up, proceed; from this, a common noun use

☐ The boss has given us the go-ahead to buy the new equipment. (i.e. we have permission to buy it)

The adjective *go-ahead* is in common use, meaning 'lively', 'progressive'.

## go along with
agree with

**1** a person

☐ I cannot go along with you on that point.

**2** an idea, a proposal etc.

☐ I am afraid I cannot go along with the party's proposals on the reorganisation of the educational system.

## go along with you
an exclamation expressive of annoyance, impatience or incredulity

☐ Go along with you! You can't deceive me. I've heard the tale before.

**Get along with you!** and **Get away with you!** have exactly the same meaning.

## go and do something
used in colloquial English to express a feeling of annoyance, disgust, disapproval, surprise etc., or sometimes amusement, at whatever is done

☐ He went and did the very thing I had warned him against.

☐ Don't go and get drunk on that whisky.

## go begging
be unclaimed and therefore available for anyone who applies or asks

☐ If you would like these two or three biscuits you may as well have them; they will only go begging otherwise.

☐ There are several valuable scholarships going begging.

## go by the board
(especially of ideas, projects etc.) be lost irretrievably

## go by the book
follow strictly instructions, regulations etc.

☐ In ministering to human needs one should use a little imagination; always to go by the book may result in the infliction of hardship on deserving people.

## go dutch
see **dutch**

## go easy
make no great exertion

☐ Go easy while you can, and reserve your strength for the more difficult part of the task.

**go fifty-fifty**
see **fifty-fifty**

**go for a burton**
be lost, not to be seen, sometimes merely broken
□ May I borrow your tape-recorder?' 'Sorry, it's gone for a burton.'
The expression was coined in the Air Force. An airman who was
presumed lost or killed was said to be enjoying Burton beer in the
after-life.

**go for a song**
see **for a song**

**go halves**
share equally (in profits, expenses etc.)
see also **fifty-fifty**

**go it alone**
pursue a course of action unaided (where one might have expected the
help or support of others)
□ Even if those to whom we had looked for help should fail us, we
shall not be deterred. We'll go it alone.

**go off the deep end**
(*off* cannot go at the end) to become argumentative; lose one's temper

**go off the rails**
take a wrong course, either in practical matters or morally
□ I can't get this calculation to work out properly. Can you show me
where I have gone off the rails?
□ He used to be a very reliable and trustworthy person, but he has
gone off the rails recently.

**go on!**
an exclamation used to express incredulity
□ 'He even offered me the loan of his cottage rent-free for my holiday.'
'Go on!'
*Go on with you* is much stronger, suggesting definite disbelief.
□ 'I shall buy that house when it comes up for sale.' 'Go on with you!
Why, you couldn't afford it.'

**go on about/at**
speak angrily or tediously and at length (*about* the matter that causes
annoyance, *at* the person to whom the remarks are directed)
□ When I left the meeting the speaker was going on about the burden
of taxation upon the middle classes.
□ You needn't go on at me like that; I'm not responsible for what has
happened.

**go one's own way**
  act independently, without taking advice
**go out of one's way to**
  take particular care to (especially when motivated by kindness)
  □ She went out of her way to make sure we had everything we needed.
**go shares**
  share (usually, but not necessarily, equally)
  □ She went shares with me in the business.
**go through**
  suffer
  □ I don't wonder he's feeling rather bitter about life, after all he's gone through.
  hence *go through it*: suffer a great deal
  □ What with all those illnesses, and two operations, and the loss of her husband, she has gone through it this year.
**go through the roof**
  lose one's temper; similar to **hit the roof**
**go through with**
  carry (a project or a task) through to the end
  □ I almost wish we had never undertaken the task, but now we've started it we shall have to go through with it.
**go to blazes***
  see **blazes**
**go to great lengths**
  take a lot of pains (to do something carefully etc.); also used with *considerable lengths*
**go to pot**
  deteriorate very badly, so as to become worthless
  □ He used to be a very good student, but his work has gone to pot lately.
  This is stronger and more slangy than the next phrase.
**go to the dogs**
  deteriorate very much (used of people, institutions, organisations, social groups etc.)
  □ According to some pessimists, the country is going to the dogs; but such people have existed in every generation.
**go to town**
  **1** spend lavishly
  □ You certainly seem to have gone to town on the decoration of your house.

**2** exercise no restraint in one's remarks, expression of opinion etc.

□ At last I've got the chance to go to town on what I think of his conduct, and I shall take full advantage of it.

**go west**

die or disappear; an older expression than **go for a burton** but with the same meaning

**go without saying**

so obvious as not to need saying

□ It goes without saying that we shall look favourably on any suggestion that will increase efficiency.

**goat**

see **get someone's goat**

**gobble (up)**

eat quickly

**godforsaken**

(of a place or part of the country) remote, dreary, and having few of the amenities of modern civilisation; often used with *dump* or *hole* (i.e. place)

**gods**

colloquial term for the gallery of a theatre: *up in the gods, a seat in the gods*

*in the lap of the gods*: unpredictable; dependent on chance

□ Negotiations have broken down; what will happen now is in the lap of the gods.

**gogglebox**

television

*Goggles* are worn to protect your eyes on a motor bike or when skiing; to *goggle* originally meant to 'move the eyes from side to side'.

**going**

**1** available; to be had; on offer

□ Is there a cup of tea going?

□ There are not many jobs going for people of my age.

**2** *hard going*: difficult

□ It's hard going to pay all the bills this year.

see also **Dutch**

**going (getting) on (for)**

nearly (of time)

□ Her son's going on (for) twenty.

□ It's going on for one o'clock.

**going strong**

active and in good health; flourishing

□ My grandfather was ninety years old on his last birthday, and he is still going strong.

**goings-on**

happenings (singular rarely used)

□ These goings-on will have to stop, or they will bring discredit on the society.

**golly!***

(also *By golly!*) an exclamation to express surprise, probably a euphemism for *God* and used more by children than by adults

□ Golly! Look at that big apple.

**gone on**

in love with or much attracted to

□ He's gone on her but she takes no notice of him.

**gonna**

vulgar for *going to* (sometimes found in direct speech quotes)

**good**

rather in excess of (amounts, measurements, distances etc.): *a good six feet*, *a good two pounds*, *a good five years*, *a good ten miles*

(Note that *a* is retained with these plurals.)

*as good as gold*: perfectly good (used mainly of a child's behaviour)

*as good as one's word*: faithfully carrying out one's promise or undertaking; keeping one's word

□ He promised to help us if we were ever in need, and he was as good as his word.

*not good enough*: unsatisfactory

□ 'My employer has promised that he will raise my salary some time in the future.' 'A vague promise like that is not good enough. You should get a definite undertaking.'

□ I am taken to task for being a few minutes late, while others may be half an hour behind time, and nothing is said. It is not good enough.

*to the good*: on the credit side

□ Five pounds to the good.

see also **as good as, get off to a good start, take the good with the bad, up to no good** and **deliver the goods**

**good at**

(+ gerund) sometimes used colloquially in a sarcastic fashion: *good at looking after himself*, *good at finding work for others*, *good at evading one's obligations*

Whether it is sarcastic or not, remember the preposition in these phrases is *at*: *Were you clever at geography? She is very poor at maths.*

**good, bad and indifferent**

of all standards and qualities

☐ We had all kinds of entries for the essay competition—good, bad and indifferent.

**good few**

a fairly large number, though not so large as would be suggested by *many* or *a lot*

☐ A good few of us disagree with the party leader on that point.

☐ That is the best performance of *The Merchant of Venice* I have ever seen; and I have seen a good few in my time.

Notice *a good few* is followed by a plural noun.

**good for you**

used colloquially with the emphasis on *you* as a compliment to the person addressed, or in commendation of something he has said or done; the sense being 'That remark (or action) of yours was very good'

☐ 'I told her that those who had had no experience of the work should not criticise.' 'Good for *you*.'

**good gracious!**

an exclamation of surprise or astonishment, probably a euphemism to avoid the use of the name of God

☐ Good gracious! What's that noise?

sometimes used to lend emphasis to a statement

☐ Stop playing with those chemicals at once. Good gracious, man, you might blow the place up.

(notice that the main meaning of *gracious* is agreeable, generous)

**good grief**

a euphemistic exclamation to express surprise, astonishment, or sometimes horror

**good heavens!**

an exclamation of surprise (note the plural form; not *Good heaven!*)

**good innings**

a long life

The metaphor is from the game of cricket, and is usually used of a person who has died at an advanced age, or of an elderly person who is expected to die.

☐ 'Old Mr Green is not likely to recover from his illness.' 'Well, he has had a good innings. He is nearly ninety.'

## good job

*it's a good job*: it's fortunate

□ It's raining. It's a good job we brought raincoats.

We can equally say *It's (just) as well we brought . . .*—though it is less colloquial to omit *just*.

## good lord!

a euphemistic exclamation of surprise, or to lend emphasis

## good one

a good joke or story (usually of a humorous kind)

□ That's a good one, that is.

## good riddance

used to express one's pleasure to be rid of someone or something

□ 'Bradley is leaving our firm at the end of the month.' 'Well, all I can say is, "Good riddance to him".'

(This is of course linked to the very important phrase *get rid of*: see **rid** and **well rid of**.)

## good sort

*a real/very good sort*: a very good-hearted chap

## goods

see **deliver the goods**

## good thing

used with an adjectival force, in the sense of 'fortunate'; the same as **good job**

□ It's a good thing we checked the time of the train, or we should have missed it.

*too much of a good thing*: something which becomes unpleasant, objectionable, or irksome when carried to excess (There is not necessarily any suggestion that in moderation it is a good thing.)

□ I do not mind working overtime occasionally, but when it comes to every night in the week, it is too much of a good thing.

## good turn

a kind or helpful act for someone

□ Boy scouts are supposed to do one good turn every day.

## good while

a fairly long time

□ They have been living in the same house for a good while now.

## goody-goody

(pejorative) good to the point of priggishness; used adjectivally (*a goody-goody kind of person*) and as a noun (*a goody-goody*), plural: *goody-goodies*

**gormless**

    lacking in common sense: *a gormless fellow*

**gosh**

    a very common exclamation of surprise, pleasant or otherwise

**got to**

    be compelled, or be obliged to do whatever is specified; preceded by
    the auxiliary verb *have*

    □ We've got to be at the station by half-past eight.

    □ Don't go out in weather like this, unless you've got to.

    When the infinitive expresses a negative idea, the negative is
    sometimes attached to the word *got* instead.

    □ We haven't got to play near the stream.

    *Got to* may also express the idea of necessity.

    □ You've got to live here a long time before the villagers will accept
    you as one of themselves.

    □ You haven't got to have a university degree to become a teacher.

**G.P.**

    a general practitioner, that is, a doctor in general practice, as opposed
    to a specialist

**grab**

    remove (something) quickly, snatch (also used of robbery, especially
    in newspaper headlines)

**gracious**

    see **good gracious**

**graft**

    corruption; bribery

    □ An inquiry is to take place into the allegations of graft in the
    administration of state enterprises.

**grand\***

    nothing to do with size but commonly used meaning 'excellent',
    'splendid'; now dated or regional

    □ This is a grand little car—I shan't sell it in a hurry.

**granny**

    grandmother; used mostly by children, and sometimes adults when
    speaking to children

    □ Granny's coming to see us tomorrow.

    When a child has two grandmothers living, the surnames may be
    added to distinguish one from the other: *Granny Jackson, Granny
    Simmonds.*

    see also **nana** and **teach one's grandmother to suck eggs**

**grandpa**
grandfather, used similarly to **granny**

**grapevine**
*I heard about it on the grapevine.* I heard about it unofficially or by rumour, overhearing others talking about it. It was originally used by and of criminals, but now used of any organisation, or of society in general.

**grass widow**
a wife whose husband has left her for a temporary period (e.g. because of working abroad)
see also **green** and **snake in the grass**

**grease a palm**
bribe to get something done (very much the same as **oil a palm**)
see also **elbow-grease**

**great**
the modern equivalent of *grand*, originally American but equally common in Britain
see also **go to great lengths** and **no great shakes**

**great one**
*He's a great one for swimming.* He loves swimming.

**great scott!***
exclamation of surprise or astonishment, rarely used in conversation nowadays (The derivation is uncertain.)

**Greek**
*That's all Greek to me.* I simply don't understand it at all.
(more used of a whole subject than a particular word or sentence)

**green**
(of a person) ignorant or inexperienced: *a green youth* (In Dickens's novel *Oliver Twist* the Artful Dodger expressed his surprise at Oliver's ignorance of underworld cant in the exclamation, 'My eyes, how green!')
*green about the gills*: bilious-looking
*green about*: envious of
*You seem to have green fingers.* Everything you plant seems to grow well.
*The grass is always greener* (*on the other side of the fence*). Other people's lives and possessions seem more desirable than your own. (a proverb of which the first part is often spoken alone)

**grief**
see **come to grief** and **good grief**

**grim**

uncomfortable or unpleasant (of conditions)

□ The temperature in this room is pretty grim.

□ With all this frost, the roads are pretty grim this morning.

see also **hang on like grim death**

**grin and bear it**

accept difficulties, misfortunes, unpleasant conditions etc., without complaining

□ If nothing can be done to remedy the position, we shall just have to grin and bear it.

**grind**

a long tiring job/journey etc.

□ It's been a terrible grind.

**grindstone**

see **nose**

**grips**

*get to grips with*: tackle fundamentally and in earnest

□ It's about time I got to grips with the garden.

**grist**

*It all adds grist to the mill.* It all makes things/business/my job/my living more profitable. (*Grist* is an old word connected with *grind*.)

**grit one's teeth**

make oneself strong to accept something; steel oneself (like **grin and bear it**)

□ You won't like working in these conditions. I'm afraid you'll have to grit your teeth.

**groggy**

in rather poor health

**groovy**

the same as **cool 1**

**grotty**

of poor quality

□ They live in a grotty area.

**ground**

see **cut the ground from under someone's feet**, **down to the ground**, **ear** and **get off 5**

**grub**

(slang; uncountable) food

*Grub's up* is often used to announce a meal is ready. Note that *grubs* and *a grub* give the meaning of 'maggot(s)'

**grubby**
rather dirty

**grumpy**
bad-tempered

**guess**
*anybody's guess*: unpredictable; uncertain
□ What will happen now is anybody's guess.
*Your guess is as good as mine*. I've no more idea of the answer to that question than you have.
□ As to what will happen next, your guess is as good as mine.

**guinea pig**
From its widespread use in experiments, this little animal's name is now used for people being submitted to an experiment. A teacher may say to a class 'I've worked out a new exercise. I hope you won't mind being guinea pigs!'

**gum up the works**
make something go quite wrong

**gumption**
(uncountable) common sense
□ The job is not so difficult as all that, if only you use a bit of gumption.
□ He lost his way, and all because he hadn't the gumption to follow the simplest directions.
It is not usually preceded by a possessive adjective. We may tell a person to use his common sense, but not as a rule to use his gumption: we should say *a little gumption* or *a bit of gumption*.

**gumtree**
*up a gumtree*: completely confused or doing it wrong

**gun**
see **jump the gun**

**guts**
courageous persistence or determination (perhaps slightly vulgar, though very expressive)
□ He's only a little fellow, but he has plenty of guts.
□ He hasn't the guts to stand up for his convictions.
A far more slangy expression is to be heard: *I hate his guts*—a strong way of saying 'I hate him'.

**gym**
(pronounced like *Jim* and sometimes spelt *gymn*) short for *gymnasium*, which is a sports hall (not a type of school)

# h

**hack**

*A hack* is anyone who offers his services especially as a 'ghost writer', who writes for someone else and the text is published under the latter's name.

**hackles**

anger, used in a few idioms

□ Don't get your hackles up.

□ This soon raised his hackles.

**had better**

used colloquially:

**1** to suggest advisability

□ You had better tell the police what you have heard.

□ We had better be starting now, before the rush-hour traffic begins.

**2** in the nature of a threat

□ 'I'll pay you the money by the end of the month.' 'You'd better.'

This common phrase is frequently used incorrectly by foreign students. Notice carefully that *to* is not used in the above examples and also notice the question and negative constructions:

□ Had I better tell the police?

□ Hadn't I better tell the police?

□ You had better not tell the police.

*Had best* also exists with the same meaning and construction but it is far less common and not colloquial.

**had it**

see **have had it**

**hail from\***

come from (slightly jocular and mainly used about a person's place of birth)

□ Judging from his speech, I'd say he hails from Scotland.

**hair**

*Keep your hair on.* Don't get angry.

*let one's hair down*: throw off restraint in one's behaviour; act in defiance of those social conventions which one is normally expected to observe

□ Those who are doomed to a life of formality for five days a week look forward to the week-end when they can let their hair down.

*a hair-do*: the arrangement of someone's hair

□ I like your new hair-do.

see also **make someone's hair stand on end**

**half**

*half the time*: a good deal of one's time (not necessarily a precise half)

□ It is no good calling at his office and expecting to see him; half the time he isn't there.

*not half* **1** used before adjectives and adverbs which normally express approval, to convey the meaning 'falling far short of'

□ This work is not half good enough.

**2** before *bad* to remove the depreciatory sense, and express the meaning 'fairly good' (an example of litotes and now sounding rather dated)*

□ Not half bad for a beginner.

□ The weather isn't half bad, considering it's January.

**3** to emphasise, or to express a high degree (stress on *half* in speaking)*

□ It isn't half hot today.

□ We didn't half enjoy ourselves.

□ Your father won't half be angry when he gets to know of this.

sometimes used as an emphatic reply in the form of an exclamation

□ 'Would you like some ice cream?' 'Not half!'

Since, though it is grammatically negative, it has the force of a positive, *not half* takes a negative tag if one is used: *not half I wouldn't*, *not half we didn't* etc. This is a bit dated now.

In all these examples *half* is always given more stress than *not*.

see also separate entry for **not half**

**4** *half six* The standard way of saying 6.30 is of course *half past six* but colloquially, this is now sometimes shortened to *half six*, which is even more confusing to students whose languages would express this with the equivalent of *half seven*. This of course applies to the other hours too, not just six.

see also **by half** and **go halves**

**half a chance**

the least chance

□ Be careful of that fellow; he'll swindle you if he gets half a chance.

**half a mo**

or *half a tick*: wait (half) a moment (i.e. a short time)

see also **mo**

**half-baked**

**1** (of a person) lacking in common sense or intelligence

**2** (of an idea, a scheme, a plan etc.) not fully thought out (always used in disparagement)

□ I don't see why we should waste our time considering such half-baked ideas.

**half the battle**

the thing that counts most in successfully carrying through a difficult task

□ Where the accomplishment of a task like this is concerned, persistence is half the battle.

**half the time**

see **half**

**ham acting**

very bad acting (more likely to be for lack of skill, in contrast to **camp 2**); to *ham something up* is to 'play for laughs' and fool about while doing it

**ham-fisted**

very awkward in doing work with one's hands

□ Never before have I come across such a ham-fisted person as he is.

**hammer**

inflict heavy losses/damage on an opponent; attack bitterly

**hammer and tongs**

(of disputing, arguing etc.) furiously; with great vigour (The metaphor is from the hammer and tongs used by the blacksmith in beating out a piece of red-hot iron.)

□ When I left, the two disputants were still going at it (i.e. arguing) hammer and tongs.

**hammer it out**

work hard at a problem or discuss a disagreement till the difficulties have been overcome

**hand**

*get one's hand in*: get some initial practice; learn how to do something

□ You won't find the work difficult, once you get your hand in.

similarly, *keep one's hand in*: keep in practice

□ I don't play much golf nowadays, though I have an occasional round, just to keep my hand in.

*have one's hands full*: be burdened with work, responsibilities etc.

□ Mrs Barton had her hands full, what with three children, an invalid husband and an aged mother to look after.

*not much of a hand at*: not very skilful at (not confined to things performed with the hand)

□ I'm not much of a hand at painting.

□ He's not much of a hand at explaining things to others.

similarly, *a good hand at*, *a poor hand at*

*take a hand in*: have a share in (arrangements, plans etc.)

□ The negotiations were going quite smoothly until he took a hand in them.

similarly *have a hand in*:

□ The arrangements are sure to go wrong if he has a hand in them.

*on the other hand*: used to introduce a point to consider on the other half of an argument (Notice neither *side* nor *part* can be used for this.)

*try one's hand at*: attempt to do (something)

*live from hand to mouth*: have so little money that all that is earned must immediately be spent on food

*hand in glove with*: in very close relationship with

see also **chuck, dab hand, free hand, give someone a big hand, give someone a hand, high-handed, old hand, out of hand** and **throw one's hand in**

## hand it to someone

admit that someone is the superior

□ All right, you've got me beaten there. I hand it to you.

## hand over fist

very rapidly or in many different ways (used only of the making of money)

□ He's making money hand over fist.

## handful

a child, an invalid, an elderly person etc. who is difficult to manage

□ Poor Mrs Brown! Those children of hers are a handful.

## handle

see **fly off the handle**

## handy

skilful: *quite handy with her needle, handy with a screw-driver, handy at repairing clocks*

also note: *It'll come in handy*. It'll be useful.

see also **come in (for)**

## hang

*get the hang of something*: get the general idea of it

□ I have explained the plan as clearly as I can, but he still hasn't got the hang of it.

☐ I couldn't get the hang of his argument.

*Might as well be hanged for a sheep as for a lamb.* If one is to be punished, or to suffer, in any case, it might as well be for a serious fault as for a trivial one.

**hang on**

wait a moment (especially common on the telephone but also in other situations)

**hang on like grim death***

different from the above expression; used in a situation of great danger:

☐ As the wave crashed over me, I hung on the rail like grim death.

**hang-up**

an obsession or fear

*I've got a real hang-up about this essay now.* I've developed a complex about this essay I'm trying to write. (*I've got a thing about* is also used.)

**hanging matter**

a serious matter (usually used in the negative, *not a hanging matter*)

☐ It is unfortunate that you made that mistake, but don't worry; it's not a hanging matter.

**hangover**

the after-effects of over-indulgence, especially in alcoholic liquor

☐ I woke up with a hangover, as a result of last night's party.

see also **morning after the night before**

**hanky**

handkerchief (*Hanky* was originally a child's word but is now used by adults; the longer word is still usual in writing.)

**hanky-panky**

(uncountable) trickery, dishonest dealing

**happy-go-lucky**

allowing nothing to worry one; taking nothing seriously

☐ He's a happy-go-lucky man; he has a happy-go-lucky disposition.

**hard at it**

**1** working hard

☐ I've been hard at it all the morning, and I'm not half-way through the job yet.

**2** drinking heavily

☐ He's been hard at it for several months now, and nothing we do can restrain him.

see also **at it**

**hard-boiled**

(of a person) unsentimental; lacking in finer feelings; not easily shocked

□ When you spend the greater part of your working life amongst squalor and foul language, you tend to become quite hard-boiled.

**hard done by**

treated harshly or unfairly

□ Because he did not get as much as he expected under his father's will, he felt himself hard done by.

**hard lines***

hard luck

**1** as an exclamation, or a comment on a situation

□ 'I failed to get the prize by only a couple of points.' 'Hard lines!'

**2** followed by *on* to indicate the person who experiences the hard luck

□ If he acted so foolishly he deserved to be discharged from his employment, but it's hard lines on his wife and family.

**hard of hearing**

rather deaf

**hard put to it**

having difficulty (followed by an infinitive)

□ You would be hard put to it to find a pleasanter spot than this.

**hard up**

having insufficient money

□ If you're hard up, it's no good applying to me for a loan.

Followed by *for*, it may also denote an insufficiency of things other than money: *hard up for time*, *hard up for sugar*, *hard up for qualified staff*. It is the opposite of **well off**.

**hare along**

one of several verbs used for rapid movement, and with other adverbs or prepositions: *up* (*the road*), *down* (*the street*), *into* (*the building*)

see also **dart/dash**, **scorch**, **tear**

**harum-scarum**

thoughtless; scatter-brained; unable to keep one's mind on one thing for very long

□ He's a harum-scarum young fellow.

**has-been**

a person or a thing that is past his/its best

□ Twenty years ago she was the centre of attraction in social circles; now she is just one of the has-beens.

## hash

*hash something up* or *make a hash of something*: spoil it; make a mess of it

□ A clumsy man like Jack is not the person to be entrusted with a delicate task; he's sure to hash it up.

Also the noun formation a *hash-up* is to be heard.

## hassle

as a noun, an argument; as a verb, to attack verbally, harass

□ He's hassling me again.

## hat

*keep something under one's hat*: keep it secret and confidential; not mention it to others

□ Whatever you know about this business, be careful to keep it under your hat.

*pass the hat round*: take up a collection (usually on the spur of the moment)

see also **eat one's hat**, **knock into a cocked hat**, **old hat** and **talk out of one's hat**

## hat-trick

originally a term used in cricket, but now used of other games etc., when someone manages to do something very difficult three times in succession

## hatchet

see **bury the hatchet**

## hate

see **guts**

## have

(+object+adverb or adverb phrase) cause whatever or whoever is mentioned to be in the position specified

□ You'll have the car in the ditch if you are not careful.

□ Look out where you kick that ball, or you'll have it through the window.

□ You'll have that pram over if you don't take more care.

## have a bash

make an attempt (perhaps nearly slang, but it has been in use for many years)

## have a bone to pick

see **bone**

## have a crush on someone

see **crush**

## have a date

have an engagement or appointment (a phrase of American origin)

□ I am afraid that evening would not be very convenient, as I have a date with a friend.

*make a date* (*with*): fix an appointment, especially with a girl or boy friend

*date a person*: take out a girlfriend or boyfriend

□ He used to go out with Mary, now he's dating Sue.

## have a down on someone

see **down**

## have a go

have or make an attempt; have a turn at doing something

see **go** *(n)*

## have a head for

see **head**

## have a/no/one's say

see **say**

## have a shot

see **shot** *(n)*

## have a time of it

experience an unpleasant or an arduous time

□ I'm sorry for poor Mrs Robinson; she does have a time of it with that drunken husband of hers.

But *a rare old time of it* means a very wild (and amusing) time, sometimes even the party rather getting out of control.

## have an eye for

be endowed with the ability to appreciate visually whatever is mentioned

□ She has an eye for beauty.

*have an eye for the ladies*: be attracted by good-looking or smartly dressed women

## have fun

amuse yourself, have a good time

## have got it in one

have the capacity, capability, inclination etc. as part of one's character (usually used in the negative)

□ He is not the kind of person for a leader in a difficult situation: he hasn't got it in him.

also followed by an infinitive in apposition to *it*

□ He hasn't got it in him to stand out in defiance of public opinion.

**have got someone there**

usually *You've got me there!* I can't answer your question.

**have got to**

see **got to**

**have had it**

*You've had it, he's had it, it's had it* etc. are used colloquially to signify that the people or things in question have arrived at a point where nothing further can be done for them.

☐ If poison of this kind gets into your system, you've had it.

☐ I shall have to get a new pair of shoes; these that I am wearing have just about had it.

It may also express the idea that disaster is imminent, or that unpleasant results are likely to follow.

☐ The dogs seem to have picked up our scent; I'm afraid we've had it now.

**have had one's chips**

usually heard as *You've had your chips* meaning 'you have no more chances'

The expression presumably comes from gambling, since *chips* are the tokens which are used in casinos etc. (You should notice however that the normal meaning of *chips* is fried potatoes, while the thin flaky potato slices eaten cold are called *crisps*.)

**have it**

**1** have the advantage

☐ As a means of cooking and heating, electricity is very convenient, but where price is concerned, gas has it every time.

**2** for *you've had it*, see **have had it**

**have no call (to do something)**

see **call**

**have no time for**

have no patience with; be intolerant of

☐ They've no time for people of that sort.

☐ He's got no time for idlers.

☐ I've no time for people who make promises and then don't keep them.

**have not the faintest**

see **faintest**

**have one's bellyful**

have more than one desires (always used to express disgust, dislike or disapproval, and likely to be considered rather objectionable)

□ I've had my bellyful of listening to other people's complaints.

**have one's cake and eat it**
enjoy the advantages of two alternatives which are usually mutually
exclusive (generally used in the negative: *you can't have your cake and
eat it*)

□ If you *will* have an expensive holiday, it's no good complaining
afterwards about having nothing left in your bank account: you can't
have your cake and eat it.

**have one's day**
see **day**

**have one's fling**
indulge in wild behaviour

□ Even the most sober-minded person will have his fling now and
again.

□ Let the children have their fling while they are young.

**have one's hands full**
see **hand**

**have one's work cut out**
see **cut out 2**

**have second thoughts**
see **second thoughts**

**have someone**
1 cheat or deceive someone

□ He had me over that bargain.

also passive

□ I was had over that bargain.

2 entrap or catch out

□ He claimed to know my father quite well, but when I asked him how
they came to be acquainted, he had no reply. I had him there.

**have someone doing something**
*He had us all* (*singing folk songs, painting his flat, laughing* etc.)
This is a common expression, often overlooked by dictionaries (or at
least hard to find!), meaning 'with his encouragement, guidance, help
and (possibly) teaching, we all (sang folk songs, painted etc.)'.

**have something up one's sleeve**
hold in reserve some device, trick or piece of information, which, if
necessary, can be produced and used to one's advantage

□ I should be very cautious in any dealings you have with that fellow,
for however honest he appears to be, you can be sure he has something
up his sleeve.

152

□ It is advisable to have something up your sleeve, in case you have exhausted the main subject of discussion before the time is up.

**have the edge on**
see **edge**
**have the face to**
see **face**
**haven't a clue**
see **clue**
**haw**
see **hum and haw**
**haywire**

in a state of confusion; (of a person) crazy, having absurd ideas

□ You mustn't take too seriously anything he says; he's haywire.

□ Our carefully made plans have gone all haywire.

The origin is thought to be the coils of wire used years ago in America to tie up hay, which often became hopelessly tangled.

**hazy**

confused

*I'm a bit hazy about it now.* I don't remember (it) clearly now.

**head(s)**

*get it into one's head that*: get an idea or belief that it is difficult to rid oneself of

□ He has got it into his head that some of his relatives are trying to cheat him out of his inheritance.

*have one's head screwed on* (*the right way*): be knowledgeable or intelligent.

□ It would take a clever person to improve upon Bob; he may look youthful, but he's got his head screwed on the right way.

*heads I win, tails you lose*: whatever the outcome, it will be to my advantage (The metaphor is from tossing a coin.)

□ I shouldn't agree to those conditions; it's a case of 'heads I win, tails you lose'.

*not know whether one is on one's head or one's heels*: be in a state of mental confusion

□ It was all so chaotic, I didn't know whether I was on my head or my heels.

*have a head*: often means 'have a headache' (literally, but see **headache** below)

*have a* (*good*) *head for*: be clever/good at (also *a bad head for* for the opposite)

□ I don't have a head for maths.

*be head over heels in love with*: love very dearly, especially used of people who have just fallen in love

*have one's head in the clouds*: not know what is happening round one (rather like *absent-minded*)

see also **clouds**

*I can't make head (n)or tail of it.* I simply don't understand it.

see also **bite someone's head off**, **eat one's head off**, **keep one's head**, **laugh one's head off**, **put heads together**, **off one's head** and **standing on one's head**

## headache

a problem; a worry

□ It's not for me to say how we are to raise the money; that's your headache.

## headlines

see **hit the headlines**

## heaps of

a large number or large amount of: *heaps of opportunities*, *heaps of money*, *heaps of time*, *heaps of room* etc.

Although the word *heaps* itself is plural, it takes a singular verb when it refers to non-countables and a plural when it refers to countables.

□ There is heaps of time.

□ There have been heaps of opportunities.

## hear someone out

listen to someone till he has said all he wants to say

## hear! hear!

an exclamation expressing approval of what has been said (used mainly by members of the audience at a public meeting)

## hear tell

(followed by *that* or *of*—*that* for the fact that is stated, *of* for the person or people concerning whom the statement is made) hear (it) said in general; similar to *hear say that* (which is less common)

□ I've heard tell that women can't keep a secret, and now I believe it.

□ I've heard tell of him that he was once well off, but that he squandered his money on reckless living.

## heart

*one's heart in one's mouth*: terrified; expecting an imminent calamity

□ As we dashed along at that reckless speed, my heart was in my mouth.

*one's heart sinks into one's boots*: one becomes very despondent

*wear one's heart on one's sleeve*: display or proclaim publicly one's deepest feelings—especially those which savour of tenderness or virtue (often said of someone who falls in love easily)

*to one's heart's content*: as much as one wants to

☐ Come to the seaside with us, and you can swim to your heart's content.

The second syllable of *content* is stressed.

*one's heart isn't in it*: *My heart isn't really in this job.* I have to do it but I'm not enthusiastic about it. It doesn't seem worthwhile.

*take heart from*: be encouraged by

☐ Take heart from the promise of promotion.

*after one's (own) heart*: to one's taste and liking

☐ She's a girl after my own heart.

*not have the heart to*: find it cruel or unkind to (be critical etc.)

*take something to heart*: be much affected by (someone's comments/criticism)

*have one's heart in the right place*: have sincere and kind feelings

☐ He looks bad-tempered but he has his heart in the right place.

*with all one's heart*: very willingly; very much

## heart and soul

all one's energies and interest

☐ His heart and soul are in his work.

also adverbially, applied to a person

☐ He is heart and soul in his work.

*with all one's heart and soul*: the same as *with all one's heart*,

see **heart**

## heat

see **dead heat**

## heaven(s)

see **good heavens!**

## heel

*take to (one's) heels*: run away

*well-heeled*: originally said of shoes which are not worn down, but now used to mean having plenty of money

*Down at heel* is exactly the opposite of *well-heeled*.

see also **head(s)**, **hot on** and **kick one's heels**

## hell

*The hell* may be used as an emphatic term

(a) after semi-interrogative, semi-exclamatory words such as *what, where, when, who, how*:

☐ What the hell do you think you're doing?

☐ How the hell are we going to find the money?

(b) before nouns:

☐ We had the hell of a time in Paris.

NOTE *The hell of a time* usually expresses pleasure or approval and is much less common than *a hell of a time* which usually expresses displeasure or disapproval; so does *merry hell*.

These two expressions using *like hell* are scarcely objectionable, but convey different meanings:

**1** *He ran like hell.* He ran as fast as he could.

**2** *Like hell I will.* I absolutely will not.

## hell for leather

at a furious speed (of riding, running etc.)

☐ We saw two horsemen riding hell for leather across the plain.

The origin is uncertain. It has been suggested that it is a corruption of *all of a lather*. But it seems worthwhile asking whether it is perhaps not what we may call a de-euphemised euphemism. That is to say, it starts with the simple word *hell* (*ride like hell*); later this is felt to be profane, so the aspirate is dropped, and the word is pronounced like the name of the letter *l*. To make sure there is no mistake about it, the tag *for leather* is added—just as we might say *b for beef*, *a for apple* etc. As the final stage, the aspirate is restored, but the tag *for leather* remains.

## helluva

In written forms of conversations, this spelling of *hell of a* is often used as an emphatic form.

☐ He's spent a helluva lot of money on that house.

## help a lame dog over a stile

help someone out of a difficulty

## help but

(+verb stem) *As she spoke rather loudly we could not help but overhear what she said.* This kind of construction is very common in the speech of northern parts of England, and is not unknown elsewhere. It seems to be a mixture of the older and more formal idiom 'could not but overhear' and the more normal modern idiom 'could not help overhearing'.

## help someone off/on with his coat

assist to take off or put on his coat

## hen party

a party (as a social function) consisting entirely of women; one consisting entirely of men is known as a **stag party**

**hen-pecked**
used of a man who is dominated by his wife

**here and there**
scattered about in odd places

**here goes**
often used just when you are going to try to do something

**here, there and everywhere**
in many different places, widely scattered
□ I'll do my best to keep an eye on the place, but you can't expect me to be here, there and everywhere.
□ Usually you scarcely see a single policeman around here; today they seem to be here, there and everywhere.

**here today and gone tomorrow**
said of a person who never stays long in one place or one post
□ I don't think we should rely on Smith's helping us in what is essentially a long-term task; he's here today and gone tomorrow.

**here you are**
said when
**1** presenting something to a person
**2** pointing out something to a person, or calling his attention to it
**3** directing a person's attention to a position or a predicament
□ You *would* squander your money, despite the warnings of your friends, and here you are, with scarcely enough to feed and clothe yourself.
**4** putting a suggestion to someone
□ Here you are, what do you think of this idea?

**here's to**
the formula used in proposing a toast: *Here's to absent friends/the bride and bridegroom.*

**het up**
(jocular) heated up temperamentally

**hideout**
a place in which one hides to escape detection, arrest or discovery (of criminals, fugitives etc.)

**higgledy-piggledy**
an adverb or adjective meaning that a line of things or people is not at all straight, or that things are jumbled and untidy
□ Don't leave those desks all higgledy-piggledy.

**high**
having a strong, unpleasant smell

157

☐ That cheese is getting rather high.

also in reference to drugs, said of someone who is under the influence of a narcotic

see also **fly high**

**high and dry**

(originally *home high and dry*) safe, out of danger; probably coming from getting a boat well up on the beach out of reach of the waves

**high and mighty**

important and powerful (often used with a touch of sarcasm)

☐ He's very high and mighty now, but I can remember the time when he was a mere nobody, with scarcely a penny.

also as a noun:

☐ Only the high and mighty can do that sort of thing and get away with it!

**highbrow**

a person of intellectual pretensions (often applied disparagingly)

It is also used as an adjective (*highbrow pursuits*, *highbrow music*) and predicatively.

☐ I never listen to Radio 3, it is too highbrow for me with all those operas and talks.

see also **lowbrow**

**high-falutin(g)***

(the *g* is not pronounced even when it is written) said of remarks/ideas which sound important but are really without sense; pompous

**high-flyer**

see **fly high**

**high-handed**

exercising power insensitively or tactlessly

☐ It was high handed of him not to consult his colleagues.

**high horse**

*on one's high horse*: arrogant

**high jinks**

noisy and hilarious merry-making

☐ When all the family get together on a festive occasion, we have high jinks.

You can say *there was* or *there were* high jinks.

**high jump**

see **jump**

**high-powered**

originally used of motors etc., it is now used both of people who are

influential and of conversation, lectures, books etc. which are
intellectual

**high spirits**

*in high spirits*: very cheerful (*In low spirits* is the opposite.)

**hippie**

a social rebel of the 1960s and early 1970s, identifying himself or
herself with the 'alternative society', and believing particularly in a
rejection of material values and return to a simpler and more natural
life

**hippo**

shortened colloquial form of *hippopotamus*

**hit**

a book, film and especially a record which is a great success

□ It will be a hit.

**hit below the belt**

act so as to take an unfair or mean advantage of someone (The
metaphor is from boxing.)

**hit by**

upset or distressed by

□ I was rather hit by the news.

**hit it off with someone**

*He has never hit it off with his father.* He has never been able to agree
with his father, or have a happy relationship with him.

**hit the headlines**

be reported prominently in the newspapers

**hit the jackpot**

taken as a phrase from a big win, e.g. in gambling, now also used to
mean 'discover a way of making a lot of money'

**hit the roof/ceiling**

lose one's temper suddenly

□ He hit the roof when he found the money had gone.

**hitch-hike**

see **lift**

**hobby-horse**

someone's favourite subject

□ Don't get him on his hobby-horse! He'll never stop talking about
it.

**hobnob**

associate and talk with on familiar terms (often used with a slight
sense of sarcasm or disapproval)

□ At any social gathering where he was present you were sure to find him hobnobbing with the rich and influential.

□ What are you two hobnobbing about?

## Hobson's choice

in reality, no choice at all

It is taken from a famous Cambridge character who hired out horses in the 17th century. His customers always had to take the horse which had rested for the longest time and he never allowed them to have a favourite.

## hocus pocus

(uncountable) deception, hiding the truth

## hog the floor

(at a meeting) persist in talking and prevent others from taking part and contributing

## hold

(of weather, climate conditions etc.) continue as it is, without a change for the worse

□ We should be able to finish the job in about another couple of days, if the weather holds.

## hold down a job

manage to do a job (often despite difficulties) and retain it; also *hold a job down*

## hold it

(commonly used in the imperative) Wait a moment, don't rush into it!

## hold one's tongue

remain silent

□ The secret is out now, and all because someone could not hold his tongue.

## hold-up *(n)*

**1** an armed robbery

**2** an expression for a (mild) traffic-jam

## hold water

(of arguments, excuses, theories etc.) stand up to a critical examination; usually used in the negative

□ That theory won't hold water.

□ It's a very ingenious explanation, but it won't hold water.

## hold your horses

Wait a moment! the same as *hold it* (taken from the Horse Artillery)

## holding the baby

see **baby**

## hole

*be in a hole*: be in a difficult or awkward position
□ If we don't receive the money by the end of the month, we shall be in a hole.
*burn a hole in someone's pocket*: (of money) be available and ready to spend (often used when there's no opportunity to spend it)
□ It's Sunday, everything's closed, and there's Bob with £10 burning a hole in his pocket.
*make a hole in someone's savings*, *bank account* etc.: deplete them considerably
□ The cost of these repairs to the house has made a big hole in my bank account.
*pick holes in*: find fault with; point out imperfections in
□ It is rather discouraging, when you have spent much time and trouble on a piece of work, to have someone pick holes in it.
NOTE also the use of *hole* as a depreciatory or contemptuous reference to a place
□ I shall be glad when we get away from this wretched hole.
□ The village was a sleepy little hole.

## home

see **come home with the milk** and **nothing to write home about**

## homework

*do one's homework*: consider a matter carefully; collect and take into account all the relevant facts or information
□ If that is the speaker's opinion, it is quite clear he has not done his homework.

## honest woman

(now usually humorous) *He made an honest woman of her*. He married her after they had been living together for a time, or when she was pregnant.

## honestly

frequently used in moments of exasperation
□ Honestly! You should have told me before!

## hooey

(uncountable) rubbish, nonsense

## hooha

*make a hooha*: make a lot of fuss

## hook, line and sinker

Usually combined with *swallow* (*it*), the phrase comes from fishing, and means someone is gullible—ready to believe anything.

161

□ George will swallow your story hook, line and sinker.

see also **by hook or by crook**

**hooked (on)**

addicted (to); first used about drugs, but now often used in a jocular way for being 'addicted' to anything

□ I'm really hooked on guitar music.

**hoot**

*It was a hoot.* It was uproariously funny

**hoover**

verb and noun: (to clean with) a vacuum cleaner (from a famous trademark)

**hop**

*on the hop*: unprepared; unawares (chiefly in the expression *catch someone on the hop*)

□ Our visitors arrived early, and caught us on the hop.

*hop in* (*the car*): get in(to the car), often used in the imperative

□ Just hop in!

*hop along*: get along

□ You'd better hop along, or you'll be late.

*hop it**: go away (rather stronger than *hop along*)

□ Hop it, or I'll set the dog on you!

**hopefully**

The original English use of this word (*he opened the letter hopefully*) had in the early 1970s a second use added to it (*hopefully we'll arrive in time for lunch*). This came from America, where large numbers of German immigrants transferred their own use of the similar word into English. Many older British speakers resist the new usage, but it seems here to stay. (Formerly *all being well* or *I hope* expressed the idea.)

**hopes**

for *some hopes*, see **some**

**hopping mad**

very angry, i.e. mad to the point of hopping in rage

**horns**

see **draw in one's horns**

**horror**

*a horror*: a person (especially a child) who horrifies one by his behaviour

□ Julia is a very likeable child, but her brother's a horror.

*the horrors*: a strong feeling of horror and revulsion (used mainly in the expression *to give someone the horrors*)

□ He creeps round like a ghost, making ugly grimaces; it gives me the horrors to see him.

**horse**
*horse-trading*: bargaining (uncountable)
*look a gift horse in the mouth*: examine a gift critically (A horse's age is known by looking at marks on its teeth.)
*a dark horse*: a person of unknown capabilities or intentions
see also **back the wrong horse, flog, high horse, hobbyhorse, hold your horses, put the cart before the horse, straight from the horse's mouth** and **strong as a horse**

**hot**
*be hot stuff*: various uses of approval
□ He's hot stuff at maths.
Simply by saying *she's hot stuff*, a man will mean a girl is very attractive and sexy.
*get hot*: come near to discovering the answer to a riddle or puzzle, or to locating something hidden
□ That's not quite the right answer, but you're getting hot.
*Warm*, *cool* and *cold* (no good!) are also used.
see also **make it hot for someone**

**hot air**
(uncountable) empty, meaningless talk
□ He spoke for almost twenty minutes, but most of what he said was just hot air.
The verbal idiom is *talk hot air*, not *speak hot air*.
□ He just talks a lot of hot air.

**hot and bothered**
see **bother 4**

**hot cakes**
see **sell like hot cakes**

**hot on**
**1** pursuing closely and unremittingly
□ The police are hot on his trail
also *hot on someone's heels*
**2** having a good knowledge of; well versed in: *hot on astronomy*, *hot on modern poetry* etc.
**3** keen or enthusiastic about: *hot on football*, *hot on jazz* etc.

**hot under the collar**
nervously worried or angry
□ He soon gets hot under the collar if anything goes wrong.

☐ Keep calm; there's no need to get hot under the collar.

**hot water**

trouble (the idioms are *be in hot water* and *get into hot water*)

**hotch potch**

(countable) a mixture of different things

**house**

see **eat someone out of house and home**, **on the house** and **safe as houses**

**how about?**

**1** used in making a suggestion and asking another person's opinion of it

☐ We ought to invite the Coopers to dinner. How about Friday?

☐ How about taking two days for the journey and staying at Bath overnight?

**2** to present, in the form of a question, something that in the opinion of the speaker disproves or refutes a previous assertion

☐ 'The twentieth century has produced no great statesmen.' 'How about Sir Winston Churchill?'

☐ 'I have never had an accident while driving.' 'How about that time you ran into a lamppost?'

**3** to make a suggestion that amounts in substance to a request or an invitation

☐ How about paying back some of that money you borrowed from me?

☐ How about coming to stay with us for a few days when you are in the district?

NOTE *What about?* can be equally used in all these cases.

**how come**

how does/did it come about (that)

☐ How come that a lion was wandering around the streets of Rome? (an actual question asked during a discussion of Shakespeare's play *Julius Caesar*)

☐ 'I lost my wallet on the train.' 'How come?'

**how do you do?**

This is a form of greeting on first meeting a person. It can be used only in the second person, and as a direct question. We cannot ask 'How does your wife do?', 'How does your father do?', 'How does Charley do?' etc., nor can we say 'He asked me how I did' or, in answer to the salutation, reply 'I do very well'. The correct response is to repeat *How do you do?* to the person we are meeting.

## how-d'ye-do*

(compound noun) **1** affair; business; concern; happening
(depreciatory or ironic: *a pretty/fine/poor how-d'ye do*)
**2** a fuss: a strong expression of concern or indignation

## how goes it ?

clearly a very old form but widely used meaning 'How are things going
for you?'

## how is it ?

Why is it? What is the reason?
□ How is it that you can never get here on time?
similarly in the indirect form, except that *how is it?* becomes *how it is*
□ I don't know how it is that all the awkward jobs fall to me.

## how it is

what the position is: what the facts are (*That's how it is* follows the
explanation, *this is how it is* precedes it.)
□ 'After the death of their father there was a quarrel over the
property, and they have had nothing to do with each other since.' 'Oh,
that's how it is, is it?'
□ I should like to get another job, but if I give up my present one I lose
the pension rights attaching to it, that's how it is.

## howler

a blunder; a very bad or laughable mistake

## howling success

a great success (perhaps from a successful stage play, which produces
howls of laughter from the audience; no longer confined to the
theatre, however, or to something producing laughter—often applied
to people and their conduct)
□ As a social figure she thinks herself a howling success.

## huff

a mood of strong displeasure and resentment
□ After having his proposal voted down, he left the room in a huff.
□ He very easily gets in a huff if things do not go his way, or if anyone
disagrees with him.
The adjective is *huffy*.

## hullo

**1** a salutation used on meeting a person
**2** an exclamation expressive of surprise at the sudden sight or
discovery of something unexpected
□ Hullo! what's the matter here?
□ Hullo! the light's gone wrong.

## hum

*make things hum*: cause much activity and liveliness

□ For years the village had been a sleepy little backwater, but the new vicar soon began to make things hum.

## hum and haw

talk at some length and around the point, without arriving at any definite conclusion

□ After almost half an hour of humming and hawing they were no nearer reaching a decision than when they started.

□ He just hummed and hawed, and finally refused to commit himself.

## humdrum

very dull, boring or commonplace: *a very humdrum life*, *a humdrum task*, *humdrum work*

## hump

*get over the hump*: manage to pass the most difficult stage of doing something

## hunch

a premonition: an idea that comes to a person through intuition, and of which he can give no rational explanation

□ I had a sudden hunch that I should meet him at the club that day.

□ Hunches are unsafe guides in investment; occasionally they come off, but more often they do not.

## hurly burly

(countable) a lot of movement and noise

## hurry

see **in a hurry**

## hurt

*it wouldn't hurt someone*: used

**1** to suggest the idea that someone could well afford to do what is suggested

□ It wouldn't hurt him to give fifty pounds to the fund.

**2** to suggest that someone ought to do what is referred to

□ You've got some spare time on your hands this week. It wouldn't hurt you to cut that old lady's lawn for her.

## hush-hush

secret; confidential; not to be spoken about

□ The proposal was so hush-hush that very few people knew anything about it until it was an accomplished fact.

□ Why can't the management be more open with us? This hush-hush policy tends to breed suspicion.

**hush money**
>money paid to a person as a bribe to ensure that he keeps secret certain facts or information that he knows

# i

**ice**
>*We'll have to put that idea on ice*. We must lay it aside, postpone action on it.
>see also **cut no ice**

**iceberg**
>see **tip 3**

**idea**
>*The idea of it!* is an exclamation expressing disgust or disapproval
>□ 'He actually suggested that I should lend him my car for his summer holiday.' 'The idea of it!'
>*What's the idea?* What is the purpose or intention of what you are doing?
>□ You seem to be very busy with all those gadgets. What's the idea?
>sometimes (semi-humorously) *What's the big idea?*

**if it weren't for . . .**
>(some people use '*wasn't*') an elliptical expression which many students fail to understand
>□ I'd like to live there permanently, if it weren't for the local politics.
>(i.e. only the local politics discourage or dissuade me from wanting to live there)

**if you like**
>added to a statement or observation to emphasise it
>□ That's a tall story, if you like.
>NOTE *Like* is always stressed in this use.

**if you please**
>used colloquially to express surprise or indignation
>□ He spent about twenty minutes belittling my efforts, and then, if you please, asked to borrow a pound note.

**I'm sure**
>often added to *I don't know* as a confirmatory tag
>□ 'How much would you have to give for a house like that?' 'I don't know, I'm sure.'
>□ I don't know who that person is, I'm sure.

**imp***

rascal

□ That child is a real imp!

**imperative preceded by** *you*

In spoken English the subject *you* is often expressed before an imperative to give it the force of a suggestion or an invitation rather than a command.

□ There seems to be a noise coming from under the floor; you listen.

*You wait* may convey a threat.

□ I'll get my own back for this: you wait.

*You see if* suggests that a statement regarding the future is likely to come true.

□ I shouldn't rely on his promises. He'll let you down at the last minute, you see if he doesn't.

**in**

(used as an adjective) smart, fashionable

□ This is the in thing to wear at the moment.

□ Boots are in this winter.

It is also used of books, music, activities, ideas etc.

**in a bad way**

**1** in very poor state of health or repair

□ Mrs Coleman is in a bad way; the doctors cannot do much.

□ Our car's been in a bad way—first the steering went and now there's something wrong with the transmission.

**2** in a precarious position financially

□ That used to be quite a flourishing little business, but it's in a bad way now.

*In a poor way* has a similar meaning, though perhaps not quite so serious as *in a bad way*.

**in a cleft stick**

see **cleft stick**

**in a fix**

see **fix** *(n)*

**in a flap**

see **flap**

**in a hole**

see **hole**

**in a hurry**

In the sense of *in haste* this is, of course, normal English, but there is a colloquial use of it in such sentences as the following:

☐ I shan't do that again in a hurry.

Here the idea is 'for a very long time', often with the implication of 'never'.

**in a jam**

in a difficult position

☐ You'd better not resign from your present post until you're sure you've got another, or you may find yourself in a jam.

**in a mess**

in a state of dirtiness, untidiness, confusion, chaos, disorganisation etc.; hence *make a mess of something*: (a) cause it to be in such a state, as *make a mess of the carpet, the table cloth, one's overcoat*; (b) bungle (a task or undertaking)

**in a minute**

see **minute**

**in a nutshell**

very briefly and concisely, without going into details

☐ Can you give me the facts of the case in a nutshell?

**in a pickle***

see **pickle**

**in a state**

used colloquially to mean

**1** in a bad state

☐ His clothes were in a state!

☐ Her nerves must be in a state for such a small thing to frighten her like that.

**2** a state of worry or anxiety

☐ The poor woman was in a state until the lost child was found by the police.

**in a stew***

in a state of worry, anxiety or agitation

☐ Mrs Thomas is in such a stew. She's lost her purse, with about ten pounds in it.

**in a way**

in one respect; from one point of view

☐ In a way, I'm glad you made that mistake, for it will serve as a warning to you.

**in aid of**

sometimes used colloquially, in questions, to inquire the purpose of something, where no question of aid, in the real sense of the word is implied

# in (at) one ear and out of the other

□ We've not seen you for ages. What's this unexpected visit in aid of?

**in (at) one ear and out at the other**

said of any spoken information, advice, remarks etc. that are taken no heed of

□ Whatever you say to him goes in (at) one ear and out at the other.

**in black and white**

stated plainly in writing

□ We cannot accept the conditions unless we have them in black and white.

**in case**

This important phrase has two uses, but first note that it is used without *the* and without *that* (*in the case that* is totally wrong).

**1** with a verb following—*I'm taking my mac in case it rains*: because perhaps it will rain (You may also say *in case it should rain* but this is not necessary.) Notice this is quite different from saying *if it rains*.

**2** with a noun following

(a) *There are fire extinguishers in the corridor in case of fire*: in case there is (a) fire

(b) You can often see the instructions by a phone in Britain *In case of emergency, dial 999*. This clearly means 'if there is an emergency'. In addition to these, colloquially, *in case* is often added at the end of a statement without saying what might happen, and you must infer from the context what is implied; *just* is often used before it.

□ I'm taking my mac, (just) in case.

This corresponds to the meaning of **1** above but in some languages there is a totally different translation.

**in clover**

in a comfortable or fortunate position (probably from a horse browsing in a field of clover)

□ If once you get a job like that, with such a good salary, you're in clover.

**in for**

destined to receive or experience: *in for a shock*, *in for a surprise*, *in for a good time*

□ It looks as though we are in for a storm/a spell of fine weather.

*in for it*: in for punishment, an unpleasant experience etc.

□ One of these days all these petty misdemeanours will be discovered; then you'll be in for it.

**in good form**

see **form**

**in hot water**
see **hot water**
**in-joke**
not a fashionable joke in the sense of *in* as an adjective, but a private joke (only amusing a select group—a so-called *in-group*)
□ I didn't understand their college play, it was full of in-jokes.
**in-laws**
the parents of one's wife or husband
□ We're spending next week-end with my in-laws.
**in luck's way**
unexpectedly or unusually lucky
□ That's the third profitable venture we've managed to pull off this morning. We're in luck's way today.
**in no time**
very quickly; in a very short period of time (an example of hyperbole)
□ You can get from London to New York in no time by one of the latest jets.
**in on something**
taking part in it; having something to do with it
□ If there's any mischief afoot, young Daniel Jackson is sure to be in on it.
**in (one's) seventh heaven**
supremely happy (The medieval Cabbalists taught that there were seven heavens through which the spirit had to pass after death. Not until one reached the seventh did one attain perfection, and therefore supreme happiness.)
□ The little fellow was in his seventh heaven, playing with the other children on the beach.
**in one's stride**
see **stride**
**in one's time**
**1** during one's lifetime
□ I've had a good many disappointments in my time.
**2** in that part of one's life which is left to one
□ Men may one day be able to travel to the moon with as much ease as they now travel to the other side of the world, but that is not likely to be in my time.
**3** during that part of one's lifetime that is implied by the context
□ Students are much better provided for nowadays than they were in my time. (i.e. when I was a student)

**in . . . out**

*day in, day out*; *year in, year out* etc.: from one day/year etc. to another, without a break

□ I have done this journey, day in, day out, for the last ten years.

**in someone's bad books**
**in someone's black books**

in disfavour with someone

□ I don't want to see Susan—she's in my bad books because she broke my record player.

□ The assistant had a feeling that he was in the manager's black books, though he did not know why.

**in someone's line**

the kind of thing with which someone is concerned, in which he is interested or of which he has special knowledge

□ Is stamp-collecting in your line?

□ If you want any information on art, it's no good asking me; that's not in my line.

**in the air**

not in a settled and definite form; existing merely as an idea

□ It is impossible to give any details of the plan for rebuilding the town centre. At this stage it is only in the air.

**in the altogether**

see **altogether**

**in the bag**

see **bag**

**in the cart**

in an awkward situation

□ We had better realise our assets while we can get a good price for them. If we hold on to them and the price declines, we may find ourselves in the cart.

**in the end**

finally, eventually, ultimately (These are all near synonyms.)

NOTE *At the end* is rarely used alone, but followed by *of the day/party/story* etc.

□ I am sure that everything will turn out all right in the end.

□ We shall have to agree to their demands in the end, so we may as well agree now.

**in the first place**

**1** at the very beginning

□ We ought not to have trusted him with the money in the first place.

☐ We should have fared much better if we had adopted this method in the first place.

**2** as the first reason

☐ There are several reasons why I am opposed to the scheme. In the first place, it is too costly. In the second . . .

## (in) the kitty

(in) the reserves (of cash) upon which one can draw if necessary

☐ When we've paid all the outstanding accounts, there won't be much left in the kitty.

Literally, the *kitty* is the name given to the pool of money in some gambling games.

## in the know

see **know 3**

## in the land of the living

alive; still living

☐ It is over twenty years since I saw him, and he was pretty elderly then; I shouldn't think he's still in the land of the living now.

## in the pink*

in perfect health

☐ All the family is in the pink.

## in the red

in debt; owing more than one has the immediate means of paying (in banking and accountancy a debit balance is entered in red ink)

☐ If he doesn't pay me what he owes by the end of this month, I shall be in the red.

## in the soup

see **soup**

## in the swim

having a full and up-to-date knowledge of what is taking place in a particular sphere and taking part in it

☐ Investment is a hazardous business; even those who are in the swim sometimes come a cropper.

## in the thick of

in the most strenuous or active part of

☐ I am very busy just at present, for we are in the thick of re-organising the company.

☐ I cannot accept any social engagements for the next few weeks, while we are in the thick of examinations.

## in the way of

coming under the classification of

□ Have you anything in the way of fruit drinks?
□ In that small village there was very little in the way of entertainment.

## in (or into) trouble

a colloquial euphemism for *pregnant* (An unmarried girl who is pregnant is said to be *in trouble*; she *gets into trouble*; the man who is responsible *gets her into trouble*. It is not, of course, applied to a married woman.)

## in with

on very friendly terms with; closely associated with
□ He's in with all the well-known people in the entertainment world.
The usual combinations are *be in with*, *get in with* and *keep in with*.
□ I've had nothing to do with him since he got in with that rather disreputable crowd.
□ He takes care to keep in with those who he thinks can exercise influence in the party.
*Well in with* is probably commoner than *in with*. It denotes an even closer degree of association or intimacy.
□ He is well in with the management.
*Well in* may also be followed by *at* instead of *with*, when it denotes a place with which persons are associated:
□ He is well in at headquarters.

## indeed

note the sarcastic use of *indeed* to deny or rebut a statement or allegation made against one
□ 'I should be more likely to believe you if you weren't such a liar.' 'Liar indeed!'

## individual

used colloquially for 'person', but usually in a derogatory sense: *an odd sort of individual, a loud-mouthed individual, a shifty individual*

## influence

see **under the influence**

## innings

see **good innings**

## ins and outs

details
□ I can give you a general account of the case, but I don't know all the ins and outs of it.

## inside (a period of time)

in rather less than that period

☐ I shan't be away long: I'm hoping to be back inside two hours.

**intercom**

short for *intercommunication system*, as in an aircraft

**into the bargain**

see **bargain**

**into someone's shoes**

*step into someone's shoes*: succeed to the position another person occupies

☐ I am hoping to step into my father's shoes when he retires.

see also **shoes**

**inversion**

In colloquial English when a statement has a pronoun as a subject, in order to attract attention to it or to emphasise it, the verb and the noun-equivalent of the pronoun are repeated, in inverted order, at the end of the statement. Except with *to be*, *to have*, *can*, *will* and *must*, the verb *do* is used.

☐ He always liked his joke, did your father.

☐ He was never very keen on dancing, was my brother John.

**inviting**

attractive, tempting, welcoming: *an inviting bar*, *an inviting meal*

**irons in the fire**

undertakings in which one is engaged

☐ The family business is not his only interest; he has several irons in the fire.

☐ You can't give anything the attention you should, if you have too many irons in the fire.

see also **strike**

**it**

**1** *It* is used as an object with no clearly defined meaning after certain verbs: *hop it*, *catch it*, *walk it*, *ask for it*. Usually the whole combination makes a single compound verb, with a meaning of its own.

**2** *of it*: used for purposes of emphasis in such expressions as *a hard life of it*, *a tiring day of it*, *an easy time of it*; *of it* has a limiting or restrictive function, applying the description to the particular life, day or time in question.

see also **at it** and **for it**

**it was like this**

This is/was the position; these are the facts. (used to introduce an explanation)

☐ How did we get to know each other? Well, it was like this. I had booked two seats for the theatre, and my companion failed to turn up, so I offered my spare ticket to a young lady who had not been able to get one ... (and so the explanation continues)

**itch to do something**

be impatient to do it

also *itch for something* (*to happen*)

see also **dying**

**itchy feet**

*She's always had itchy feet.* She's restless and has always been keen on travelling.

# j

**jabber**

talk quickly, perhaps rather loudly, and in a way difficult to understand, often with *away*

☐ She was jabbering away with her friend.

**Jack of all trades**

This is rather a disparaging description of a person who undertakes many kinds of work, but is not expert, or really qualified, in any; sometimes expanded to *Jack of all trades, master of none*.

see also **every man jack**

**Jack Robinson**

*before you could say 'Jack Robinson'*: very quickly, in a very brief space of time

☐ Before you could say 'Jack Robinson', he had disappeared.

It is not known who Jack Robinson was. It is not the shortest name to pronounce.

**jackpot**

the largest (money) prize to be won, e.g. in a quiz, when a lot of money has accumulated from competitors who have won nothing

see also **hit the jackpot**

**jam on it**

If someone has a very easy job, and yet complains about it, someone may say to him 'What do you want, jam on it?' Notice this is very different from (being) in a jam.

see also **money for jam**

**jaw\***
(noun and verb) talk
□ Have a good jaw.
□ They have been jawing away there for the last quarter of an hour.

**jell**
literally, to set like a jelly, but used of groups brought together who may be expected to settle down together and become integrated; also used of theories and ideas becoming established

**jet lag**
the tired, dazed or sometimes overactive state produced by long journeys by jet, often lasting for a few days and known to be undesirable if decisions have to be taken or work done efficiently.

**jet set**
(usually taking a plural verb) the fashionable wealthy people of the world, who supposedly spend much of their time travelling in jet aircraft

**jib**
**1** (of an animal or a piece of mechanism) stop and refuse to go on
□ The horse jibbed at the journey.
□ The engine jibbed at the foot of a steep hill.
**2** (of a person) show unwillingness to go any further in some activity, be reluctant to have anything to do with an idea or suggestion
□ He jibbed at the suggestion that they should falsify the accounts.

**jiffy**
a very short time: *in a jiffy, it won't take a jiffy*

**jigger\***
*Well, I'm jiggered!* a euphemism for *Well, I'm damned!*
□ Well, I'm jiggered! Who would have thought of meeting you here?

**jiggery-pokery**
(uncountable) secret, dishonest, shady or underhand work
□ There has been so much jiggery-pokery in this affair that it is impossible to know exactly what the true facts are.

**jinks**
see **high jinks**

**jinx**
supposedly a curse, said of something constantly going wrong
□ I reckon there must be a jinx on this wretched machine.

**jitters**
a state of extreme nervousness (The principle idioms are *have the jitters, get the jitters, give one the jitters.*)

**jittery**

having the jitters

□ What's the matter with you? You seem all jittery.

□ Don't get jittery; that won't help you.

**job**

**1** The use of *job* for any kind of work, task, post, position etc. has ceased to be a colloquialism, and has become accepted informal English: *look for a better job*, *have a well-paid job*, *have an interview for a job*, *find someone a job to do*, *entrust someone with a job*.

**2** a difficulty; a difficult task

□ We had a job to find the house.

□ It was a job getting through the traffic in the High Street.

**3** *make a job of* (some task or piece of work): do it properly

□ There's no point in just patching it up; we may as well make a job of it while we're at it.

**4** see **good job**

There is also the expression *a bad job*: something to be deplored

□ It's a bad job about that train crash, isn't it?

**5** *(that's) just the job*: (that is) exactly what we need

see also **cushy job**, **hold down a job**, **soft job** and **put-up job**

**jobs for the boys**

good positions for one's associates, one's friends or those in one's favour

□ One sometimes gets the impression that in these large commercial organisations the more responsible and better-paid posts do not go by merit; it's a matter of 'jobs for the boys'.

**jog someone's memory**

help someone to remember something

□ You won't need to jog his memory—he never forgets anything.

**jogging**

running practice (known as 'footing' in many languages but not in English)

**joint**

**1** an organisation, association, club, hotel etc. (usually derogatory)

□ I shouldn't want to stay at that joint, judging from what I have heard of its reputation.

**2** a marijuana cigarette

**joke**

*no joke*: no easy task; no light matter

□ It's no joke, carrying a heavy suitcase nearly two miles.

**jolly**
> used adverbially, in the sense of *very*, but with rather more emphasis, before adjectives and adverbs: *jolly good*, *jolly hot*, *jolly quickly*, *jolly soon*

**jolly someone along**
> encourage someone, sometimes more particularly if you hope for his help later

**jolly well***
> used with verbs or participles, to give force to a statement
> ☐ I shall jolly well do what I like.
> ☐ It serves you jolly well right.
> ☐ He was jolly well made to pay.

**jot**
> **1** a word to strengthen a negative
> ☐ He doesn't care a jot.
> ☐ It doesn't make a jot of difference.
> *Jot* means 'the smallest amount' and is derived from *iota*, considered to be the smallest letter in the Greek alphabet.
> **2** *jot down*: write down quickly

**joy-ride**
> a ride for amusement, originally used of rides on roundabouts etc. at a fair, but now often heard of youths taking a car illegally, having a ride in it and then abandoning it

**jump**
> *He's for the high jump*, originally taken from athletics, subsequently meant 'He is faced with a difficult task', but lately, it is more commonly used to mean 'He is going to be reprimanded' and even 'sacked/fired'.

**jump the gun**
> anticipate something for which a time has been set
> ☐ The report is to be published next Thursday, and I don't want to jump the gun by telling you any of its contents now.
> taken from running races, when one or more of the competitors start to run before the starting gun has been fired

**junk**
> (uncountable) rubbish; discarded materials or articles
> ☐ It's about time we got rid of all that junk of your grandmother's in the box-room.

**just a minute!**
> Wait just a minute! used:

**1** to intimate that the speaker cannot comply with a request immediately

□ 'George, could you come and unlock this door for me?' 'Just a minute.'

**2** to suggest that one should pause or hesitate before accepting a previous reply, or a conclusion previously reached

□ I should think the best train for us to go on would be the 10.12—but just a minute; is that a 'Saturdays only' train?

**just about**

almost exactly; not quite, but nearly: *just about three o'clock*, *just about five miles*, *just about five pounds*; also before adjectives and past participles used adjectivally: *just about finished*, *just about worn out*, *just about ready*, *just about due*, *just about fed up*, *just about done for* (also with finite verbs)

□ The accident just about finished him as a footballer.

**just as well**

sometimes used colloquially in the sense of 'fortunate' or 'a good thing'

□ It is beginning to rain; it is just as well we brought our raincoats with us.

see also **good job**

**just in case**

see **in case**

**just like**

see **like**

**just now**

**1** a short time ago

□ I do not know where Miss Austin is. She was here just now, but she seems to have disappeared.

**2** But in such a sentence as *I cannot see you just now*, *just now* means 'this very moment'.

**just on**

just exactly; as near as makes no difference

□ It is just on twelve o'clock.

□ The journey took us just on two hours.

□ The bill came to just on ten pounds.

**just one of those things**

see **one of those things**

**just so**

in perfect order; as things should be

☐ She was a very house-proud woman; everything in her home was just so.

**just this minute**

only a very short time ago

☐ Don't trample mud from your shoes on to the carpet; I've just this minute swept it.

NOTE The perfect tense is used, not the preterite.

**just too bad**

see **too (bad) 4**

**just what the doctor ordered**

said jocularly to express one's appreciation of something that is very welcome to one

☐ Should I like a whisky and soda? I certainly should; that's just what the doctor ordered.

# k

**keep**

*That story will keep.* There is no need to tell that story now; it can be kept for another occasion.

*You can keep your* (Gorgonzola cheese/vodka/rural bliss etc.). You may like it, or think highly of it, but I don't.

**keep an eye on**

see **eye(s)**

**keep body and soul together**

*I don't know how you manage to keep body and soul together* is used of someone earning very little money, barely enough to buy food and keep alive.

**keep on at**

*I don't want to keep on at you, but* you really must mend the fence. I don't want to pester or nag you, to worry/annoy you, but you really ...

**keep one's ears open**

listen intently; be on the alert so far as one's hearing is concerned

☐ You can often pick up useful tips if you keep your ears open.

**keep one's end up**

maintain one's position in the face of opposition or adverse circumstances

    □ Things are not so easy for us as they used to be, but we manage to keep our end up.

**keep one's eyes open**
    be very watchful (a similar meaning to *keep one's ears open*, but concerned with eyesight instead of hearing)
    □ As we go through the town, keep your eyes open for a post office or a letter box.

**keep one's eyes skinned**
    watch very intently and closely; be constantly on the look-out
    □ Keep your eyes skinned for any suspicious-looking characters.
    *Peeled* is also heard sometimes instead of *skinned*.

**keep one's fingers crossed**
    By the superstitious this is regarded as a charm to ward off misfortune or ill luck; hence the expression has come to be used colloquially as a warning against over-confidence.
    □ I think the experiment will turn out to be successful, but I'm keeping my fingers crossed.

**keep one's hair on**
    see **hair**

**keep one's hand in**
    see **hand**

**keep one's head**
    remain calm in a crisis (the opposite is **lose one's head**)

**keep one's mouth shut**
    *Keep your mouth shut* for 'Hold your tongue' is vulgar; to say that a person *cannot keep his mouth shut*, when we mean that he cannot resist telling other people anything he knows, is a colloquialism.
    □ He is the last person I should confide in. He is a decent enough fellow, but he cannot keep his mouth shut.

**keep one's weather eye open**
    be vigilant; be on the look-out (a nautical metaphor)

**keep oneself to oneself**
    be rather reserved; not associate with, or confide very much in, other people
    □ No-one knew very much about the two maiden sisters, for ever since they had come to live in the neighbourhood about five years ago they had kept themselves to themselves.

**keep someone on his toes**
    cause someone to maintain an alert attitude
    □ The new boss keeps us all on our toes.

**keep something under one's hat**
  see **hat**
**keeps**
  see **for keeps**
**kerfuffle**
  see **caffuffle**
**kettle**
  see **pot**
**kettle of fish**
  situation, state of affairs; found in the phrase *that's another kettle of fish*: that's a very different matter, that's something else entirely
  with other adjectives, used sarcastically:
  □ That's a pretty kettle of fish. (i.e. an unpleasant situation)
  similarly with *fine, nice*
**kibosh**
  (first syllable pronounced to rhyme with *cry*) *He'll put a kibosh on our plans.* He'll put an end to our plans.
**kick** *(n)*
  *have a kick in it*: have a pleasantly stimulating effect, especially as appreciated by the palate
  □ I don't care very much for fruit drinks; I like something that has a kick in it.
  *get a kick out of something*: get enjoyment or pleasurable excitement from
  □ It is still assumed that kings and queens get an enormous kick out of being kings and queens. (*Observer* Supplement, 2 Oct. 1966)
  *a kick in the pants*: (somewhere between slang and colloquial) an unexpected rebuke or reprimand
  □ He was expecting a compliment, or at least an expression of gratitude, when all he got was a kick in the pants.
  see also **kicks**
**kick off**
  start; begin an activity (a metaphor from the start of a football match)
  □ We kicked off with soup, and then went on to duck and green peas, followed by ice cream.
  □ It might be a good idea to kick off with a few folk songs.
**kick one's heels**
  idle about and pass the time, with nothing particular to do
  □ Having missed the train, we were left kicking our heels for just over an hour, until the next one went.

## kick oneself

reproach oneself for something one regrets doing

☐ No sooner had I uttered the words than I could have kicked myself, as I knew they would displease him.

☐ I could kick myself for selling those shares; if only I had kept them a day or two longer I should have made nearly another hundred pounds on them.

## kick the bucket*

(slang) die (It is probably an allusion to a person who, when hanging himself, climbs on to a bucket to reach the noose and then kicks it away when the noose is round his neck.)

☐ Hasn't old George kicked the bucket yet?

## kicks

*do something for kicks*: do it for excitement, a thrill (usually used of people doing something regarded as antisocial, such as speeding or breaking windows)

## kid

**1** The noun form is used for a child or young person. *Kiddy* is a more affectionate form, but is applied only to younger children: *a kiddies' party*, *a kiddies' outing*.

**2** (verb) deceive

☐ Don't you believe him; he's kidding you.

☐ She managed to kid them that her father was an admiral.

## kill (the) time

*What on earth did you do to kill (the) time?* How did you spend the time in such a boring situation?

## kill two birds with one stone

accomplish two tasks, or achieve two purposes, by a single effort

☐ By selling some of the books we don't want, we can kill two birds with one stone: make room on our shelves for new books, and raise some money for a deserving charity.

## killing*

humorous; enough to cause one to kill oneself with laughter

☐ She was a wonderfully clever mimic; it was killing to watch her.

## kind

**1** *These kind* and *those kind*, often condemned in English textbooks, are widely used, in colloquial English. Thus you may hear *I never read those kind of books*. Similarly with *sort* (but not *type* so often): *Those sort of people get on my nerves*.

**2** *Kind of*, used adverbially, is accepted in colloquial English: *he kind* *of sniggered, I felt kind of dizzy*. In direct speech it is sometimes even written *kinda* (and similarly *sorta*, but never *typa*). The meaning here is that the following verb is not quite accurate but 'something like it' is wanted.

see also **of a sort**

## king

one who stands out far beyond others in some pursuit or accomplishment

□ 'I didn't know Atkinson was interested in cross-country running.' 'Why, he's the cross-country king in this area.'

## kinky

jokingly used to refer to someone who has unusual habits or interests, generally somewhat sexual in content, and often referring to clothes

## kip

*have a kip*: have a short sleep (like **forty winks**)

## kittens

*have kittens*: be very frightened, taken aback, shocked

□ Mum'll have kittens if I suggest going away on holiday by myself.

## kitty

see **(in) the kitty**

## knack

a gift or ability to do something well

□ She has a knack for expressing herself.

□ You have to get the knack of writing essays for exams.

## knife

*have/get one's knife into someone*: be unforgiving; have a long-standing grudge against someone

□ He began to suspect that the reason he never got promotion was that the manager had got his knife into him.

□ Once he gets his knife into you, you will never please him, whatever you do.

## knock

see **take a knock**

## knock into a cocked hat***

be far superior to

□ You may be only an amateur painter, but your pictures can knock mine into a cocked hat.

## knock someone back

cost (someone)

□ 'How much did that knock you back?' 'It knocked me back £8.'

## knock someone down with a feather

astonish, but not of situations so unpleasant as **kittens**
□ When I saw Simon after all those years, you could have knocked me down with a feather!

## knock the daylights out of

give someone a severe beating, so as to render him helpless
□ If I find him bullying small children again, and I can lay my hands on him, I'll knock the daylights out of him.
*Living daylights* is as commonly heard.
(*Daylights* is an old colloquial term for eyes.)

## knock up

**1** make as a total, when all the individual amounts are put together
□ On top of his wages, he manages to knock up about nine or ten pounds a week in tips.
**2** make ill
□ You'll knock yourself up, if you go on working at this rate.
**3** wake someone up (often at night, bringing him to the door because of an emergency of some kind, but sometimes in the morning to make sure he isn't late)
**4** make a girl pregnant (This American usage is understood by some British speakers; it may become more current in Britain in which case the three uses given above may decline.)
**5** build, construct
□ They knocked up the platform yesterday evening.
This is a little slangy and suggests the work was not as hard as may be expected; it may also be affected by **4**.

## know

Notice that *it* can only follow *know* in the sense of **3** (a) and (b), and must be in (h).
**1** *I know* (a) to introduce a sudden idea
□ I know; we'll pretend to be commercial travellers, and gain admittance that way.
(b) to express probability in the light of what one would do oneself in a similar situation
□ He might object to such a suggestion: I know I should.
(c) in a conditional clause, to express the grounds for a statement
□ If I know John, he's not likely to be late.
(d) *not that I know of*: not as far as I know
□ 'Has anyone called to see me while I've been out?' 'Not that I know of.'

**2** *I don't know* (a) *Well, I don't know!* expressive of surprise
□ Well, I don't know! Fancy his doing that, when I'd expressly told him not to.
(b) I am not sure
□ I don't know that I care for that picture.
□ I don't know that I can get there by five o'clock.
□ I am willing to give him any advice I can, but as for lending him money, I don't know so much about that.
(c) *for I don't know how long*: so long that I cannot remember
□ I haven't seen him for I don't know how long.
similarly, *since I don't know when*
**3** *you know* (a) to introduce an instruction or an explanation by relating it to some place which the speaker assumes is known to the other person
□ You know St James's Church? Well, the bus stop is a few yards farther down the road.
(b) to introduce a subject regarding which the speaker is about to make a statement
□ You know the large white house at the corner of South Street and Matfield Lane? Well, I understand there was a fire there last night.
(c) to make clear, or explain, something the speaker thinks is already clear to the other person, but which apparently is not
□ 'What film are you referring to?' 'You know, the one we saw last Wednesday.'
(d) to remind a person of something which he should know, and presumably does know, already (usually appended to a statement)
□ I can't afford to pay all that for a house. I'm not a millionaire, you know.
□ Don't start ordering people about like that. You're not at the office now, you know.
(e) to emphasise or impart a fact which the speaker wishes someone to know, but which probably he does not
□ There is not much hope of getting another job at my age. I'm over sixty, you know.
□ Did you say they asked five pounds for it? That's quite cheap, you know.
(f) in the form of a question, to introduce, in a striking fashion, a statement of a fact which the listeners cannot already know
□ Do you know, I think I'll accept the invitation, in spite of what I said just now.

☐ Do you know, I thought I felt a spot of rain just then.

(g) *Do you know what?* is used to announce something the speaker considers interesting/important/amusing. (There is no satisfactory answer to it!)

(h) *you'll know it*: used to convey the notion of severity or painfulness as a result of something one does or that happens to one

☐ Don't speak to me like that again, or you'll know it.

☐ If you hit your head on that beam, you'll soon know it.

(i) *What do you know?* is spoken quickly in answer to some surprising remark; often *Well, what d'you know!*

(j) *be in the know* (the only case of *know* being used as a noun): have information that is unknown to other people; also *having inside information*

(k) *know your onions*: know your facts

see also **from A to Z**

## know-all

a person who imagines he knows everything, and is ready to give 'authoritative' information and advice on a large number of subjects

☐ He has many good points to his credit, but I'd think more highly of him if he were not such a know-all.

## know-how

(uncountable) skill, expertise; knowledge of the way things are done

## know it all

know everything there is to know (usually in a particular field or on a particular subject) generally used sarcastically

☐ You can't teach that fellow anything; he thinks he knows it all.

## know which side one's bread is buttered (on)

This rather clumsy expression is not uncommon, meaning a person knows where his interest and advantage lie.

☐ I'm not going to complain to the boss now—I'm up for promotion in three weeks' time and I know which side my bread's buttered.

## knuckle

*Near the knuckle* is said of remarks coming close to being embarrassing and tactless.

## knuckle under

submit

☐ For a long time he maintained an aggressive and defiant attitude, but he had to knuckle under in the end.

## kowtow *or* kotow

adopt an obsequious attitude (by origin a Chinese word, denoting the custom of bending low and touching the ground with the forehead in the presence of an important person)

□ I cannot feel much respect for a person who is always kowtowing to the rich or to those in positions of authority.

**kudos**

(uncountable) a curious borrowing from Greek (though not used in modern Greek): glory; credit; honour

□ Now you've gained a lot more kudos.

# I

**lab**

abbreviation of *laboratory*, usually used in informal spoken style instead of the full word; hence attributively: *lab coat*, *lab assistant*, *lab boy*, *language lab*

**lad**

a young man, a youth (usually, though *an old lad* is also used); not an offensive word, more common than the corresponding *lass* for a girl although they are both really North country words

*a bit of a lad*: a man (of any age) who is keen on girls and is (probably) successful with them

**lag**

see **old lag**

**lamb**

see **mutton dressed as lamb**

**lame duck**

see **duck** and also **help a lame dog over a stile**

**land of the living**

see **in the land of the living**

**land on one's feet**

see **fall on one's feet**

**landed with**

usually with *get/got*: *Why did you get landed with this awful job?* Why did they give it to *you*? Why must *you* do it? (the implication being that no-one else would do it)

also *lumbered with*, *saddled with*

**large**

*as large as life*: used to express surprise at someone's presence in a particular place or on a particular occasion

□ Not for a moment did I think he would be there, after the embarrassment that he had caused on the previous occasion, but there he was, as large as life.

**lark** *(n)*
a joke; a piece of fun
□ We didn't mean to annoy anyone; we just did it for a lark.

**lark about** *(v)*
play about; fool about
□ Near the bus stop there was a gang of youths larking about.

**lash out**
spend a lot of money; be extravagant

**lashings**
(of food and drink) great quantities

**last**
see **see the last of**

**last legs**
see **leg**

**last straw**
an elliptical reference to the saying *It's the last straw that breaks the camel's back. Well, that's the last straw* will be spoken by someone in exasperation.

**last thing (at night)**
see **first thing**

**last word**
**1** the very latest; all that could be desired: *the last word in comfort, the last word in central heating*
**2** the final retort in an argument

**late in the day**
see **day**

**latest**
*the latest*: the latest news or information (not necessarily the latest in the strict sense of the word, but the latest of interest)
□ Have you heard the latest? Susan has had £50,000 left to her.

**laugh on the other side of one's face**
change one's laughter to sorrow or regret
□ It's all very well for you to laugh, but if the same thing ever happens to you, you'll laugh on the other side of your face.

**laugh one's head off**
indulge in loud and prolonged laughter
□ We laughed our heads off at the antics of the comedian.

sometimes used to denote great amusement, and not audible laughter
□ I laughed my head off when I heard of his embarrassment in front of all those people.

**laugh up one's sleeve**
laugh secretly; laugh without revealing it
□ The conceited youth thought he was making a great impression; little did he realise that most of the company were laughing up their sleeves at him.

**lay-about**
a shiftless, idle person
□ He used to be quite a respectable and reliable man; nowadays he seems to have become just a lay-about.
□ That pub is the haunt of all the lay-abouts in the district.

**lay it on thick**
use too much flattery

**lazy-bones**
a lazy person

**lead**
see **swing the lead**

**leaf**
see **take a leaf out of someone's book**

**lean over backwards**
go to extreme limits to try and satisfy someone or achieve one's purpose
□ We have leaned over backwards to persuade him to change his mind, but all to no avail.
sometimes *bend over backwards*

**lean time**
a time when one has to economise, or be very careful in one's expenditure, owing to lack of money
□ We've had a pretty lean time these last few months, with my husband out of work.

**leaps and bounds**
see **by leaps and bounds**

**leather**
see **hell for leather**

**leave out in the cold**
see **cold** and also **by your leave** and **french leave**

**left feet**
see **two left feet**

## leg

*not a leg to stand on*: nothing by which one can justify one's position

□ If you took the matter to court, you wouldn't have a leg to stand on.

*on one's last legs*: (of people) looking very ill; by extension of business or organisations when they seem near to closing down

## leg-pull *(n)*

see **pull someone's leg**

## leg-up *(n)*

**1** assistance given to a person to help him to climb up by hoisting him by the leg

□ I think I can climb over that wall if you will give me a leg-up.

**2** metaphorically, assistance given to a person to help him surmount a difficulty, or to rise to a higher position

□ I am always willing to give a deserving person a leg-up if I can.

## lemon

*The answer's a lemon* is a meaningless reply to an impossible question or riddle.

## lend someone a hand

see **give someone a hand**

## lengths

see **go to great lengths**

## lesser of two evils

the choice or decision which has to be taken in a dilemma, where one alternative is slightly less dreadful than the other

□ Let us hope this action will be the lesser of two evils.

NOTE *Evil* is usually uncountable.

## let alone

much less

□ It is not all of us who are born with the gift of handling normal children, let alone those of subnormal intelligence. (*Times Literary Supplement*, 30 June 1966)

Less idiomatically, *let me alone* means 'stop bothering me'; in contrast, *please don't leave me alone* means 'please don't go away, I'm frightened of being alone'. (You can easily remember this by the *ea* in *please* and *leave*.)

## let bygones be bygones

let us finish our quarrel/disagreement and be friendly from now on

## let-down

From the phrasal verb *to let someone down*, a *let-down* is a disappointment.

**let it ride**
    see **ride**
**let one's hair down**
    see **hair**
**let oneself (*or* someone else) in for**
    (often followed by *it*)
    *You've let yourself in for it*. The work you have agreed to do is very
    tiring/difficult.
    *You've let Jean in for a lot of extra work*. You've caused her to have
    it—not directly, but by being ill, late, inefficient etc.
**let's see**
    see **see**
**let the cat out of the bag**
    disclose a secret
    □ We've kept the matter confidential until now, but sooner or later
    someone is sure to let the cat out of the bag.
**let the side down**
    If you *let someone down*, you fail to do your duty or what is expected
    of you. By extension, in sport, if you *let your side down*, you fail to
    support your side or team, and this is now used of situations such as
    arguments or disputes.
**let up**
    **1** slacken one's effort
    □ We are making good progress, but we must not let up until we have
    achieved our object.
    **2** It now also means 'relax' and is even used as a noun.
    □ You need a bit of a let-up after all that hard work.
**level best**
    the very best that one can (The usual idioms are *do one's level best* and
    *try one's level best*.)
    □ I've done my level best to persuade them to co-operate with us, but I
    have had no success.
**lick someone's boots**
    adopt a very obsequious or servile attitude towards someone
    □ I look for politeness and courtesy from my subordinates, but I do
    not expect them to lick my boots.
**lid**
    see **put the lid on it**
**lie in**
    stay in bed late in the morning

**lie in one's teeth**
   tell an obvious lie
**lie low**
   hide, remain inconspicuous
**life**
   *for the life of me*: even if my life were to depend on it
   □ Not for the life of me can I remember where I put that parcel.
   □ I couldn't do that for the life of me.
   NOTE *for the life of me*, not *for my life*
   *in all my life*: added to *never*, to emphasise or strengthen it
   □ Never in all my life have I known such a disgraceful exhibition of
   behaviour.
   for *not on your life*, see **not on your nelly**
   see also **dog's life**, **large**, **never 4** and **time of one's life**
**life and soul**
   that which keeps something in a state of liveliness (used chiefly in *the
   life and soul of the party*)
   □ He was the life and soul of the party.
**lift**
   *give someone a lift*: take a person somewhere in a car
   *get a lift*: be offered (and accept) a lift by car
   These phrases may be used for *lifts* between people who are already
   acquainted or those who are not. *Hitch-hike* is only used in the latter
   case. (Remember that *autostop* really means nothing in English.)
**lift a finger**
   do the slightest thing (usually in negative sentences)
   □ They wouldn't lift a finger to help us.
**light-fingered**
   an adjective used of someone who steals (usually unimportant) things
**like**
   **1** used to inquire about the state of something
   NOTE *How* and *like* are not combined. You can say: *How was the
   party?* which is more colloquial than *What was the party like?* but
   English speakers do not say *How was the party like?*
   □ What's the weather like?
   □ What's it like out? (i.e. outdoors)
   □ What's it like in town? (i.e. the state of the weather, or the state of
   the traffic)
   **2** *that's just like him*: characteristic of him; what one would expect of
   him

□ That's just like Jim; you can never rely on him to keep a promise.

**3** *the like(s) of*: people of the same kind as

□ Such hotels are not for the like(s) of us (because they are too expensive).

**4** (substandard use) appended to a verb, to signify an activity resembling that mentioned: *I hesitated, like. He coughed, like.*

also after adjectives, for a similar purpose: *I felt drowsy, like.*

Sometimes, when used in an explanation, the word is superfluous, and adds nothing to the meaning.

□ I had a day off from work, like, so I stayed in bed a bit later in the morning.

**5** *I like it but it doesn't like me.* I would like to eat that food, but it would make me ill.

**6** *nothing like so ... as*, as in *She's nothing like so pretty as you.* You are much prettier than she is.

**7** *as like(ly) as not*: see **likely**

**8** *the like(s) of it*, as in *I've never seen the like(s) of it before.* I've never seen anything like it before.

see also **something like**

### like a shot

very quickly; without waiting

□ As soon as he heard the news he was off like a shot to see them.

### like anything

a meaningless comparison, used to suggest 'very much', 'very fast' etc.: *spend money like anything, run like anything, laugh like anything*

### like hell

see **hell**

### like mad

as if one were mad; furiously, wildly

□ He dashed down the road like mad/shouted like mad.

### like this

see **it is/was like this**

### like wildfire

very rapidly

□ The news spread like wildfire.

### likely

*as likely as not*: probably

□ As likely as not, they have heard the news already.

*Not likely!* is a strong or emphatic way of expressing a denial or a refusal (an example of litotes)
□ Do you think I'm going to pay all that money for a small cottage, especially when it needs so many repairs? Not likely!

**limb**
*be out on a limb*: find one's ideas/outlook to be different from other people's; be out of touch/isolated

**limelight**
*be in the limelight*: receive a lot of publicity; originally referring to the spotlights used in a theatre

**limit**
the most remarkable or astonishing thing I've known or heard (usually used with a suggestion of disapproval or disgust)
□ I've known people make some extraordinary requests, but that's the limit.
also of people: *he/she's the limit*

**line(s)**
*on these/those lines*: of this kind
□ I think the boss is going to suggest introducing some new rules or something on those lines.
see also **drop a line**, **hard lines**, **in one's line** and **sign on the dotted line**

**line of country**
sphere of interest and/or knowledge
□ Church organs? Well, I'm afraid they're not really my line of country.

**lined up for**
(also sometimes *in line for*) in mind for, or in prospect for, a task or a position
□ The management have got him lined up for the secretaryship.
□ There are several people lined up for that job.

**linen**
see **wash one's dirty linen in public**

**lino**
a colloquial abbreviation of *linoleum*

**lip***
(uncountable) impolite answers
□ Don't give me any of your lip.
□ I don't want any of your lip here.
see also **stiff upper lip** and **pay lip service**

**live and let live**

be tolerant of others' shortcomings or failings, in the hope that they will be similarly tolerant of yours

□ We shall never get anywhere with all this criticism and fault-finding. I believe in the principle 'Live and let live'.

**live from hand to mouth**

see **hand**

**live wire**

(used of a person) one full of energy and enthusiasm

**living**

see **in the land of the living**

**lo and behold**

an archaism preserved in semi-jocular use in colloquial style; expresses surprise at something or the appearance of someone who was not expected

□ Lo and behold, who should be there but Aunt Matilda.

**loads**

commonly used for *lots*

□ There were loads of fish in the lake.

*Masses* is used in the same way.

see also **heaps** and **get a load of this**

**loaded question**

a question with an ulterior motive, such as:

□ 'Are you free tomorrow evening?' 'Yes, I think so.' 'I was wondering if you could possibly come and help me to move my things to my new flat.'

**loaf**

waste time; often *loaf about/around* (A *loafer* is someone who doesn't work.)

see also **use your loaf**

**local**

**1** the local public house, but not a night club or restaurant

□ The team's unexpected victory was the one topic of conversation in the local that evening.

**2** a local person, generally of a village; a native

**3** a local newspaper

□ Do you read the local regularly?

It is also commonly referred to as the *local rag*.

**lock, stock and barrel**

entirely; completely

☐ They sold the business lock, stock and barrel.
(The metaphor is from the parts of a gun.)

**log**

**1** an abbreviation of *logarithm*; also attributively, as *log tables*

**2** (verb) travel (a distance)

☐ I suppose we logged a good 9000 miles all told (altogether).

**loll**

(usually *loll about/around*) lean against walls or furniture and do nothing

**lollipop man** *or* **lady**

a person who guides children across a busy road to and from school, carrying a sign looking like a lollipop

**lolly**

abbreviation of *lollipop*: a sweet (somewhere between slang and colloquial)

More commonly, it means 'money' (slang).

**loner**

**lone wolf**

an individual who seems to avoid company and who has very few friends

(*Loner* has become more common in the last few years.)

**long and short of it**

all that it amounts to when the facts have been considered

☐ He made out a very plausible case to excuse himself, but the long and short of it is that he never intended coming from the very beginning.

**long chalk**

see **by a long chalk**

**long** *(adv)* **for**

not destined very long for; chiefly in the expression *not long for this world*: not likely to live much longer

**long in the tooth**

elderly

**long sight**

for *by a long sight*; *a long sight* + comparative, see **sight**

**long way**

see **by a long way**

**long-winded**

verbose; (of a person) given to speaking at great length; (of a speech, address, sermon etc.) delivered at great length, and in a great many words

## loo
a useful word in common use since the 1960s for W.C., lavatory; welcome, as it is inoffensive, not funny, and seems comparatively classless

## look
see **picture 2**

## look at
consider
□ He wouldn't even look at the suggestion.
□ The house may be in good repair, but I couldn't look at it at that price.

## look big
look important in the eyes of other people
□ He can't really afford to stay at the best hotels wherever he goes; he just does it to look big.

## look down (one's nose) at/on someone
look at a person in a scornful/superior way
□ I have the uncomfortable feeling that he is looking down his nose at us all the time.
□ Those people look down on you.

## look here
used to introduce and lead up to (a) a suggestion or proposal, (b) a protest or threat
□ Look here, suppose we accept the goods on trial first, and then see whether they will be suitable?
□ Look here, do you think you can treat me like a schoolboy?

## look in *(n)*
an opportunity of participating in some activity, or of giving one's attention
□ After the lecture one or two people monopolised the discussion, so that no-one else could get a look in.

## look like
seem as if
**1** talking of the weather, using a noun, to say what is expected or likely
□ It looks like rain/snow.
**2** followed by a gerund
□ The rain does not look like stopping.
□ He looks like failing his exams.

**look-out** *(n)*
**1** prospect
□ If the company can't pay its dividend, it's a poor look-out for the shareholders.
**2** responsibility; fault
□ If your application is not considered because you failed to send it in on time, that's your look-out.

**look over one's shoulder**
nervously keep a careful watch on others, for fear one might be noticed or overheard
□ What a relief it is not to have to look over your shoulder before you speak to a companion in a café or any similar public place.
NOTE *Over* cannot be put at the end of this or the following phrase.

**look over someone's shoulder**
keep a careful watch on someone
□ It is embarrassing to have someone looking over your shoulder while you're at work, as though you could not be trusted.

**look sharp***
be quick
□ Look sharp; don't dawdle about like that.
□ You may just manage to catch the bus if you look sharp.
see also **by the look of it** and **dirty look**

**loop-hole**
frequently used to refer to a way of avoiding a rule or law because of some imprecise wording in it

**loose-endish**
bored, unable to decide what to do next
□ The children are so loose-endish today.
see also **at a loose end** and **on the loose**

**lose face**
lose prestige or esteem in the eyes of others
□ He knew he was wrong, but would not admit it, for fear of losing face.
cf. **save one's face**

**lose one's head**
see **keep one's head**

**loss for words**
unable to find anything to say (because of embarrassment, shock, confusion etc.)
□ I was simply at a loss for words.

**lot** *(n)*
all (when preceded by *the*)
□ The waitress dropped the tray of cups and saucers, and smashed the lot.
□ The greedy little boy ate the lot, and then asked for more.
see also **take a lot of**

**lots**
many; much
When the reference is to number (*many*), *lots*, in normal idiom, takes a plural verb; when it is to amount or quantity, it takes a singular verb (*lots of people are, lots of butter is, there are lots of people, there is lots of time*). But in colloquial English, after the formal subject *there*, a singular verb is sometimes used with a plural noun when the individual ones are thought of collectively.
□ There's lots of apples on that tree.

**loud-mouthed**
used of someone who shouts, particularly if he swears a lot and noisily

**lousy**
literally infected with lice but now used (emotively) to mean 'very bad'

**love** *(n)*
In the local speech of certain parts of England, especially London, Yorkshire and Lancashire, *love* is widely used as a polite form of address (mainly by women) to children and adults alike, irrespective of sex, and irrespective of whether they are known to the speaker or not. No kind of affection is implied.
□ Good morning, love.
□ Thank you, love.
□ Could you oblige me with some small change, love?
often written 'luv' in this use
*for love (n)or money*: by any means whatever (The words *love* and *money* are not to be taken literally.)
□ You can't get servants nowadays for love or money.
□ That watch has a sentimental value for me; I wouldn't part with it for love nor money.
*There is no love lost between them*. They do not like each other; they are not on friendly terms with each other.
□ I wouldn't say they are enemies, but there is no love lost between them.

**lowbrow**
the opposite of **highbrow**

If you like classical music, you may consider pop-music to be *lowbrow*, but you won't think of classical music as *highbrow* of course! So you are only likely to use the word about the opposite extreme to the one you enjoy. In fact, *middlebrow* is also sometimes used.

**low-down**

confidential information

□ Give me the low-down on John's wife.

**low-key** *(adj, adv)*

not showing emotion though the situation could easily lead to it

□ I tried to treat the whole delicate matter very low-key.

**low profile**

*keep a low profile*: remain quiet and try to be as little noticed as possible, in order to escape criticism

**low spirits**

see **high spirits**

**luck**

see **down on one's luck** and **in luck's way**

**lucky**

In itself it is not colloquial, but envy is often colloquially expressed by: *you lucky thing/beggar*, without the usual unpleasant associations these might have.

**lug something about**

drag or, more often, carry something heavy from place to place; also *lug in/into*, *lug outside*, *lug up* etc.

**lukewarm**

In itself, this is a very old term meaning 'tepid' but it is common to talk of a *lukewarm attitude/response*, meaning 'unenthusiastic'.

**lumbered with**

□ Poor old George *got lumbered with* all the heavy boxes: he had to carry them all (very similar to **landed with**)

**lurch**

usually to *leave someone in the lurch*: leave him in a difficult situation

# m

**mac(k)**
abbreviation of *mackintosh*, in conversational English used more often than the full word
□ You'd better take your mac(k) with you.
Waterproof material used for the coats was invented by a Mr Mackintosh who died in 1843.

**mad**
cross; annoyed
□ I do feel mad about making that stupid mistake.
*mad about* something that has happened, *mad with* a person
see also **like mad**

**-mad**
(as a suffix) mad on whatever is mentioned: *football-mad*, *theatre-mad*

**mad as a hatter**
**mad as a march hare**
These are conventional expressions, meaning 'scatter-brained', 'unpredictable in one's behaviour', 'having strange ideas'. Hares are particularly wild in March which is their rutting season. The original mad hatter was a certain Robert Crab, of very eccentric behaviour, who set up in the trade at Chesham, in Buckinghamshire, in the latter part of the seventeenth century; but it was Lewis Carroll who made the phrase a household word, in his character of the Mad Hatter, in *Alice in Wonderland*.

**mad on** *or* **about**
wildly enthusiastic about (*mad on football*, *mad on pop music*, *mad about motor bikes*)

**madam**
used colloquially to characterise a young girl who is somewhat precocious, or a woman who is inclined to be dictatorial
□ Susan is only eight, but she is quite a madam.
□ Mrs Sharp is not exactly popular with the other members of the society; she is such a madam.

**mag**
short for *magazine* (periodical)

**make** *(n)*

Remember we talk in English of the *make* of a car, radio etc. (not *mark*)

see also **on the make**

**make a bee-line**

see **bee**

**make a clean sweep**

get rid of everything (or every one of the things specified)

□ They made a clean sweep of the flowers in the garden, and planted fresh ones.

**make a fool of**

*He doesn't mind if he makes a fool of himself.* He doesn't mind if other people laugh at him—even unpleasantly.

*Don't make a fool of Tim.* Don't laugh at him.

**make a fuss**

see **fuss-pot**

**make a go of something**

make a success of it

□ His father set him up in business, but he couldn't make a go of it.

**make a hash of**

see **hash**

**make a hole in**

see **hole**

**make a song about**

speak continually about (often also *make a song and dance about*)

□ I am sorry to hear of your bad luck, but you needn't make a song about it.

*nothing to make a song about*: something rather trivial

□ Our victory over a team considerably inferior to our own was nothing to make a song about.

**make a splash**

do something on such a scale as to create a sensation, or attract attention

□ He determined to make a splash on the occasion of his daughter's wedding, so he spent £2500.

**make an honest woman of her**

see **honest woman**

**make (both) ends meet**

keep expenditure within the limits of income

□ With a large family of growing children to feed and clothe, my mother had difficulty in making (both) ends meet.

**make eyes at**

gaze amorously at

□ He sat in the corner of the room, making eyes at the girls.

**make it hot for someone**

treat someone severely (usually by way of punishment, or to show one's displeasure at his conduct)

□ If I find anyone trespassing on my land, I'll make it hot for him.

**make no bones about**

see **bones**

**make off with**

*Make off* is 'hurry away', so *he made off with my dictionary* means he took my dictionary and perhaps he has actually stolen it.

**make oneself scarce**

see **scarce**

**make quick work of**

**make short work of**

dispose of, get rid of quickly (see **rid**)

□ The hungry children made short work of the jam tarts.

□ A bulldozer can make short work of a brick wall.

**make someone at home**

help someone to be relaxed in your own home

**make someone think**

cause someone to reflect on a matter in a more serious light than he has done before

□ When you hear of such serious accidents being caused by such simple things, it makes you think.

□ I suggested that he should put himself in the place of the other fellow before condemning him. That made him think.

**make someone's blood boil**

make someone very indignant or angry

□ The selfish way in which that young fellow treats his mother makes my blood boil.

**make yourself at home**

an invitation to be relaxed and not stand on formalities

**make the most of**

profit as much as possible from

□ Make the most of your time at college.

This is a common and easily learnt phrase; its significance lies in the fact that it is the only place in English where the three words *the most of* come together. If you want to express the idea 'the greater part of the people', you can say *most people* or *most of the people*. (*The most* is of course used in superlatives.)

**make tracks**

depart; leave

□ It's nearly midnight. It's about time we were making tracks.

The place to which one is going may also be specified: *make tracks for home*, *make tracks for the office*, *make tracks for the railway station*

**make whoopee***

**1** rejoice wildly (from the exclamation *whoopee!*)

□ After hearing of the victory of our side, we spent the whole of that evening making whoopee.

**2** make love (Because of this meaning, foreigners are not recommended to use it in the original meaning.)

**man**

used as a form of address to express feelings, such as surprise, impatience, annoyance etc.

□ Come on, man, don't stand hesitating like that.

see also **old man**

**man jack**

see **every man jack**

**man-size**

of the size suited to a man: *a man-size job*, *a man-size salary*

**man-to-man talk**

This is a serious conversation between two men; in comparison, a *tête-à-tête* (which is used in English) suggests a more light-hearted or gossipy conversation. A man-to-man conversation is often unpalatably frank.

**manger**

see **dog in the manger**

**map**

see **off the map**

**marge**

abbreviation of *margarine* (pronounced to rhyme with *large*; hence the final *e* in the spelling, though in the full word the *g* is followed by an *a*)

**marines**

see **tell it to the marines**

**mark**

*mark my word(s)*: take notice of what I say

□ Mark my word: he'll let you down, as he has let down other people.

*quick (slow) off the mark*: quick (slow) in making a start

□ Smithers must have been quick off the mark. He was due to leave at 4.30, and it's scarcely a minute past that now.

*up to the mark*: up to the required or expected standard

□ This work is scarcely up to the mark.

Where one's health is concerned, *not up to the mark* usually means 'not very well'.

□ I've not felt up to the mark for the last two or three days.

see also **wide of the mark** and **make** *(n)*

**masses**

see **loads**

**mate**

a very widely used (substandard English) vocative, usually to someone whose name you don't know (It may be spreading slowly up the social scale and always implies a relationship of equality.)

**maths**

short for *mathematics*

**matter**

see **for that matter**

**may/might as well**

used to put forward a proposal without enthusiasm, because there is nothing better to do

□ If you don't want any more coffee, we may as well go home.

*Might as well* gives the same meaning.

see also **as well**

**meal**

see **square**

**mean to say**

*do you mean to say ...?* used to express incredulity

□ Do you mean to say you actually lent him the money without any security?

(*Well*) *I mean to say* expresses surprise, disgust, incredulity etc. as a comment to the speaker's remarks.

**means**

see **by all means** and **by any manner of means**

**measly**

contemptibly small: *a measly little thing, a measly little sum of money*

**meaty**

intellectually substantial: *a meaty lecture/book/programme*

## media

short for *mass media* of communication, i.e. the press, radio and television (strictly a plural)

□ The media will soon get hold of this story.

## memo

short for *memorandum*, a written note as a record or to remind someone to do something

## memory

see **jog one's memory**

## menace

Literally a threat, but in colloquial speech the noun is much weakened and means 'nuisance'.

□ My three-year-old son is a real menace.

## mend

*be on the mend*: be getting better from an illness

## mercy

*it's a mercy*: something to be thankful for

□ It's a mercy he wasn't killed, dashing in front of a car like that, without looking.

## mess *(n)*

A *mess* is a dirty or untidy state of affairs; hence *in a mess*, *make a mess*. *Make a mess of* may also mean 'spoil by doing imperfectly'.

□ No matter what you ask him to do, he makes a mess of it.

A *mess-up* is also often used.

see also **in a mess**

## mess about

**1** trifle; not be seriously employed (often used to express the speaker's contempt for an occupation which he regards as trifling, but which may not actually be so)

□ We spent the whole morning just messing about.

□ He's been messing about with that motor bike for the last hour or more.

**2** interfere (with)

□ Don't mess about with that typewriter.

## messy

such as is likely to make one in a mess

□ Cleaning and oiling a bicycle is a messy job.

□ It is so messy in the garden, after all this rain.

## micky

see **take the micky (out of someone)**

**middle name**
in ordinary colloquial English a name of such a kind is bestowed
jocularly or sarcastically on a person on a particular occasion to
express the speaker's opinion of him
□ Your middle name's Scrooge. (i.e. you are mean)
(Scrooge is the classic miser character in Dickens's *A Christmas
Carol*.)

**middle of the roader**
**1** used (mainly in an academic context) of a person of average ability
and performance; rather better than **also-ran**
**2** someone whose political stance is not extreme

**middlebrow**
see **lowbrow**

**middling**
moderately good; moderately well (used especially of a person's
health)
□ 'How are you feeling today?' 'Middling.'
*Middling* expresses a qualified satisfaction; *only middling* expresses a
certain degree of dissatisfaction or disappointment. *Fair to middling*
implies lukewarmness.
□ 'How is your wife?' 'Fair to middling.'
see also **fair**

**might**
**1** followed by a perfect infinitive to express mild reproach for
something one has omitted to do
□ You might have told me you were going to be late for dinner!
**2** similarly to reproach oneself
□ I might have known this would happen
**3** in a question, in place of the plain *do?*, *is?* or *are?*, to express
sarcasm
□ Who might you be? What might you want?
□ Your friend Mr Jenkins? And who might he be?

**mighty**
very (usually used ironically or sarcastically: *mighty fine*, *mighty
smart*, *mighty soon*)
□ He thinks himself a mighty clever fellow.
□ A mighty fine thing it would be, wouldn't it, to have the family
name dragged in the dust?
□ You'll have to do it mighty soon, or it will be too late.
see also **high and mighty**

**mike**
   **1** abbreviation of *microphone*
   **2** abbreviation of the name *Michael*, as in the rather mild oath *for the love of Mike* (i.e. St Michael)
   □ For the love of Mike, stop your grumbling.
**mile**
   see **stick out a mile**
**milk**
   see **come home with the milk**
**mill**
   see **grist**
**mince one's words**
   choose one's words carefully so as not to give offence, or at least so as to tone down their import (usually in negative sentences)
   □ I told him what I thought of him, and I didn't mince my words, either.
**mind how you go**
   take care of yourself; be careful
**mind one's step**
   see **watch one's step**
**mind you**
   used colloquially to draw attention to a statement and emphasise it
   □ I didn't believe him, mind you.
   □ Mind you, I would always investigate a case pretty thoroughly before I gave any monetary help.
   Sometimes *mind* alone is used:
   □ I wouldn't do that for everyone, mind.
   see also **give someone a piece of one's mind**, **never mind**, **to my mind** and **weight off someone's mind**
**minute**
   a short period of time (not strictly a minute as reckoned by the clock)
   □ Wait a minute.
   □ I shan't be a minute.
   □ Lunch will be ready in a minute.
   see also **just a minute**, **just this minute**, **mo** and **half a mo**
**misfit**
   a person who cannot adjust to society or his/her position; in itself, not very colloquial but quite often used jocularly or sarcastically
**miss**
   see **give someone (*or* something) a miss**

**mistake**

*and no mistake*: added to the end of a statement as a strong affirmative

□ We have had a wretched summer this year, and no mistake.

*make no mistake about it*: added to the end of a statement, or occasionally prefixed to it, as a kind of warning that the statement is to be taken seriously

□ We shall insist on having every penny that is due to us, make no mistake about it.

**mixture as before**

(always used after *the*) Strictly, this is a formula used by a doctor or a pharmacist in instructions written on a bottle of medicine. In an extended and more colloquial sense, it is applied to a number of provisions, instructions, regulations, proposals etc. that do not differ greatly from those that preceded them.

□ At first sight the new budget looks very much like 'the mixture as before'. (i.e. there are very few changes from the previous one)

**mo**

a common shortening of *moment*

□ Wait a mo. He'll be back in a mo.

see also **half a mo**

**moan**

complain

□ I cannot bear a woman who is always moaning.

□ For goodness' sake, stop moaning about misfortunes.

**mod cons**

an abbreviated form of *modern conveniences* (in a house), originally (and still largely) an auctioneer's or a house agent's term; from there passing into colloquial English and used for the ordinary conveniences and refinements of civilised life, such as piped water, proper sanitation etc.

□ It was a small cottage in a remote village, with few mod cons.

**moment**

(used with *the*) as soon as; perhaps being a shortening of *at the moment when*

□ The moment he saw me, he ran away.

see also **at the moment**

**money**

*have more money than sense*: spend money in a foolish way

□ She's got more money than sense.

see also **hush money**

**money down the drain**
  see **down the drain**
**money for jam**
  money that is very easily earned
  □ If you've had the job offered you, take it; it's money for jam.
**monkey** *(n)*
  a mischievous child
  □ He's a monkey, that child is.
  also *a little monkey* and *a young monkey* (The latter is often used good-humouredly when addressed to a child: *What are you doing there, you young monkey?*)
**monkey about** *(v)*
  indulge in mischief; interfere mischievously with (something)
  □ Someone's been monkeying about with this lock.
  □ Stop monkeying about with that typewriter.
**monkey tricks**
  **1** mischievous tricks
  **2** practices to which one objects
  □ If he comes any of his monkey tricks with me, I'll soon tell him off.
**month of Sundays**
  a very long time
  □ You haven't cleaned the car in a month of Sundays.
  There is no real reference to Sundays and idiomatically the preposition is usually *in* and not *for*.
**mooch**
**moon**
  walk about idly and in a slovenly manner: *mooch down the street, just mooch about, mooning around the house*
**moonlight flit**
  a secret removal from one house to another under the cover of night (The implication is often that it is done to avoid paying the rent or other debts; it is sometimes shortened to *do a moonlight*.)
**moonlighter**
  a person who does one job by day and a second job in the evening or night (which may not be admitted or declared openly)
**moonshine**
  nonsensical ideas or talk; ideas that are for the most part merely visionary, with no foundation on fact
  □ All that he says sounds attractive enough, but it's just a lot of moonshine.

Notice that *moonshine* and *moonlight* are quite different and both are uncountable.

**more like it**

*That's more like it* expresses approval after someone has done better or produced more exactly what was ordered.

**morning after the night before**

the morning following a night of revelry, when the after-effects are felt

□ 'You don't seem very energetic this morning. What's the matter?' 'I'm afraid it's the morning after the night before.'

closely associated with a **hangover**

**most of**

see **make the most of**

**mother's boy**

a boy who is doted on and spoiled by his mother

**mountain out of a molehill**

*Don't make a mountain out of a molehill.* Don't exaggerate the importance of this matter.

**mouth**

see **down in the mouth, heart, horse, keep one's mouth shut** and **take the words out of someone's mouth**

**move**

Notice the difference among the following idioms:

*I must make a move.* I must leave. (e.g. a group of friends—temporarily)

*I'm thinking of moving.* I'm considering that I may change my job or the place where I live.

*It's my move.* My turn is next (in a game, or more metaphorically, in the 'game' of business, human relationships etc.)

□ The boss told me the job would be coming up so it's my move now (so it's up to me to apply for it).

*I must get a move on.* I must hurry (up).

The first and last of these are especially common colloquially.

**much**

see **up to much**

**much of a muchness**

very much alike; closely resembling each other

□ I don't see that there is anything to choose between the two patterns; they're much of a muchness.

**muck**

dirt, filth, rubbish; hence *mucky*: dirty, filthy (But it is only used of material dirt or filth. We can talk about a dirty story, or a filthy story, but not a *mucky* story.)

☐ His shoes were all mucky, because he had been in the pig-sty.

**muck about**

fool about; play rather boisterously and aimlessly

☐ Someone had been mucking about with my bicycle.

☐ Now you boys, stop mucking about there.

**mud**

see **clear as mud** and **stick-in-the-mud**

**muddle**

as a noun, similar to *mess* (Both words are countable.)

*muddle-headed*: unable to think clearly

*muddle through*: manage somehow

☐ We haven't got much money left but we can muddle through.

**mug**

**1** (slang) face

**2** a foolish person; one who is ignorant or incompetent

☐ I object to your treating me as though I'm a mug.

☐ He's a mug where chess is concerned.

*no mug*: an intelligent or clever person (understatement)

☐ 'Gavin's just got in to Cambridge.' 'I thought he was no mug.'

see also **game** *(n)*

**mugging**

attacks on pedestrians etc. often in large cities, usually involving robbery (A *mugger* is a youth who does this.)

**mum**

*Mummy* is mainly used by young children, *mum* is used as the vocative by older people and *mother* is used more when talking of her to others (mostly outside the family).

cf. **dad(dy)**

There are still families where *mother* and *father* are used in the vocative and probably *mother* is more common than *father*.

**mumbo jumbo**

(uncountable) meaningless talk or jargon

**mum's the word**

keep quiet; say nothing

**murder**

see **get away with murder**

**muscle in**

**1** intrude or force one's way in (followed by *on*)

□ 'Muscling in on Matron's World.' (headline to an article on men as matrons in hospitals, in the *Observer*, 8 Sept. 1965)
**2** take advantage of a situation to turn it to one's own account
□ All the drug firms are muscling in on this scare about an influenza epidemic.

**must**
(countable) a necessity; something that is considered indispensable
□ Binoculars are a must when you go on holiday.

**mutton dressed as lamb**
something ugly or old disguised to look attractive or young

**my!**
an exclamation expressing surprise or admiration (probably an abbreviation of *my word!*)
□ My! That's a big apple.

**my foot!**
see **foot**

**my word!**
an exclamation to give emphasis to a statement or a command
□ My word! you'd better not do that.
□ Did she really say that? My word!


# n

**nab**
one of several colloquial synonyms for 'steal', see **whip**, **nick**, **pinch** and **rip off**

**nag**
complain persistently, especially within a family
□ Jan nagged me for days about forgetting to mend the window.

**names**
for *call someone names*, see **call**; for *drop names*, see **drop**

**nana**
This has perhaps since the early 1960s replaced **granny** in many children's speech.

**nap**
a short sleep

**narrow squeak**
a narrow escape; an attempt that succeeds by only a very narrow margin

☐ You had a narrow squeak there; if that car had not pulled up just when it did, you would have been knocked down.

☐ We just managed to catch the train, but it was a narrow squeak.

see also **straight and narrow**

**natter**

**1** indulge in idle talk or conversation

☐ Those two women have been standing there nattering for the last twenty minutes.

**2** complain; grumble petulantly

☐ I know it's annoying to have to alter your plans at the last minute, but don't keep nattering about it.

**natty***

neat and elegant

**near the bone**

see **bone**

**near the knuckle**

see **knuckle**

**near thing**

a narrow escape; something achieved only by a narrow margin (see **narrow squeak**) The idiom is *it (or that) was a near thing*, not *you had a near thing*.

**neck**

*stick one's neck out*: expose oneself to criticism

see also **dead from the neck up** and **get it in the neck**

**needle**

*Why do you keep needling me like that?* Why do you keep trying to irritate me with such remarks? (Probably more sly and subtle than *nag*.)

**neither here nor there**

of no significance; of no relevance to the matter under discussion or consideration

☐ There is a difference of just on two pounds between the two estimates, but that's neither here nor there when we are dealing in thousands.

☐ The fact that the defendant was awarded four medals in the last war is neither here nor there where a charge such as this is concerned.

**nelly**

see **not on your nelly**

**nerve**

*Have a nerve* is the same as *have a cheek*. Similarly *What a nerve!* and

*Of all the nerve!* are exclamations to express shocked disgust at someone's impudence.

**nervous of**

*She's always been nervous of spiders.* Notice carefully that this everyday use does not mean 'agitated' or 'angry' or 'excited' but 'afraid (of)'.

**nervy**

Many languages use a word (resembling *nervous*), which as you see from the above entry is a false friend. In English, there are a remarkable number of expressions to supply this idea, and they are gathered here rather than being scattered through this book. They are not exact synonyms: the one which best describes a person who is constantly like this is *highly-strung*. The remainder, grouped according to their similarity of construction, are more usual to describe someone's temporary state.

To be flustered/bothered/agitated; to be edgy/jittery/nervy/tense/upset/uptight; to be in a dither/flap/flat spin/pother/state/stew/tizzy; to be (all) hot and cold/(all) hot and bothered/(all) on edge/all of a dither; to go to pieces/up the wall/spare; have/get the wind up; have a fit/butterflies in the stomach.

This list covers the range of meanings of being angry, confused, harassed and worried.

**nest-egg**

a sum of money which has been saved up

**never**

**1** used as an emphatic negative in making a denial

□ I never said any such thing. (i.e. I did not say . . .)

□ 'You promised me a watch for my birthday.' 'I never did!'

**2** used as an exclamation to express incredulity

□ 'What do you think? That old miser has given five pounds to the fund.' 'Never!'

**3** used to express a mingling of incredulity and reproof

□ You never let him have the money, did you?

□ You surely never signed the document without reading it?

**4** *never on your life*: expresses a strong negative

□ 'You'd willingly accept a reduction in salary, wouldn't you, Jack?' 'Never on your life.'

**5** *Well, I never!* an exclamation expressing surprise or astonishment

□ Well, I never! Here's that ring I lost two or three months ago.

**6** *Well, I never did!* an expression of surprise mixed with disapproval (an ellipsis of *Well, I never did hear of such a thing*)

□ 'After all the unpleasant things he's said about me, he's now asking for my assistance.' 'Well, I never did!'

**never mind**

**1** much less

□ I can scarcely afford to live in the house I have at present, never mind a bigger one.

**2** disregard; leave out of account; take no notice of

□ Do what your doctor advises you; never mind what other people say.

□ Never mind what you paid for it. What is it worth now?

□ He goes for a walk every Sunday morning, never mind what the weather is.

**never-never**

(used with *the*) a satirical colloquialism for the hire-purchase system (The suggestion is that the buyer never finishes paying for the goods.) You buy goods *on* the never-never just as you buy them *on* hire purchase.

**new leaf**

see **turn over a new leaf**

**news**

*That's news to me.* I hadn't heard that. (almost showing disbelief)

NOTE *News* (though it always needs as -*s*) is uncountable, so all associated words must be singular: *this news is good.*

**next door to**

almost; almost like; almost as good or as bad as

□ If taking advantage of a person's gullibility is not dishonesty, it's next door to it.

**next to no time**

very little time

□ I can do that in next to no time.

**next to nothing**

very little

□ This old bicycle has been very useful to me; and I got it for next to nothing.

see also **what next?**

**nice**

**1** used ironically to express disapproval

□ That's a nice thing to say to your aunt.

**2** *nice and* (+ adjective or adverb) expressive of pleasure or satisfaction on account of the characteristic stated

☐ It's nice and warm in this room.

☐ I'm glad you've arrived nice and early.

Many students use *nice* too much. It can sound distinctly unenthusiastic without an adverb. Thus *She's an extremely nice person* is acceptable, but otherwise *pleasant* or *agreeable* may be a safer word.

**nick** *(n)*

*do something in the nick of time*: manage to do it just before it is too late

**nick** *(v)*

steal but used of small things, like **pinch** and **whip**

☐ Who's nicked my pencil?

**nifty**

smart, clever: *a nifty bit of work*, *a nifty gadget*

**niggling**

*niggling details*: small, unimportant but irritating details which take up so much time

**night-hawk**

a person who stays out very late at night (used either disparagingly or jocularly)

**nines**

see **dressed up to the nines**

**nineteen to the dozen**

used of very rapid, almost non-stop talk

☐ She was rattling away nineteen to the dozen. We couldn't possibly have said anything.

**nip** *(n)*

*There's a nip in the air*. It is rather cold.

The adjective is *nippy*.

**nip** *(v)*

move quickly

☐ Nip out and buy some bread.

☐ He's just nipped into the street.

**nit**

an abbreviation of *nit-wit*

☐ You treat me as though I'm a nit.

**nitty-gritty**

the essentials/fundamentals of a subject/problem

☐ Now we're getting down to the nitty-gritty.

## nitwit

a person wanting in intelligence; often used by way of insult

□ That's not the way to do it, you nitwit.

## no

*take 'no' for an answer*: accept a refusal or denial (used chiefly in negative sentences)

□ He's so persistent that he will not take 'no' for an answer.

□ He would not take 'no' for an answer, so in the end I had to accede to his request.

Some speakers put *no* at the beginning of a sentence with the meaning 'As I was saying . . .' 'To go back to what I was saying . . .'

## no end

a great deal (The idea is that of no limit.)

**1** adjectivally, followed by *of*

□ We went to no end of trouble.

□ There are no end of exciting opportunities for young people nowadays.

□ There was no end of traffic in the High Street.

NOTE *No end of* is treated as singular or plural according to the number of the noun that follows it.

**2** adverbially, qualifying a verb

□ We enjoyed the party no end.

**3** followed by the indefinite article and a singular noun, to convey the meaning 'a very great'

□ There will be no end of a row over this mistake.

□ He thinks himself no end of a humorist.

## no fear!*

a strong way of expressing a negative, a denial or a refusal (The sense is 'There is no fear of that!')

□ 'You didn't accept his offer, did you?' 'No fear!'

□ 'Do you intend complying with my request?' 'No fear!'

## no great shakes

not very good or satisfactory

□ He's no great shakes as an actor.

□ I have heard that place highly spoken of as a pleasure resort, but I did not think it was any great shakes.

## no mistake

see **mistake**

## no sort (*or* kind) of

used colloquially to express disapproval of whatever is under discussion

□ This is no sort of job for a person of your abilities.

☐ That is no sort of way to speak to a visitor.

☐ Ten thousand pounds a year is no sort of salary for a post with such responsibility attaching to it.

**no time for**

see **no use for** and also **in no time**

**no use for**

a colloquialism for expressing disapproval

☐ I've no use for people who squander their money and then expect others to help them.

*I've no time for* has a similar meaning.

**nobody**

a person of no importance; also *a mere nobody*

☐ I'm not going to kowtow to a mere nobody like him.

**non-event**

an event which everyone has looked forward to, but which is in the end a failure or an anticlimax

**none too**

(+adjective or adverb) not quite, but almost, the opposite of that denoted by the adjective or adverb

☐ The weather was none too good.

☐ My father was none too pleased with my school report.

☐ The doctor arrived none too soon.

**nose**

*get your nose to the grindstone*: start doing some really hard work

see also **cut off one's nose to spite one's face**, **look down (one's nose) at someone** and **turn up one's nose**

**nosey** (*or* **nosy**)

inquisitive about things that do not concern one

(cf. **poke one's nose into**)

☐ She's a likeable woman, if only she were not so nosey.

**nosey-parker***

a name for a person who is nosey

☐ She would be better liked if she were not such a nosey-parker.

There has been much speculation about the identity of the original Parker whose name is perpetuated in this idiom, but none of those suggested seem satisfactory. Might an additional suggestion be made? That it does not refer to a person at all, but is a deliberate and facetious corruption of *nose-poker*?

**not a bit (of it)**

see **bit 3**

## not a patch on
far inferior to
□ As a scholar he is not a patch on his predecessor in the post.

## not half
**1** for the emphatic use of *not half*, as in *it didn't half rain, he wasn't half angry*, see **half**

**2** closely allied to this is the enthusiastic use
□ 'Did you enjoy yourself?' 'Not half!'
□ 'Would you like a game of tennis?' 'Not half!'

## not likely/not on your life
less slangy ways of saying **not on your nelly**

## not on your nelly
certainly not
(Somewhere between slang and colloquial. It is a curious development of Cockney slang; *nelly* is short for *Nelly Duff*, which is 'rhyming slang' for *puff*, meaning 'breath' or 'life'. So it just means 'not on your life'.)
□ 'Do you think I'm going to swallow that story?' 'Not on your nelly.'

## not so
(+ adjective) used as a mild understatement, or as a grudging admission, of the idea denoted by the opposite adjective
□ 'How are you feeling today?' 'Not so bad.' (i.e. fairly well)
□ It's not so warm outdoors. (i.e. rather cold)

## not so sure
a hesitant or guarded way of expressing doubt or dissent
□ I am not so sure that I agree with you there.
□ 'I rather like that picture, don't you?' 'I'm not so sure.'
□ I'm not so sure that I can come.

## not to worry
you/we etc. must not worry
□ 'I've run out of money.' 'Well, not to worry—I can lend you some.'

## nothing if not
used before an adjective to convey the meaning 'very', 'excessively' or 'above all else'
□ She's nothing if not polite.
□ We're nothing if not up to date in this office.
(usually a touch of sarcasm is implied)
occasionally used before a noun which denotes some quality or characteristic:
□ He's nothing if not a gentleman.

**nothing like so**
    see **like**
**nothing to write home about**
    not remarkable or outstanding; not of any special interest
    □ 'What did you think of the exhibition?' 'It's not bad, but it's nothing to write home about.'
**nous**
    (uncountable and rhyming with *house*) common sense
    □ Use your nous, Fred!
**now and then**
    see **every now and then**
**now**; **now then**
    used by way of admonition
    □ Now, you boys, stop fooling about.
    □ Now then, do what you're told.
    *Now!* alone may be used to reprimand or check someone.
    □ Now! I thought I told you not to do that.
    see also **for now** and **just now**
**number one**
    oneself
    □ He certainly knows how to look after number one (i.e. himself).
**nutcase**
    (from the old slang *nuts* meaning crazy) *He's a nutcase* can now be used more seriously: mentally unbalanced, needing psychiatric care
**nutshell**
    see **in a nutshell**

# O

**ocean**
    for *drop in the ocean*, see **drop**
**odd**
    (appended to a statement of number or amount) approximately the number or amount stated: *twenty-odd, five pounds-odd*
**odd man out**
    the one who is different from all the others in a group or gathering
    □ He did not easily mix with others, with the result that on most social occasions he was the odd man out.
**odds**
    *the odds are that* . . .: it is probable or likely that . . .

□ The odds are that he will be disqualified.

*it makes no odds*: it makes no difference; it doesn't matter

□ It makes no odds whether he comes or not.

*What's the odds?* (a) What difference does it make? What does it matter? (note the singular verb)

□ The pay is good: and even if the hours are irregular and uncertain, what's the odds?

(b) *What's the odds that . . .?* What is the likelihood that . . .?

□ What's the odds that they don't come after all?

*The odds are even.* They are evenly matched.

□ 'Which team do you think will win the match this afternoon?' 'I shouldn't care to say. The odds are just about even between them.'

*at odds*: in a state of disagreement

□ Those two brothers are always at odds with each other.

These curious phrases are based on the fact that *odds* is a term used in betting and refers to the probability of an event.

## odour

*be in bad odour*: have offended someone who is consequently unfriendly

(Be **in someone's bad/black books** is similar.)

## of a sort

**1** a kind of whatever is stated, though not as the word is normally understood

□ A veterinary surgeon is a doctor of a sort.

**2** an inferior kind of whatever is stated

□ 'Do you run a car?' 'Well, a car of a sort.'

□ 'What did you have for lunch?' 'Roast beef of a sort.'

*Of sorts* is also used, similarly *of a kind* and *of kinds*.

## of it

for *a rough time of it*, *lead one a life of it*, see **it**

## off

**1** cancelled

□ I understand the football match is off.

**2** putrid, rancid, sour

□ Don't eat any of that pork; it's going off.

**3** reprehensible (of one's conduct); not in good taste; below the standards of behaviour that one would have expected; inconsiderate

□ It's a bit off, his asking you to give him a lift home when he knows it will take you two or three miles out of your way.

see also **bit** (d)

**off the cuff**
**4** short for *off duty*

□ When do you come off this evening?

□ She's off all day tomorrow.

The opposite is *on* (*duty*).

**5** *be off something/someone*: not like it/him/her any more

**off-beat**

unconventional

**off-chance**

a remote chance; a chance of which one cannot be certain

□ We did not make an appointment, but as we were passing we called on the off-chance that you might be able to see us.

**off colour**

slightly unwell

□ I am feeling off colour this morning.

**off day**

**off days and on days**

see **day**

**off-hand**

**1** (adjective) lacking politeness/respect

□ He had a distinctly off-hand manner.

**2** (adverb) from memory

□ 'What is the train fare to London?' 'Sorry, I can't tell you off-hand.'

**off one's head**

crazy, mad

□ The poor fellow's worries finally drove him off his head.

**off one's own bat**

see **bat**

**off one's rocker**

the same as **off one's head**

**off pat**

*He's got his part off pat.* He has learned his lines (in a play) perfectly by heart.

**off-putting**

deterring; such as is likely to put one off from doing something

□ No matter how experienced a speaker you are, and how well you have prepared your speech, such a noisy reception as that is apt to be very off-putting.

**off the cuff**

impromptu; given on the spur of the moment, without reference to evidence or verification of facts

225

□ That is not the kind of question that one can answer off the cuff.
the same as **off-hand 2**

**off the map**

descriptive of a place: (a) very remote, (b) small and insignificant

**off the mark**

see **mark**

**off the peg**

applied to a ready-made suit of clothes (The peg is that on which the clothes hang while they are in the shop.)

□ He bought a suit off the peg.

□ It's an off-the-peg suit.

**off the rails**

see **go off the rails**

**off the record**

confidentially: not intended to be recorded or officially put down in writing

□ What I am telling you is off the record, so keep it amongst yourselves.

**off the top**

*go off the top*: lose one's temper; fly into a passion

□ She'll go off the top at the slightest provocation.

**offing**

*Another conference is in the offing.* It is going to be held soon. This was originally a shipping expression, of a ship *off-shore* waiting to come into harbour.

**oh dear (me)!**

an exclamation expressive of grief or regret (from the Italian, *Dio mio*)

**oil a palm**

the principal idiom used for bribery

□ 'How did he manage that?' 'I expect he oiled someone's palm.'

the same as **grease a palm**

**ointment**

see **fly in the ointment**

**O.K.**

all right

Two origins are now offered:

**1** It was brought to America by West African slaves. In Wolof, two words are combined to mean 'certainly' which sound very much like O.K.

**2** When Martin van Buren (who became the 8th U.S. president) went on political campaigns, his supporters used as their rallying slogan the initials of his town or constituency, which was Old Kinderhoek, near Albany in New York State. This was later supposed by other people to stand for 'oll korrect'.

□ That's O.K. Will it be O.K. if I finish work half an hour earlier today?

*give one the O.K.*: give one the signal that things are O.K.

□ Don't come out of your hiding-place until I give you the O.K.

□ As soon as those in authority give us the O.K. (i.e. signify their approval) we can go ahead with the project.

From this last has come the use of O.K. as a verb (*to O.K. a proposal or a suggestion*). It is often spelt *okay* in all uses, but especially when used as a verb.

## old

(before a personal name) used colloquially without any reference to age, and may even be applied to a child or someone who is not yet an adult

□ Old Thompson came bottom of the form in the terminal examination.

It usually expresses some kind of attitude or feeling, viz. familiarity (*old Joe*, *old chap*), affection (*Old Bill*) hostility or dislike (*I hate old Johnson*). *You old silly!* usually expresses good humour.

see also **Adam**

## old

(followed by a person's age) looking more than the real age

□ She's an old forty. (i.e. she is forty, but she looks rather older)

## old battleaxe

see **battleaxe**

## old bean*

see **bean**

## old chap

see **old man**

## old codger

a strange, eccentric or bad-tempered old man

□ Mr Bones is a funny old codger.

## old crock

**1** an old motor-car (sometimes some other piece of mechanism) in a bad state of repair

□ I shouldn't want to drive an old crock like that.

**2** (in a special sense) an old and obsolete model of a motor-car, but kept in a good state of repair as a curiosity: *the annual Old Crocks Race from London to Brighton*

**3** a person whose health is breaking up

□ As a young man he was very athletic, but by his middle fifties he was just an old crock.

**old fogey**

see **fogey**

**old geezer***

a rather sarcastic or disrespectful way of referring to an elderly person

□ I'm fed up with entertaining those old geezers all the evening.

**old girl**

a rather sarcastic or disrespectful way of referring to a woman

□ The old girl was delighted when she heard the news.

□ Who was that old girl you were speaking to just now?

sometimes also used as a familiar way of addressing a woman, especially by way of consoling her (slightly vulgar)*

□ Come on, old girl, cheer up.

**old hand**

someone who is experienced or well practised in whatever is stated

□ He's an old hand at bluffing people.

**old hat**

(only used after the verb *to be*) old fashioned

□ These mugs are rather old hat nowadays, aren't they?

**old lag**

one who has spent a good deal of his time in prison; one who has been in prison repeatedly (The standard word is *recidivist*.)

**old man***

**1** used by some young people to refer to their fathers

□ I'll have to get my old man's permission before I can promise to come.

**2** used by some women to refer to their husbands

□ My old man did not come in till past midnight.

**3** used by sailors, to refer to the captain of their ship, and thence by some workmen or members of an office staff, to refer to the person in charge

□ Has anyone seen the old man today?

**4** a familiar way of addressing a man or a boy, and here *old chap* can equally well be used (*Old thing* can be used of men or women.)

□ Could you lend me a cigarette, old man?

**old stager**

one who has been in a particular profession or occupation for a long

time (from an actor whose stage career has lasted for a long time)
□ When I went back to visit my old school, most of the staff were
quite new to me, but there were still one or two of the old stagers left.

**old thing**

see **old man 4**

**old wives' tales**

old stories or beliefs, usually superstitious

**old woman**

a derogatory term applied to a man with very little initiative
□ How can we expect any bold measures of town-planning, when the
Councillors are just a lot of old women?
also used by some men to refer to their wives

**on**

**1** at the expense of
□ The next round of drinks is on me.
see also **on the house**

**2** *on* (*duty*): see **off 4**

**3** *It just isn't on.* What you suggest is quite impossible.

**on about**

*What is he on about?* What is he saying? (implying incomprehension)

**on all fours with***

on a par with in every respect (most frequently used in the negative)
□ This case is not on all fours with the other one, so no analogy can be
drawn between them.

**on and off**

intermittently
□ It rained all day on and off.

**on appro**

abbreviation of *on approval*
□ We have the goods on appro for a week. (We can keep them or
return them after a week if we don't want to buy them.)

**on earth**

**1** added for emphasis after an interrogative word
□ What on earth is it?
□ How on earth did he do that?
□ Where on earth are they?
□ When on earth shall we get there?
In all these *the hell* can replace *on earth* but it is stronger.

**2** After negative words like *nothing*, *no-one*, *nobody*, *nowhere*, the
phrase *on earth* makes the negative absolute.

☐ Nothing on earth could persuade him to do what he thinks is wrong.

Sometimes it is used for exaggeration, especially when a person's appearance is concerned.

☐ He looks like nothing on earth, dressed up in that way.

☐ Aren't you feeling well this morning? You look like nothing on earth.

**on edge**

see **edge** and **nervy**

**on end**

continuously; without a break: *three days on end*, *miles on end*, *hours on end*

see also **make someone's hair stand on end**

**on form**

see **form**

**on-going**

unfinished, taking place now

**on ice**

see **ice**

**on one's beam ends**

almost without money

☐ By the time I get to the end of the month, and another salary cheque is due, I am just about on my beam ends.

**on one's plate**

see **plate**

**on one's toes**

on the alert; active

☐ A family of lively children keeps you on your toes.

used of mental, besides physical, alertness

☐ In some of these guessing games you need to be on your toes all the time.

**on someone's tracks**

pursuing, with the intention of catching someone; seeking someone out, with the purpose of reprimanding him

☐ Don't damage those trees, or you'll have the farmer on your tracks.

**on spec**

abbreviation of *on speculation*, though the full form is very rarely used in conversational English

☐ We knew nothing about this hotel when we booked; we just came here on spec, but it has turned out to be all that one could desire.

**on the**

(+adjective). *On the cheap*, *on the quiet*, *on the sly*: these phrases have the force of an adverb, but usually carry a certain depreciatory connotation. *To get things on the cheap* suggests an element of meanness or niggardliness, which the simple adverb *cheaply* does not; and similarly *to do something on the quiet* implies secretiveness.

**on the**

(+verb stem)

Such phrases express the general idea of a present participle. They fall into two main classes:

(a) those that mean 'on the point of doing something', or 'just beginning to do something': *the kettle is on the boil*, *his health is at last on the mend*

(b) those that denote a permanent state or position

□ She is always on the moan.

□ I have been on the go from morning till night.

□ The lawn is on the slope.

similarly *on the prowl*, *on the march*, *on the trot*, *on the look-out*, *on the run*

**on the ball**

mentally alert; seeing straight to the main point of a statement or the implication of an argument

□ The great value of Jack as a committee man is that he is always on the ball.

**on the brain**

obsessed with the idea that is specified

□ Ever since a house a little further down the road was burgled, Mrs Everson has had burglars on the brain.

**on the cards**

see **card**

**on the carpet**

before one's superior for censure or reprimand

□ He's been on the carpet several times about his carelessness.

**on the cheap**

see **on the** (+adjective)

**on the dot**

see **dot**

**on the hop**

see **hop**

231

**on the house**
>at the expense of the house (primarily a business or commercial house, but extended also to any kind of body or organisation)
>☐ The refreshments are on the house tonight.
>☐ He used his car for business purposes, and many of the minor repairs were done on the house.
>Other less idiomatic words can be used here, like *firm*, *company* etc.
>see also **on**

**on the loose**
>(used of people or animals usually not free for various reasons) free; at large
>☐ There's a criminal on the loose from the prison.
>☐ Jim's on the loose now his wife's away.

**on the make**
>aiming to make money
>☐ I have never known him do a disinterested action; he's always on the make.

**on the mend**
>see **mend**

**on the other hand**
>see **hand**

**on the Q.T.***
>a colloquial abbreviation of *on the quiet* ('secretly'): *do something on the q.t.* (*or Q.T.*), *tell one something on the q.t.*

**on the rocks**
>**1** in financial difficulties
>☐ I understand that that company is on the rocks.
>also used of a person
>**2** also used of drinks served with ice blocks: *a Scotch on the rocks*

**on the shelf**
>A spinster who is beyond the normal marriageable age is sometimes said to be *left on the shelf*.
>☐ She refused several offers of marriage, and then, at the age of forty, found herself left on the shelf.

**on the side**
>see **side**

**on the sly**
>secretively

**on the stocks**
>used of a project on which work has already commenced or which has

already been commissioned (a term from ship-building)

□ Before he had finished one historical novel, he had another on the stocks.

**on the tip of one's tongue**

on the point of being pronounced or uttered (of a word, phrase etc.)

□ I cannot think of the word I want; and it was on the tip of my tongue a moment ago.

□ His name was on the tip of my tongue, when I remembered the warning I had been given, and stopped myself from uttering it just in time.

**on the trot**

moving about from place to place on one's feet

□ I could do with a rest for a while; I've been on the trot all the morning.

**on the upgrade**

improving

□ The quality of our production is on the upgrade.

(*On the downgrade* also exists but is less common.)

see also **upgrade**

**on these/those lines**

see **line(s)**

**on tick**

on credit (*buy goods on tick*)

**on top of**

**1** following immediately after, and adding its effects to

□ Floods, on top of famine, caused widespread distress.

**2** *things get on top of someone*: prove too much for him

□ Don't let your troubles get on top of you.

**3** in addition to; over and above

□ He has a small pension, on top of his salary.

**on top of the world**

in good health, happy, contented and alert; not to be discouraged or disheartened by anything in the world

□ It's wonderful what a little rest and fine weather will do for you. I feel on top of the world this morning.

**once in a blue moon**

see **blue moon**

**one foot in the grave**

a state of poor health from which one is not likely to recover

□ That cat's got one foot in the grave!

**one for the pot**

In making a pot of tea, many people use one more spoonful of tea than there are people to be served. This extra one they call *one for the pot*.

**one for the road**

a final drink before setting off on a journey in a car

**one in the eye**

a misfortune, a set-back

**one of these days**

see **day**

**one of those things**

one of those things that are liable to happen, though they may not happen often (often *just one of those things*)

**one over the eight**

*have one over the eight*: be slightly drunk

□ That fellow looks as if he has had one over the eight.

The eight referred to is the eight pints that make a gallon. The implication is apparently that a person can drink a gallon (eight pints) of beer without being affected, but if he has one over the eight, he begins to show signs of intoxication. (A gallon is about 4.5 litres.)

**one too many for someone***

able to get the better of the person in question (either physically or in an argument)

□ He put up a brave fight, but his opponent was one too many for him.

□ However hard you try to argue with that young lad, he always has a reply for you; he's one too many for me.

**one up on**

slightly superior to; having an advantage over

□ A student of modern languages who has a knowledge of Latin is one up on a student who has not.

**one-upmanship**

the dubious art of trying to make other people feel embarrassed or insecure (A facetious invention of Stephen Potter whose entertaining books on 'Gamesmanship', 'Brinkmanship' and 'One-upmanship' have been widely read. Of these the last seems to be the one most often referred to in conversation.)

**onions**

see **know** (i)

**only**

The following two uses of *only* in spoken English should be noted:

**1** I should have called round to see you, *only* I had a visitor just as I was about to leave home. (the reason for my not doing what I intended)

**2** Have you any shopping to do? *Only* it is early-closing day. (the reason why I ask)

**oodles***

lots (rather emotive)

□ I can stay—I've oodles of time.

□ Well, I can't because I've oodles to do at home.

**op**

short for *operation*

**open-ended**

*The discussion on the radio this evening will be open-ended.* It will not be directed along prescribed lines but will be allowed to develop as the participants wish.

**opt out**

withdraw one's support for (or involvement in) a group/job/organisation (tending to replace **back out**, but *opt out* suggests one has been given the chance to withdraw)

**option**

see **soft option**

**or**

(a question which echoes a previous statement and casts doubts upon it)

□ It's the most sensible thing to do; or is it?

□ They (a married couple) live remotely in the country, have been married ten years, have two small daughters, a cat called Caliban, and are happy. Or are they? (from a review in The *Times Literary Supplement*, 19 May 1966)

**or something**

a rather indefinite alternative used in speech when one cannot supply anything more definite or specific

□ He's a stockbroker or something.

□ Don't just idle your time away aimlessly; settle down to some reading or something.

□ 'What was that dashed across the garden?' 'A rat or something.'

**order**

see **tall order**

**other day**

see **day**

## out and out

thorough; in all respects (adjectival, usually with nouns of unpleasant or uncomplimentary associations): *an out and out villain*, *an out and out scoundrel*, *an out and out rogue*

also sometimes: *a scoundrel out and out*

## out for

having the object or intention of obtaining or achieving
followed by

(a) a noun: *out for power, position, promotion, money* etc.

(b) an infinitive (when *for* is omitted): *out to swindle people*, *out to get one's own way*, *out to enjoy oneself*

## out in the cold

see **cold**

## out of

without, owing to the supply being exhausted: *out of bread*, *out of small change*, *out of petrol*

## out of all proportion

(an ellipsis, with the *to* adjunct omitted and left to be understood from the context)

□ The pay is out of all proportion (i.e. out of all proportion to the work).

## out of hand

usually *get out of hand*: become wild, uncontrollable

□ The children were quite out of hand after the holiday.

## out of it

out of whatever is going on

□ Amongst so many distinguished people, she felt quite out of it.

like *out in the cold* (see **cold**)

## out of one's depth

literally used of swimming, but extended to finding yourself in a situation where you can't follow, manage, cope etc.

□ Jane was quite good at algebra but she was out of her depth in the geometry class.

## out of sorts

not very well in health

□ I have been feeling out of sorts for the last few days.

## out of the blue

totally unexpected; it may be pleasant or unpleasant

## out of the frying-pan into the fire

from a bad position or situation into a worse one

(*Jump* or *leap* is the usual verb used.)

□ You may not care for your present job, but think twice before you change it. You may find you have jumped out of the frying-pan into the fire.

**out of the top drawer**

out of the upper classes of society

□ They may have plenty of money, but they don't come out of the top drawer.

**out of the wood**

out of one's difficulties

□ Things are improving with the school, but we are not out of the wood yet.

**out of this world**

wonderful, magnificent

**out to do something**

(*out*+infinitive) see **out for**

**outfit**

originally used for equipment (and sometimes the clothing) for a particular activity, but increasingly used for clothing alone.

NOTE *Clothing and equipment* are uncountable but an *outfit* is countable.

**over and done with**

finished for all time; finished and not likely to happen again

□ That quarrel they had is now over and done with.

**over and over again**

repeatedly

□ I have told you over and over again that I cannot do what you are asking.

**over the hump**

see **hump**

**overnight**

an adverb used both literally (*We'll stay here overnight*) and also to mean 'suddenly':

□ You can't expect him to be a reformed character overnight.

**Oxbridge**

This is the accepted term to refer to the universities of Oxford and Cambridge, in contrast to other British universities. Despite its appearance, it is not used as a joke. Few English speakers realise that a village with this name actually exists in Dorset (about 4 km south of Beaminster)!

# p

## pack in

give up doing (some activity)
- ☐ I'm packing in football after this season.
- ☐ I don't see much prospect of advancement in this occupation; I think I shall pack it in.
- ☐ I packed in smoking several months ago.

Usually the meaning is 'to give up permanently', but it may be used of a temporary cessation.
- ☐ I've had enough of this job; I think I'll pack it in for today.

An intransitive use is also possible, provided it is understood from the situation what is being 'packed in'.
- ☐ Your health has not been too good recently. Don't you think it's about time you packed in?

see also **send someone packing**

## package

Used as an adjective, it means 'inclusive' in cost, with no extras or exceptions: *package deal, package holiday*.

## packet

a lot of money
- ☐ I bet that cost him a packet.

## paddy*

a fit or outburst of temper (abbreviation of *paddywhack*) used of children only, and now a little dated.

## pain in the neck

This is a perpetual annoyance or irritation, not a physical pain. We can say either that a person *is a pain in the neck*, or that he *gives one a pain in the neck*.

see also **aches and pains**

## pal

a very close friend; hence the adjective *pally*
- ☐ Tom and Jim seem very pally nowadays.
- ☐ He's pally with several well-known people in the theatrical world.

## palaver

(countable) used formerly to mean a lot of time-wasting talk, but now more for small time-consuming jobs, such as filling in complicated forms; rather linked with *red-tape* (see **red**)

☐ Getting our visas was a frightful palaver.

☐ We had to open and close six gates to get to the farm—what a palaver!

**palm**

see **grease a palm** and **oil a palm**

**pan**

see **flash in the pan**

**pansy***

an effeminate youth or man (more strictly a homosexual, though not always used in the strict sense)

There is also an adjective *pansyish* but both words are becoming less common.

**pants**

strictly means 'underpants' but often used for 'trousers', which is an Americanism

see also **kick one's heels**

**paraphernalia**

(uncountable) collectively refers to all the equipment associated with a hobby/job etc. (like **gear**)

☐ You really mustn't leave all your paraphernalia at the bottom of the stairs—we shall trip over it.

**pardon my French**

an apology sometimes made by someone who has just used a swear word

**Parkinson's laws**

These are a number of laws of economics which sound perverse but are in fact often surprisingly true; e.g. 'Work expands to fill the time available to do it.'

**part and parcel of**

an integral part of (the whole)

☐ Translation lessons are part and parcel of everyone's timetable.

**pass out**

faint, lose consciousness

**pass the buck**

pass the responsibility or blame to another person

**passion**

see **fly into a passion**

**past master**

one who is well practised in some kind of behaviour or pursuit; in normal English usually used of creditable things, but colloquially more often the opposite: *a past master at getting one's own way, a past master at wriggling out of difficulties, a past master at shifting the blame to other people*

It is used of women as well as men. There is no expression *a past mistress* for a woman—at least, not in this sense.

**pasting**

a beating with the fists (it rhymes with *tasting*)

□ Two or three of the boys set on the bully and gave him a pasting.

**pat**

see **off pat**

**pat someone on the back**

congratulate or praise someone

□ Children like to be patted on the back for their achievements.

Hence (a) *to give someone a pat on the back*

(b) *to pat oneself on the back*: to indulge in self-praise or self-congratulation

□ He's too good at patting himself on the back.

**patch**

see **not a patch** and **sticky patch**

**patch up (a relationship)**

try to re-establish good terms with someone after a disagreement or quarrel

**patent**

(of methods, implements etc.) clever, ingenious, special to oneself

(The suggestion is that the thing in question deserves to be patented but has not been.)

□ Come and see my patent device for washing floors.

□ I've got a patent method of my own for working out long calculations like that.

The word is not only used humorously or facetiously, as of course it can be used of a device which really is patented.

**pathetic**

basically means 'provoking pity', but now frequently used in an exasperating situation to express impatience, especially with inefficiency in business or poor quality goods

□ That firm took three weeks to answer my letter. Isn't it pathetic?

**pay lip service**

be servile, flatter

□ He pays lip service to the good work of the staff, but I know he doesn't think much of them really.

**peanuts**
   **1** a matter of no importance
   **2** a comparatively small sum of money
   □ Five pounds may be peanuts to you, but it's a welcome addition to my savings.

**peckish**
   rather hungry
   □ I am beginning to feel peckish; I've had nothing to eat since breakfast.

**peeved, peevish**
   He looked *peeved*: irritated
   He's rather *peevish*: irritable

**peg**
   see **off the peg, square** and **take someone down a peg (or two)**

**penny**
   *a penny for your thoughts*: what are you thinking about? (i.e. I would give a penny to know what your thoughts are) said to a person who appears to be deep in thought
   *he hasn't a penny to his name*: he is without money (often used as a form of exaggeration, with the meaning 'he has barely more than enough to live on', 'he has no savings or money of any kind behind him')
   □ He was a self-made man, and very proud of the fact, and so he was annoyed at the idea of his daughter's marrying, as he said, a fellow who hadn't a penny to his name.
   *Without a penny to his name* is also used.
   *a pretty penny*: a large amount or sum of money
   □ I had the house completely redecorated before I went in, and a pretty penny it cost me.
   *in for a penny, in for a pound*: having once embarked upon a project, one must carry it through to the end, no matter what the expense
   *Hasn't the penny dropped?* Can't you see the joke (or understand what I'm trying to say)?

**pent-up**
   one of several expressions similar in meaning to **nervy**

**pep**
   energy (*put some pep into one*), hence the verb *pep up*:
   □ Take some of this tonic; it will pep you up.
   possibly an abbreviation of *pepper*

**pep pill**
pill or tablet intended to put energy into one

**pep talk**
a talk, lecture, address etc. intended to put courage, spirit or determination into those to whom it is addressed

**perfect**
complete; used of nouns where there is no logical sense of perfection: *a perfect fool, a perfect ass, a perfect nuisance, a perfect right to do it* similarly with the adverb *perfectly*: *perfectly absurd, perfectly crazy, perfectly true*

**perisher**
rascal; naughty child

**perk up**
brighten up, become more cheerful/energetic
□ A cup of coffee will perk us up.

**perks**
a colloquial abbreviation of *perquisites*, very much commoner than the original word
□ Besides the salary, there are several perks attached to the job.

**perm**
**1** abbreviation of *permanent wave* (from ladies' hairdressing); also as a verb
□ Who perms your hair?
□ You should get your hair permed.
**2** *Perm* is also used as a short form of *permutation*.

**pernickety**
same meaning as *fussy* (see **fuss-pot**)

**pest**
The association with *plague* is virtually lost. It expresses impatience in sentences like:
□ That child is a perfect pest. Look how dirty his room is.
(perhaps linked in many people's minds with the verb *pester*)

**pet**
(adjective) applied to things to which one is very closely attached and from which it is difficult for one to break away: *pet theory, pet aversion, pet phrase*
Remember, as a noun, a *pet* is usually a dog or a cat. It is also often used as a term of endearment, especially to children.

**peter out**
Originally used in mining (when a deposit becomes thinner and finally

comes to a stop), so *peter out* is used of something getting less and less until it disappears.

☐ The association petered out after a year or so.

**petticoat government**

domination of the home by women, to whom the men there have to submit

**pew**

strictly, a seat in a church, but used facetiously for a chair

☐ Just take a pew for a minute, I'll soon be back.

**phone**

see **telephone**

**phoney**

not real or genuine (similar to **bogus** and **fake**)

**physical jerks**

physical exercises involving the stretching of the limbs and muscles

☐ We do a few physical jerks each morning before breakfast.

**pick holes in**

see **hole**

**pick someone to pieces**

find fault with, like *pick holes in* (see **hole**) but this is more aggressive

**pick someone's brains**

ask informally for information

☐ Can I pick your brains for a moment? I believe you've had trouble of this kind too.

**pick up**

**1** improve (of the weather, one's health, trade, business etc.; intransitive)

☐ Business is at last beginning to pick up.

**2** The transitive use in reference to a person (*to pick someone up*), in colloquial English may mean to make a casual acquaintance with a view to sexual relations.

☐ A middle-aged man was waiting rather aimlessly at the street corner, probably thinking that a likely place to pick someone up.

**3** *Pick someone up*, despite **2** above, is still used frequently with the sense of calling for someone by car and going on together (to the theatre, to work etc.)

**4** *pick something up*: (a) fetch or collect it

(b) find and buy it (in a shop etc.)

**pickle***

*be in a pickle*: be in an awkward situation (Sometimes *a sad/sorry pickle* may be heard.)

**picnic**

*no picnic*: not an easy or pleasant task or experience

□ We gathered a good deal of valuable information from our expedition, but it was no picnic, I can tell you.

**picture**

**1** *put someone in the picture*: bring someone up to date with the essential information

□ I do not know precisely what stage negotiations have reached. Could you put me in the picture?

similarly *keep someone in the picture*: keep someone supplied with information

**2** A common but surprising construction also occurs using *look* without a preposition: examples are in **sight 1** and **sketch**. Similarly, *she looked a picture* means 'she looked as pretty/attractive as a picture' (also used of gardens). By extension, someone can be said to *look* or *be a picture of health*: appear to be in excellent health.

**pictures**

the cinema: *go to the pictures, I saw that story at the pictures* (perhaps a little dated)

**pie**

for *easy as pie*, see **easy**; for *have a finger in the pie*, see **finger**

**piece**

see **give someone a piece of one's mind** and **say one's piece**

**piece of cake**

*a piece of cake*: very easy

□ That exam was a piece of cake.

**piffle***

senseless or rubbishy talk

□ Don't talk such piffle.

**pig**

see **buy a pig in a poke** and **guinea pig**

**pigeon**

(*my pigeon, your pigeon* etc.) one's affair, concern, business etc.

□ How we are going to raise the money to pay for all these renovations does not come into my department; that's your pigeon. This comes from a corruption of the word *business*, as we find in the term *pidgin English*. It's nothing to do with birds.

**pigeon-holes**
   the usual (if not official) word for boxes where letters and messages are
   placed (usually alphabetically) in schools, hotels etc.

**pile-up**
   a multiple crash on a motorway, usually in fog and successively
   involving many vehicles

**pill**
   Although *pill* is still used for any medical pill, it is also short for a
   contraceptive pill and the phrase *to be on the pill* will refer to this.
   see also **gild the pill**

**pillar**
   see **from pillar to post**

**pin**
   see **for two pins**

**pinch** *(n)*
   *at a pinch*: if absolutely necessary, by stretching the resources
   □ I can lend you £10 at a pinch.
   (This is quite different from **take it with a pinch of salt**.)

**pinch** *(v)*
   steal; see **nab**

**pink**
   see **in the pink** and **tickle**

**pint**
   see **quart**

**pipe**
   see **put that in your pipe and smoke it**

**pipe-dream**
   an unrealistic plan or idea

**pipeline**
   If something is *in the pipeline*, its delivery is awaited. It was originally
   only used of goods but now of forthcoming plans, application for
   jobs, changes in administration etc.

**pitch into someone**
   assail him, either with blows or verbally
   □ The young fellow calmly and deliberately removed his jacket, and
   pitched into his opponent.
   □ When it came to question time, a man at the back of the hall rose to
   his feet and pitched into the speaker.

**plain**
   (*plain silly*, *plain stupid*, *plain daft*) *Plain* is quite idiomatic before these

adjectives; it has a different meaning from *plainly*. *Plainly silly* would mean 'obviously silly'. *Plain silly* means 'silly and nothing but silly' —the idea is expressed by the plain, unadorned word.

**plane**

This is the usual short form for *aeroplane*, and much more commonly used; you should note that *aircraft* is being increasingly used, especially in *jet aircraft*.

**planted with**

similar to **lumbered with**

**plastered**

**1** *I plastered him*. I hit him hard.

**2** *He was plastered*. He was very drunk.

**plate**

You've already got too much *on your plate*. You've already far too many commitments/things to do.

**play**

see below, and also **card 3**, **game** *(n)*, **trump** and **second fiddle**

**play it cool**

under-emphasise a matter

□ Where that matter is concerned, I should advise you to play it cool if you wish to make any progress in the negotiations, for several of the delegates are known to be strongly opposed to the idea.

**play someone up**

make oneself an annoyance or a nuisance to someone

**1** (of a person)

□ Those children do play their parents up.

**2** (of a pain or ailment)

□ My rheumatism plays me up during this damp weather.

**3** (of some non-animate thing, such as a piece of mechanism)

□ The engine of this car is playing (me) up again.

There is also the idiom *to play up on someone*.

□ That mischievous young boy plays up on his mother.

**pleased**

note two comparisons:

□ As pleased as Punch. As pleased as a dog with two tails.

There seems to be no real difference between them in use. The first occurs more frequently (perhaps because of the alliteration).

**plod on**

literally 'continue walking when tired' but also used of continuing to work

246

☐ She's plodding on with her thesis.

**plonk**

**1** *plonk it down*: put it down heavily, or in such a way as to show displeasure

**2** (uncountable) *Plonk* is used to mean (cheap) wine. This is apparently a corruption of the French (*vin*) *blanc*.

**plough exams***

fail school/university exams

**plucky**

courageous, brave

**plug something**

keep it constantly before people's notice, in order to popularise it

☐ Party headquarters want us to plug that idea for all we're worth. It is especially commonly used of the repeated playing of new pop records on the radio.

**plumb**

(the final *b* is not pronounced)

**1** *land plumb in the middle*: in the exact middle

**2** *plumb crazy*: totally crazy, quite mad

**plump**

*plump for something*: choose something

**po-faced**

humourless, unsmiling and maybe priggish

**pocket**

**1** Of course the verb means 'put something in your pocket' but it often comes to mean 'steal'. (similar to **pinch** as a verb)

**2** two useful phrases to note together:

*be in pocket*: profit

*be out of pocket*: lose (financially)

see also **hole**

**point**

an important word in many idioms:

**1** *You have a point there.* What you say is valid (and it hadn't come to my mind before).

**2** *Point taken.* This is similar to **1** usually acknowledging a correction.

**3** *That's not one of my strong points.* That is not a subject I know much about. (similarly *a weak point of mine* etc.)

**4** *What's the point (of doing that)?* What is the good of it, what purpose will it serve? Why do that?

**5** *the point is*: spoken to introduce an important statement

**6** *point-blank*: blunt(ly), frank(ly), without a tactful introduction
□ She made me a point-blank refusal.
□ They asked me to lend them £100 point-blank.
**7** *I don't see your point*. I can't understand the essence of what you're trying to say.
**8** *a pointed remark*: a comment directed specifically at someone or his/her behaviour
**9** *He made a point of doing it*. He did it because he considered it to be important; he was careful not to forget to do it.
**10** *It is pointless to do that*. It will serve no purpose.
**11** There is a preference for *point in* with negatives (with the same meanings as **4**): *There is no point in doing that. I don't see any point in doing that*.

## poke one's nose into

be curious about, or interfere in (affairs that do not really concern one)
□ Don't poke your nose into other people's business.
see also **nosey-parker**

## poker-faced

expressionless, not showing feeling

## poky

(of a room, building etc.) small; inconveniently lacking in size
□ He's having to live in that poky bed-sitter at the moment.

## polish

see **spit and polish**

## poly

short for a *polytechnic institute/college*

## pool

To *pool resources* or *money* is to put everything together, in a common general fund. In the football *pools* (see below) the money (paid in by the people trying to foretell the match results) is all pooled to be used for prizes.

## pools

in full, *the football pools*, a popular and highly organised system of betting on the results of football matches

## poor show

(*A*) (*jolly*) *poor show!* an exclamation expressing disappointment or dissatisfaction

## pop

(as in *pop music, pop singer* etc.) This started as a colloquialism (an

abbreviation of *popular*), but it can scarcely be regarded as so any
longer.

**pop in/out**

similar to **dart/dash**

□ He popped out into the garden.

**pop the question**

put a proposal of marriage

**porn**

short for *pornography*

**posh**

smart; fine; luxurious: *a posh hotel, live in a posh neighbourhood, all
these posh people*; hence as a verb, *to posh oneself up*: to smarten
oneself up (Both adjective and verb are on the borderline between
slang and colloquial.)

**post**

see **as deaf as a post** and **from pillar to post**

**posted**

usually (We'll) *keep you posted*: write to you, keep you informed

**pot**

(uncountable) marijuana (The phrase **go to pot** is much older and
has no reference to this drug.)

*the pot calling the kettle black*: a person criticising someone else for the
fault(s) which he himself possesses

□ Don't you talk to me about being late—where were you at nine
o'clock yesterday? It's a case of the pot calling the kettle black.

see also **one for the pot**

**pot-bellied**

having a protuberant belly

**pot-boiler**

This is a book or article (occasionally a painting) produced without
much inspiration, merely to earn money. It implies the person has
produced works of greater merit.

**pot luck**

*take pot luck*: take whatever one can get, or whatever chance brings
one's way; originally of a meal (whatever luck brings out of the pot),
then applied over a wider field

□ If you don't book your accommodation in advance, you may find
that all the best places are full, and you'll have to take pot luck.

**potter (about)**

do small jobs without haste, e.g. in the house or garden

**potty***

rather silly (not so strong as *crazy*)

**pounce on**

literally, jump on (a cat may *pounce on* a mouse) but often used of conversational situations where one person may *pounce on* what another has said

**powers-that-be**

a phrase used when you can't name the exact (public) authority responsible for something or as a general term for those in authority
□ When are the powers-that-be going to get some more car parks built?

**pow-wow***

(usually jocular) discussion or conversation

**pram**

This is a baby's *perambulator*; the full word is practically never used nowadays.

**precious**

used colloquially with an emphasising force
□ A precious fool I should look, shouldn't I, if I did that?
□ A precious lot (i.e. very little) you care, don't you?
Before *few* or *little*, *precious* emphasises the paucity or scarcity:
*precious few opportunities*, *precious little time*

**prefab**

abbreviation of *prefabricated house* or other *building*

**prep**

(uncountable) short for *preparation* (the same as *homework*)

**press on regardless**

continue to work without considering what others may say or what else may happen
see **regardless**

**pretty well**

almost; nearly (used before verbs, participles, and certain adjectives)
□ She was pretty well drowned when they dragged her out of the swimming pool
see also **well**

**price**

see **at any price** and **what price**

**priceless**

literally, of such great value that a price cannot be specified; in conversation also 'extremely amusing'

**pricey** *or* **pricy**
very expensive

**prick one's ears up**
become suddenly attentive (The figure is from a dog's erecting its ears when it listens intently.)
□ At the mention of that name I pricked my ears up (*or* pricked up my ears).

**pro**
abbreviation of *professional* (noun)
□ He's a pro golfer.

**prof**
abbreviation of *professor*
□ You had better take the advice of your prof.

**prom**
**1** promenade, usually by the sea
□ Take a walk along the prom.
**2** promenade concert
□ Are you going to the prom tonight?
□ When do the proms open for this season?

**prop**
short for theatrical 'property', i.e. the clothes, furniture etc. needed for a stage production—except the scenery
□ Some of the props are missing.

**proper**
**1** complete; on a very large scale
□ He made me look a proper fool.
□ The room was in a proper mess.
□ There will be a proper row about this.
□ Their wedding reception was a proper do.
**2** typical; what one might expect of whoever or whatever is mentioned (usually before the name of a person, group or place)
□ That's a proper Charlie Scott trick. (i.e. the kind of thing one would expect Charlie Scott to do)
□ That's a proper Lancashire pronunciation. (i.e. typically Lancashire)
**3** Used after the noun, it means 'in the strict meaning of the word'.
□ He's not a teacher proper in the school; he works in the admin most of the time, and does odd lessons when other teachers are away.

**properly**
completely (see **proper 1**)

☐ You've messed things up properly now.

☐ He was properly tricked, despite his supposed smartness.

**proud**

see **do someone proud**

**pub**

abbreviation of *public house*; not regarded any longer as colloquial, but as the normally accepted term in spoken English at all levels but the most formal

**pub-crawl**

(also *pub-crawling*) going from one pub to another, drinking at each one

☐ Their evening's outing ended up in a pub-crawl.

**public**

see **wash one's dirty linen in public**

**puffed out**

out of breath

**pull someone's leg**

tease someone; deceive someone in joke

☐ Don't take what he says seriously; he's only pulling your leg.

hence *a leg-pull*: a joke

☐ I only intended it as a leg-pull.

The phrase is never used with *leg* in the plural. It is interesting to note that the phrase comes from a culprit sitting in the stocks, where you could have your revenge on him even by pulling only one leg, which would be very painful!

**pull one's punches**

exercise moderation

☐ When he's asked to write a report on something, he doesn't pull his punches. (i.e. he is quite frank)

**pull out all the stops**

(originally used of organ playing) make as great an impression as possible

**pull strings**

exercise your influence to arrange something which normally can't be done

☐ If you want to see round the factory, I've got a friend who can pull some strings and arrange it for you.

(The plural is more usual than the singular. The phrase goes back to the marionette master who directs his puppet by strings. Note that in most other contexts, *string* is uncountable.)

**punch-up**
 a fight
 □ There was a nasty punch-up outside the pub at closing time.
 see also **pull one's punches**
**punishment**
 see **glutton**
**purposes**
 see **cross purposes**
**push** (*n*)
 **1** dismissal from one's work or employment (The two chief idioms are *get the push* and *give someone the push*.)
 **2** (uncountable) determined ambition
 □ I doubt whether Simon has enough push to go into publicity as a career.
**push and shove**
 The two words mean virtually the same thing. The combination adds emphasis, and suggests repetition, with a certain amount of roughness and persistence.
 □ A small crowd was pushing and shoving at the entrance.
 □ Stop pushing and shoving, you people at the back.
**push around**
 order other people to do things bossily, and expect them to obey promptly
 □ There are some people who consider that their task in life is to push others around.
 □ I am not going to be pushed around by him.
**put a foot wrong**
 see **foot**
**put a sock in it**
 Just stop what you keep doing; shut up!
**put heads together**
 We must *put our heads together* and see if we can find a solution. We must think about it as a group.
**put in a word for**
 speak in recommendation of
 □ I've decided to apply for that post, and I wondered whether you would put a word in for me.
**put on**
 give a false impression
 □ I don't think he is really in pain; he's just putting it on.

**put one's back into it**
see **back**

**put one's best foot forward**
see **foot**

**put one's feet up**

sit or recline at one's ease, with one's feet supported, in order to give oneself a rest

☐ After lunch I like to put my feet up for about quarter of an hour.

☐ If you're feeling tired, come and put your feet up.

**put one's finger on something**

identify the crucial point (e.g. see the weakness in an argument, find what is causing a breakdown)

**put one's foot down**

assert oneself; insist on one's will being obeyed

☐ Unless you put your foot down here and now, those children will get out of hand.

**put one's foot in it**
see **foot**

**put paid to**

settle; bring to an end

☐ Let him try that game on me, and I'll soon put paid to it.

☐ 'That's put paid to it,' he exclaimed, as he dropped the vase on the floor and smashed it to smithereens.

**put someone in the picture**
see **picture**

**put someone out**

cause someone worry or trouble

☐ I should like the information now if it will be no trouble to you; but I don't want to put you out.

also used as a predicative participle:

☐ I've been so put out all the morning.

sometimes *put someone about*

**put someone up (for the night)**

give someone a bed (or at least somewhere to sleep) for the night

**put someone wise**

give someone the correct knowledge or information (in American English a colloquialism: in British English on the way to becoming one, though by most people still regarded as slang)

☐ I am not sure about the conditions one has to fulfil in order to become eligible for a grant from the fund. Could you put me wise?

**put someone's back up**
see **back**

**put that in your pipe and smoke it!**
spoken defiantly at the end of an unpalatable declaration, offering no comfort, but to reinforce its unpleasantness

**put the cart before the horse**
reverse the natural or logical order of things; do first what ought to be done second, and vice-versa

**put the clock back**
go back to an earlier state of affairs (usually used in a pejorative sense)
□ These proposed reforms would put the clock back a whole generation. (i.e. put the position back to what it was a generation ago)

**put the lid on it**
**1** provide the culminating point
□ We were confronted with difficulty after difficulty, and then, to put the lid on it, the bank refused to allow us any further credit.
**2** put an end to; stop any further progress
□ These latest regulations have put the lid on our plans.

**put-up job**
dishonestly pre-arranged affair, intended to deceive or impose on people
□ Many people suspected that the burglary was a put-up job, arranged with the intention of getting the insurance money.

**puzzle it out**
*Puzzle* is a common word, not just for crossword puzzles or jigsaw puzzles; if something is hard to understand, you may hear:
□ This puzzles me.
□ This is puzzling.
□ I'm puzzled by this.
□ I'm trying to puzzle this out.

# q

**quad**
abbreviation of *quadrangle*
□ Stephen's tutor was strolling across the quad.
used mainly by those closely associated with places and institutions that have a quadrangle connected with them

**quads**

An abbreviated form of *quadruplets*, it is normally used in the plural, but occasionally a singular (*a quad*) is heard when the reference is to one only of the four.

**quart**

*get* (or *put*) *a quart into a pint pot*: make the less contain the greater; used in the proverb *You can't get a quart into a pint pot*, or in allusions to it

□ You'll never manage it; you're trying to get a quart into a pint pot.

**queer**

The following idioms are still sometimes used, but less than formerly since *queer* means 'homosexual'.

see also **gay**

**queer someone's pitch**

make it difficult or impossible for a person to do what he had intended

□ By acting in that way you have queered my pitch.

**queer street**

**1** suspicious circumstances; a situation likely to lead to awkwardness or difficulty

□ 'For the sake of my professional reputation,' said Mr Saxton, 'I'm very careful about accepting a case. The more it looks like queer street the more I am inclined to leave it alone.'

**2** *in Queer Street(s)*: in financial difficulties

□ If he goes on spending so recklessly as this, it won't be long before he's in Queer Street.

perhaps a corruption of *queer strait(s)*, though the suggestion has been made that it is a pun on *Carey Street*, in London, where the Bankruptcy Court is situated

**question**

see **loaded question** and **pop the question**

**quick**

*cut to the quick*: offended

□ He was cut to the quick by her remarks.

**quick off the mark**

see **mark**

**quick on the uptake**

intelligent, quick to understand (*Slow on the uptake* is also used.)

**quid**

(slang) a pound (a sum of money, not a pound in weight)

□ It will cost you about a quid.

Similarly *two quid, five quid, half a quid* etc.

NOTE Idiomatically no -*s* is used in the plural, except in the phrase *be quids in*: be in a profitable position.

**quins**
abbreviation of *quintuplets*
see also **quads**

**quip**
(countable) clever quick remark

**quirk**
**1** an individual's odd habit of behaviour (or expression): *his quirk of shutting his eyes while speaking*
**2** a strange whim: *by a quirk of fate we met again*

**quite**
**1** before a noun, to suggest that the circumstances justify using the noun
□ Quite a gale blew up.
□ There was quite a row about it.
□ Quite a crowd gathered.
□ It was quite a joke to watch them.
The nouns concerned carry an adjectival notion; *gale*: strong wind, *crowd*: large gathering, *joke*: amusing sight or amusing story.
**2** used to signify agreement
□ 'I think that we ought to give praise where it is due, don't you?' 'Quite.'

**quite a few**
a fairly large number, though perhaps not enough to be called *many*
□ Quite a few people I've spoken to are of that opinion.
□ I've known that happen on quite a few occasions.

**quite a number (of)**
a fairly large number; perhaps not enough to be called *many*, but more than one might have expected.
□ There have been quite a number of changes on the staff during the last five years.

**quite a while**
a fair length of time
□ It is quite a while since I was in London.
□ Our present vicar has been here quite a while now.
The particular length of time will, of course, vary with circumstances.

**quite an amount**
a fairly large amount

□ Quite an amount of rain has fallen during the night.

**quits**

with the scores or debts between us settled

□ You owe me a pound, and I owe you one pound forty, so if I pay you forty pence we shall be quits.

*call it quits*: regard the debt as being settled

□ Don't trouble about the few odd pence; pay me the six pounds and we'll call it quits.

**quizzable**

an amusing useful new word, meaning 'available to be asked questions'.

□ I'll be quizzable after lunch.

NOTE *Questionable* does not have this meaning.

**quod**

(slang) prison, as in the phrases *be in quod*, *go to quod*, *send one to quod*; perhaps a pun upon *quad* (*quadrangle*), the prison yard (*Clink* is also used.)

**Q.T.**

see **on the Q.T.**

# r

**racket**

**1** a loud, discordant noise; a din

□ There was such a racket going on in the hall that you could scarcely make yourself heard.

**2** an organised scheme for obtaining financial or other advantages by illegal or dubious means

□ Investigations have revealed a racket in the marketing of drugs.

loosely used of proceedings of which one disapproves

□ I'll stop his racket.

**3** *stand the racket* (uncountable): put up with the rush and hurly-burly

□ I shouldn't care to live in New York for long: I couldn't stand the racket.

**4** A *racket* is of course also a tennis or squash racket (also spelt *racquet*). Don't mix it up with *rocket*.

**rag**

a newspaper; generally used in a derogatory sense: *You surely don't read that rag!* but sometimes humorously: *the local rag*

**rage**
    see **all the rage** and **fly into a passion/rage**

**rails**
    see **go off the rails**

**rain cats and dogs***
    rain very heavily
    □ When we set out there was some slight drizzle, but within twenty minutes it was raining cats and dogs.
    This book would scarcely be complete without this famous idiom but students are warned that it is not used very often; it is far more usual to say 'It was pouring with rain'.
    see also **as right as rain**

**rainy day**
    a time when one is in unexpected financial need, or is under unforeseen expense
    □ Don't be too reckless with your money. There may come a rainy day, when you will be glad of some of what you are spending now.

**raise Cain**
    raise a disturbance; be very angry
    □ He would raise Cain about the slightest mistake or shortcoming.
    In the Genesis story of Cain and Abel, Cain was very quick-tempered. The idiom means 'raise up the spirit of Cain'.

**rake-off**
    a payment received by one as a commission on business transactions
    □ He gets a rake-off on any money he collects for the firm.
    often used in a bad sense:
    □ As they got a rake-off on all money they collected, the tax-collectors used often to overcharge the unfortunate peasants.

**ram**
    He's always *ramming* new vocabulary *down our throats*. He forces us to learn it.

**ramble**
    literally, go for a country walk; colloquially, talk at great length and boringly
    □ What is he rambling on about now?

**ramshackle**
    (used of things) ready to break/collapse
    □ I keep my bike in a ramshackle shed.

**rare***
    a term of appreciation, conveying a slightly different meaning

according to the context, but with the general sense of 'exceptionally good': *a rare treat*

see also **have a time of it**

**raspberry**

a noise generally expressing disapproval, associated vaguely (but not invariably) with a fart

**rat-race**

the competitive outlook on life, pursued by some people, vying professionally/socially to be ahead of others

**rate**

see **at any rate** and **at that/this rate**

**rather***

an expression of enthusiasm in a positive reply to a question

□ 'Would you like to go to London for a few days and see the sights?' 'Rather!'

□ 'If I were offered a job at that salary I would accept it without hesitation, wouldn't you?' 'Rather!'

In this case, the stress is on the second syllable.

**rattle**

annoy; cause to feel angry

□ My persistent questioning of his story rattled him, and he refused to answer my queries.

hence the adjectival use of *rattled*: annoyed (The chief expressions are *be rattled*, *get rattled* and *get someone rattled*.)

□ In the end he got rattled (*or* we got him rattled).

**rattle away**

talk rapidly and at some length

□ She rattled away for the next ten minutes.

see also **nineteen to the dozen**

**rattling***

extraordinarily, remarkably; most frequently used before the adjective *good*: *a rattling good story*, *a rattling good game*

**rave-up**

a wild party

**raw deal**

unfair treatment

□ I feel sorry for Graham; he's had rather a raw deal ever since he's been with that firm.

**reaction**

see **spark off a (chain) reaction**

**ready**
   see **rough and ready**
**real**
   Colloquially, *real* is often used where the adverb *really* might be
   expected.
   □ It was real hard work.
   □ This is real good coffee.
   In such sentences *real* is felt to be more forceful than *really* would be.
   The noun and its preceding adjective are taken to represent a single
   idea, which the further adjective *real* then qualifies. *Real hard work* is
   hard work for which the name is justified.
**recap**
   verb and noun, short for *recapitulate* and *recapitulation*, especially
   used in quiz games; stress always on the first syllable
**reckon**
   **1** (a) think; hold an opinion of (mainly in negative sentences)
   □ I don't reckon much of that as a holiday resort.
   □ I didn't reckon much of the sermon.
   (b) think well of; appreciate; like
   □ He reckons himself doesn't he?
   □ I don't reckon that film much.
   **2** do (something) as a rule
   □ I reckon to start work at 9 a.m.
   □ What train do you reckon to catch each morning?
   □ When do you reckon to leave home?
   □ I don't reckon to go to the office on a Saturday.
   **3** suppose (often used sarcastically)
   □ What do you reckon you're doing?
   □ I reckon he'll soon be retiring.
**record**
   *for the record*: for the purpose of being recorded
   □ I'm giving you this information for the record.
   see also **off the record**
**red**
   *see red*: become enraged; lose one's temper
   □ You had only to mention the subject of pacifism in the Colonel's
   presence, and he saw red.
   (from the belief that a bull becomes infuriated at the sight of anything
   red)
   *see the red light*: see danger ahead

□ I was not at all surprised when the company went bankrupt: I had seen the red light some time before, and had taken the earliest opportunity to get out.

*red rag to a bull*: something that infuriates someone whenever it occurs or is mentioned (see *see red* above)

*redbrick university*: a provincial English university built between 1890 and 1960 (approximately)

*red herring*: a distraction from the main theme in a discussion

*red-tape*: accumulated correspondence, especially in government offices where it is said to be tied into bundles and secured with red-coloured tape (Thus the phrase is similar to *bureaucracy* and both nouns are uncountable.)

*red-handed*: in the act of committing the crime (as though blood is still on the hands)

□ They caught him red-handed.

see also **in the red**

**ref**

abbreviation of *referee* (in a game); also accepted as a colloquial term for any other kind of referee (a referee as to one's character, abilities etc.)

□ Many of the spectators accused the ref of partiality.

also used as a verb: *to ref a football match*

**refusal**

see **first refusal**

**regalia**

(uncountable) often in jocular use for a uniform or special clothing for some activity

**regardless**

an ellipsis of *regardless of . . .*

□ He spends money regardless. (i.e. regardless of whether he can afford it, or of whether it is really necessary)

□ I shall speak my mind regardless. (i.e. regardless of the consequences, regardless of whom I am speaking to etc.)

see also **press on regardless**

**regular**

real; in the full sense of the word

□ He's a regular tyrant amongst his workpeople.

□ That child is a regular tomboy.

□ It's a regular treat to have a spell of fine weather like this, after all the wet and cold that we have had.

## relative pronoun

(omission of) In standard usage the rule is that a relative pronoun may be omitted if it would be a grammatical object were it used, but not if it would be a subject. But in colloquial English this is not always observed. Sentences of the type *I've a gardener comes three days a week* are frequently heard in speech, and we feel there is nothing wrong with them. At least, they seem perfectly natural. The omission is particularly common after *here* and *there*.

□ Here's something will interest you.

□ There's nothing would please me more.

The general effect of the omission is to stress, as the really important fact, the one that is expressed in what is grammatically the subordinate clause. Thus in the sentence *I've a gardener comes three days a week*, the important fact is not that I have a gardener, but that he comes three days a week.

## rep

**1** short for *representative* (on a committee, commercially etc.)

**2** also short for *repertory* (*theatre*)

## respectable

not to be despised; not inconsiderable: *a respectable sum of money*, *a respectable salary*, *a respectable distance*, *a respectable job*, *a respectable size*

## rev

short for *revolution* of a motor; also a verb, *to rev up*: to accelerate the engine while stationary

## rhino

abbreviation of *rhinoceros*, often used in colloquial English instead of the full word

## rickety

Now that 'rickets' is rarely heard of, this adjective is used freely (without thoughts of its true origin) for anything unsafe/unstable: *a rickety table*, *chair*, *building* etc.

## rid

The usual phrase is *get rid of* but *be rid of* is sometimes used. The nearest definition would be 'free oneself of' but there are no real synonyms.

□ 'What do you do with your old clothes? You can't keep them.' 'Oh, we give them away or throw them away—we get rid of them somehow.'

see also **good riddance** and **well rid of**

**ride**

*take someone for a ride*: make someone believe something untrue; trick or deceive someone

*let it ride*: keep quiet about something and hope nothing more is said about it

**riff-raff**

the rabble; disreputable people, taken collectively

□ With his wildly revolutionary views, he found a ready following amongst the riff-raff.

□ It was mainly the riff-raff of the place that caused all the trouble.

When used as a subject it is usually treated as a singular, but a plural verb is also found: 'the riff-raff *was* delighted' or 'the riff-raff *were* delighted'.

**rig**

falsify something, especially used of politics and a *rigged election*

**rig-out**

see **gear**

**right**

*a right one*: a silly person

for *have one's heart in the right place*, see **heart**

see also **right as rain**

**right and left**

in every direction; on all sides; indiscriminately

□ It transpired that for some years he had been swindling people right and left.

sometimes *left and right*; even more commonly, *left, right and centre*

**righto** (*or* **right-oh**)*

This is a rather familiar and cheery way of conveying the idea of agreement or assent: virtually the same as *all right* in these senses. An alternative, though not quite so brusque, is *Right you are!*

□ I'll meet you outside the railway station at 10.30.' 'Righto!' (*or* 'Right you are!')

**rigmarole**

(used with *a* but not in the plural) a long, repetitive but often meaningless story or statement

**ring**

*That rings a bell*. I seem to have heard that name/word somewhere before.

see also **telephone**

**rip-off**
  a case of profiteering, swindling or stealing; a racket (see **racket 2**)
  also a verb *rip off*: to steal, cheat or swindle
  □ What a rip-off!
  □ Those market stallholders rip you off if they can.
  □ My camera was ripped off in Peru by an American con man.

**road**
  see **one for the road**

**roader**
  see **middle of the roader**

**roaring trade**
  a very brisk trade

**robbery**
  see **daylight robbery**

**rock-bottom price**
  the lowest possible price

**rock the boat**
  see **boat**

**rocker**
  see **off one's rocker**

**rocket**
  **1** a severe rebuke or reprimand
  □ If we don't get any satisfaction from him very soon, we shall have to give him a rocket.
  also occasionally used as a verb:
  □ We shall have to rocket him very soon.
  **2** the verb is commoner in a very different sense:
  □ Prices are rocketing again! (i.e. increasing very rapidly)

**rocks**
  see **on the rocks**

**roll on**
  come unceasingly nearer and nearer; used especially to express a wish for the approach of some occasion
  □ Roll on, Christmas!

**roll up**
  come; arrive
  □ People rolled up in their hundreds to see the sight.
  □ Don't trouble to fix a time: just roll up when you feel inclined.
  □ Just when we had given up all hope of their coming, they rolled up in a taxi.

**rollicking***
noisy and very happy
☐ A rollicking party of children demolished the tea we had prepared
for them.

**romance**
introduce fanciful elements into a narrative or description (not really
lying)
☐ You mustn't believe all that she says—she tends to romance a bit
sometimes.

**roof**
see **go through the roof** and **hit the roof/ceiling**

**rook**
charge unreasonably high prices
☐ Don't buy anything from that chap, he'll rook you if he can.

**room to swing a cat (in)**
see **cat**

**ropes**
rather like **know-how** (but you *have* know-how)
☐ You'll soon know the ropes.
☐ I never really learnt the ropes in that job.
probably originally the ropes of a large sailing ship

**ropy**
of inferior quality

**rot**
(uncountable) rubbish, nonsense

**rotten**
used colloquially as a strong term of disapproval, in the general sense
of *bad*: *rotten weather*, *a rotten time*, *a rotten lecture*, *a rotten teacher*, *a
rotten cold*

**rough and ready**
hurriedly and/or inadequately prepared: *a rough and ready meal*

**rough deal**
see **raw deal**

**rough house**
a state of disorder and fighting
☐ The party developed into a rough house when you left.

**rough it**
live in a rough, uncomfortable way
☐ For almost three months we had to rough it under canvas in a wild
part of the country.

**rough on**

inflicting hardship on

□ It's rather rough on Jack, having to forgo his half-day off three weeks in succession.

(more or less the same as *hard on*)

**rough passage**

*have a rough passage*: experience a time of difficulty or hardship (a metaphor from seafaring)

□ He's had a rough passage this last year, with one illness after another.

□ The bill had a rough passage through the House of Lords.

**rough time**

more or less the same as **rough passage**

see also **cut up rough**, **take the rough with the smooth** and **sleep rough**

**round about**

approximately: *round about £5, round about six o'clock, round about seven kilos*

**round the bend**

crazy

□ That noise is driving me round the bend.

□ You'll send her round the bend if you keep telling her that you don't agree.

**roundabouts**

*What we lose on the roundabouts we make up* (or *gain*) *on the swings.* What we lose on one project, or on one side of our business, we make up on another.

This strange expression comes from the fact that roundabouts usually have a cover or roof over them so customers may go on them more when it rains, and avoid the swings. When the rain stops, they may abandon the roundabouts and go for the swings!

NOTE A roundabout can be two different things:

**1** As referred to in the above idiom, it is what most dictionaries call a 'merry-go-round' (which is the usual American term), at a fun-fair.

**2** It is also a large island at a road junction where all the traffic goes round.

**row**

(rhyming with *now* and *cow*)

**1** a noise

□ Don't make such a row.

**2** a quarrel

□ They were good friends until they had a row about some trivial matter.

**3** an unpleasant fuss, involving a rebuke or reprimand

□ There will be a row about this, if it gets to be known.

The verb *to row* can be used only in the second sense, *kick up a row* in the first and third, *get into a row* in the third only.

## rubbishy

of poor quality

## ructions

uproar; a state of disturbance

□ There will be ructions when this decision comes to be known.

## rum *(adj)*

strange, odd

## rumpus

just the same as **row 1** and **3**, but only as a noun

## run-of-the-mill

Most of this week's essays were rather *run-of-the-mill*: average, nothing exceptional

## run-down

**1** declining in quality, used especially of hotels, restaurants etc.

**2** a quick résumé of information etc.

□ I gave her a run-down on the points to be discussed at the meeting.

## run into

like **bump into**, in both its meanings

## run riot

The crowd *ran riot* and looted many shops: went wild

NOTE the usual meaning of *riot*: street fighting, a violent demonstration

## run the show

manage the business

## rustle up (a meal/some food)

find and prepare food at short notice

## rusty

weak because of lack of practice

□ My French/biology/algebra is getting a bit rusty now.

## rut

(from the rut made by a cartwheel) an established and unvarying way of going on (The chief expressions are *be in a rut* and *get into a rut*.)

□ When a person gets into a rut, it is hard for him to change his ways.

# S

**sack**

dismiss from work (usually *give someone the sack*, *get the sack* and *sack someone*)

The expression comes from apprentices having a sack for their tools. If they were dismissed, they were handed the sack of tools to go and look for more work elsewhere.

To **fire** someone (originally American) is now very common too.

**saddle**

see **back in the saddle** and **landed with**

**safe as houses**

extremely safe

**sails**

see **take the wind out of someone's sails**

**salad days**

the happy days of one's youth

NOTE *Salad* alone does not mean lettuce but is the whole dish with other vegetables, served cold.

**salt**

see **take it with a pinch of salt** and **worth one's salt**

**same time**

see **at the same time**

**sandwiched between**

fitted (in the brief time) between

☐ I managed to get a game of squash sandwiched between a board meeting and the train leaving.

**sass**

be saucy; also the adjective: *sassy*

**sauce**

(uncountable) impudence

☐ Now then, not so much of your sauce.

adjective: *saucy*

☐ She's a saucy young girl.

☐ Don't be so saucy.

**save one's bacon**

save one from trouble

☐ You've just saved my bacon for me by giving me that lift; I've been late for work twice this week, and I am afraid I should have been in trouble if I had been late a third time.

**save one's breath**

not waste breath by talking

□ It's no use giving him advice. He won't take any notice of it. You might as well save your breath.

**save one's face**

see **lose face**

**save one's (own) skin**

save oneself from being killed or wounded

□ As the enemy attacked, the little band broke and fled, every man intent on saving his own skin.

**say**

The following are some colloquial expressions and uses of *say* that it seems worth drawing attention to:

*Say* + noun clause object: suppose

□ Say you were left a thousand pounds, what would you do with it?

*I say*

**1** to attract the attention of the person addressed

□ I say, Jack, bring me a book of stamps, will you, please?

**2** to express surprise

□ I say! It's nearly six o'clock.

**3** to combine surprise and warning

□ I say! there's someone coming.

*what do you say to . . . ?*

**1** what is your opinion of . . . ?

□ What do you say to that picture?

**2** what is your reply to . . . ?

□ He alleges that he was not with you at the time the accident occurred. What do you say to that?

**3** would you like . . . ?

□ What do you say to a cup of tea/a game of tennis?

In number **3**, inversion (*what say you?*) is sometimes used to convey light-heartedness or facetiousness: *What say you to a cup of tea?*

*Says you!* a sneering reply to a statement, implying disbelief of the statement in question

□ 'I would never accept any money I had not earned by my own efforts.' 'Says you!'

*that's what you say*: used to express doubt of the truth of a statement, the implication being 'we've only *your* word for it'

□ 'I've been working hard all day, with scarcely a minute's rest.' 'That's what you say.'

*so say I* (or *all of us*): a jocular or enthusiastic admission of agreement

□ 'I think we ought to give our guide our heartiest thanks for the excellent way in which he has looked after the party.' 'And so say I.'

    For he's a jolly good fellow,

    And so say all of us.

*I can't say*: a rather reluctant way of expressing a downright negative opinion

□ I can't say that I care for the decorations of the room. (i.e. I don't care for them)

*Don't say*: used to express incredulity

□ You don't say so! (i.e. surely that is not so)

□ Don't say that I've left the goods behind in the shop! (i.e. surely I've not)

□ Don't say you're going for a walk in this wretched weather!

*I must say*: I feel compelled to say

□ I must say I like your new dress.

□ I must say you've a cheek, taking the best seat without even being asked.

This idiom conveys a suggestion of apology for a remark that has not been invited.

*have something/nothing/a lot to say for oneself* (virtually the same as *have something/nothing/a lot to say*): be talkative or taciturn, as the case may be (*For oneself* focuses attention more definitely on the speaker.)

□ That young fellow seems to have a lot to say for himself.

□ It's very difficult to keep up a conversation with him, as he's nothing to say for himself.

But in some contexts *for oneself* may mean 'in defence of oneself':

□ What have you got to say for yourself now?

*there's no saying*: see **there's no** (+gerund)

*You can say that again!* strongly expresses agreement with the last remark

*I haven't had my say yet.* I've had no chance to say what I think.

for *what you say goes*, see **go** *(v)*

## say 'boo' to a goose

used almost exclusively in negative sentences such as *couldn't say 'boo' to a goose*, or *wouldn't say 'boo' to a goose*: is so timid as not to defy the slightest opposition

□ It's no good appointing a person like that to conduct the negotiations on our behalf; he couldn't say 'boo' to a goose.

The goose always had the reputation of being a very timorous bird, so that it would not take very much spirit to say 'boo' to a goose.

**say one's piece**

say what one has to say (probably from reciting (or saying) one's piece at a party)

□ He just said his piece (i.e. said what he had come prepared to say) and then made no further contribution to the discussion.

**say when**

almost invariably used by your host when pouring some drink into your glass; originally *Say when you have enough*, but most people to indicate 'enough', say as their answer 'when!'

**saying**

see **as the saying is**

**scales**

see **tilt the scales**

**scarce**

*make oneself scarce*: keep oneself out of the way; keep one's presence away from others

□ Go along and make yourself scarce for the next hour or so, while I talk to Mr Jackson.

**scared**

frightened

That which causes the fright is indicated by *of* (*scared of the traffic*, *scared of the thunder*), that which the fright inhibits one from doing is expressed by an infinitive (*scared to cross the road*).

*scared to death*: badly scared (an example of hyperbole)

*scared stiff*: so scared that one cannot move (again usually hyperbole)

*scare the life out of someone*: like *scare stiff*

**scatter-brained**

absent-minded, forgetful

**scatty**

rather crazy or forgetful, probably linked to the above entry

**scene**

*The scene* is what's going on (in a specific place or, if not specified, around one)

□ What's the scene in Paris?

*It's not my scene.* It's not pleasing to me (as a way of life, a pastime etc.).

□ Camping's not my scene, really. I'm a town girl.

**scorch**

travel at great speed (mainly of cars, bicycles and motor cycles)

□ On the motorway we were scorching along at well over eighty miles an hour when we saw the police car chasing us.

**scorcher**

a scorching hot day

□ Phew, it's a scorcher today, isn't it?

**scot-free**

without punishment

□ The magistrate let the hooligans off scot-free.

**scram**

get away, clear off etc. (usually an imperative)

**scrap**

**1** (verb and noun) fight; quarrel

□ Those youths will scrap about the slightest thing.

□ In the corner of the playground there was a scrap going on between two of the boys.

**2** (verb only) do away with; abolish

□ All the old machinery has now been scrapped.

**scrape**

a situation full of trouble or possible trouble

□ He's always getting into scrapes of one kind or another.

*a narrow scrape*: a narrow escape from trouble

□ You had a narrow scrape there; if you had been a few inches nearer that other car, there would have been a collision.

**scrape along**

manage to live in spite of difficulties

□ The survivors of the air crash could only scrape along for a week or two.

**scrape the barrel**

get the very last that is worth having

□ We have twice lowered the qualifications for entry to the profession, until by now we have just about scraped the barrel.

**scrape through**

only just manage to get through (an examination)

□ I am not feeling too confident, but I think I may manage to scrape through.

**scratch**

*start from scratch*: from the very beginning

□ We shall have to scrap all the work that our predecessors have done, and start from scratch.

(equally well used with *begin*)

*up to scratch*: up to the required standard

□ His work is scarcely up to scratch.

**scream***

a funny sight or experience; something that causes amusement

□ That clown was a scream

□ It was a scream to watch their antics.

**screw loose**

*have a screw loose*: be slightly stupid or crazy

□ I shouldn't take much notice of what he says; he's got a screw loose.

often said jocularly

see also **head(s)** and **tighten the screws**

**scribble**

strictly, (make) meaningless marks on paper as an infant may do, but used also of poor handwriting

□ I can scarcely read his scribble—can you?

□ She scribbled me a note.

**scrounge**

obtain for nothing

□ That carpenter's always scrounging cigarettes from his work mates.

hence *a scrounger*: one who scrounges; *scrounge a living*: get a living by scrounging

see also **cadge**

**scruffy**

dirty and untidy

□ I wish he would take more pride in his appearance; he always looks scruffy.

**scrumptious**

used of food, meaning 'delicious'; now often shortened to *scrummy*

**sea**

*be all at sea*: be confused, muddled

see also **devil 6** and **worse things happen at sea**

**season**

When a certain food is *in season* it is good to eat. By extension, *he cycles to work, in season and out*: he cycles throughout the year

**sec**

short for a *second* of time

□ Please wait here a sec.

compare **mo**; see also **split second**

## second fiddle

usually *play second fiddle*: take a less important part

□ She has to play second fiddle to her mother at parties.

## second thoughts

used when you have doubts about your decision

□ Are you having second thoughts?

□ On second thoughts, I think I'll stay at home.

## seconds

**1** a second helping of a course at a meal

□ I enjoyed that pie. Are there any seconds?

**2** the second course at a meal; the pudding or sweet course

□ What are we having for seconds?

## see

*let's see*: short for *let us see*, and usually addressed to oneself as a preliminary to a reckoning or calculation

□ Let's see, it's eightpence a pound, so seven pounds will be 56 pence.

□ Let's see, today is 26 February, so that means next Friday will be 3 March.

*you see*: appended to a statement to emphasise it, or draw one's attention to it, meaning 'you understand'

□ I was not twenty-one then, you see, so I didn't get the full rate of pay.

occasionally used to introduce the statement: *You see, I was not twenty-one then . . .*

## see about

attend to; take steps to ensure that something is done

□ We must see about booking our seats on the train.

This is normal English, and not exclusively colloquial. But a colloquial idiom is derived from it, namely the sarcastic use exemplified in the following

□ 'He says it's time he received an increase in salary.' 'Oh, does he? We'll see about that.' (implying 'he's not likely to get it')

## see red

see **red**

## see the back of someone

occurs mainly in the expressions *pleased/relieved/glad to see the back of someone*: glad when the person in question has gone

□ Thank goodness he is leaving at last. I shall be glad to see the back of him.

used chiefly of people, but may also be applied to non-personal things, conditions etc.

□ I am about fed up with this weather: I shall be relieved to see the back of it.

## see the last of

I hope we've *seen the last of* that chap/family/government/tax: I hope we'll never see (or have anything to do with) him/them/it again

## seedy

(of a person) **1** shabby in appearance

□ When I first knew him he was quite a smart young man, but I think he must have fallen on hard times since then, as he looks very seedy nowadays.

**2** not in very good health

□ I'm feeling rather seedy today.

□ She's looked rather seedy for the past week or so.

## sell

get others to adopt or accept (an idea, a plan etc.)

□ It is one thing for a political party to formulate an electoral programme; it's quite another to sell it to the electorate.

## sell like hot cakes

sell rapidly and in great quantity or great numbers

□ His first book sold like hot cakes.

## sell-out

(usually used of theatres, concert halls etc.) *It's a sell-out* means there are no more tickets for sale. It also has a more colloquial meaning: 'a betrayal'

## semi

short for *semi-detached house*: one of a pair built adjoining

## send someone packing

dismiss someone summarily and unceremoniously

□ If anyone comes begging at my door, I soon send him packing.

## send-up

a satirical imitation, also (in less modern speech) called a *skit*

□ Have you seen his send-up of the Prime Minister?

as a verb, to *send someone up*: to make fun of him, especially by imitating him

## sense

see **money**

**sentiments**

*them's my sentiments*: a facetious rendering of *those are my sentiments* (that's what I think too)

**separate the sheep from the goats**

separate the superior from the inferior (taken from the Bible, Matthew xxv 33)

**set off on the wrong foot**

see **foot**

**set someone back**

primarily, to cause someone to retreat; colloquially, cost (someone) money

□ 'How much did that new car set you back?' 'It set me back £2000.'

see also **dead set**

**set the ball rolling**

take the first step in starting a conversation, discussion, competition etc.

□ No-one seems inclined to ask a question, so I'll set the ball rolling.

□ In vain did the auctioneer ask for bids; none was forthcoming, until at last a person at the back of the room set the ball rolling by offering ten pounds, and from this, stage by stage, it got up to fifty.

**set the world on fire**

make a great impression (usually in negative sentences)

□ I don't think any of his ideas are going to set the world on fire.

**set-up**

The verb *to set up a business* is quite ordinary acceptable usage but to speak of an organisation, business etc. as *a set-up* may imply it is not serious or honest.

**settle for**

decide in favour of; decide to have or accept a particular thing from among several

□ From among the many things we were offered as a present, it was difficult to make up our minds which to have, but in the end we settled for a stereo player.

**seventh heaven**

see **in (one's) seventh heaven**

**shady**

basically, the adjective from *shade* but colloquially *a shady business/firm/affair* implies it is dishonest or of dubious reputation

**shakes**

see **not great shakes**

**shaky**

unstable, unreliable: (*shaky argument/case/belief/idea* etc.)

**sham**

(noun or adjective) like **bogus**; imitation

**shamble**

walk in a lazy slow way, or dragging one's feet

**shambles**

*be in a shambles*: be in terrible disorder

A former word for 'slaughterhouse', this always has -*s*.

**Shanks's pony\***

one's own legs as a means of transport or locomotion (used with slight facetiousness)

□ The only means of getting from one village to the next was by Shanks's pony.

**shares**

see **go shares**

**shark**

a person who is dishonest in business

**sharp**

see **look sharp**

**shattered**

shocked, very upset, e.g. by very bad news

**shave**

see **close shave**

**shelf**

see **on the shelf**

**shelve**

(used of questions, problems etc.) postpone, put on one side to be considered later, if at all

**shemozzle**

a fuss, disturbance

**shilly-shally**

vacillate; be undecided; constantly change one's mind

□ Don't shilly-shally: make-up your mind and have done with it.

from *Shall I? Shall I?* by analogy with **dilly-dally**

**shindy**

rather like **shemozzle** but perhaps noisier

**ship**

*when one's ship comes home* (or *comes in*): when one comes into money (no doubt from the return of a treasure ship laden with wealth)

☐ When my ship comes home I'll buy you a car of your own.

☐ I'd like a country house in the south of England, but that will have to wait until my ship comes home.

The suggestion usually is that that event is a long way off, and that there is no real reason to suppose that it will occur at all.

## shipshape

in good order

☐ At last we have managed to get the garden shipshape.

☐ Everything is shipshape.

The phrase was originally *all shipshape and Bristol fashion* (a nautical term).

## shocker

a person or thing which shocks (but the noun is more colloquial than the verb)

## shoddy

of poor quality, cheap

☐ Those shoddy shoes he bought barely lasted a month.

## shoes

*be in someone's shoes*: be in the position he is in

(generally used in negative sentences):

☐ I shouldn't care to be in your shoes/his shoes. (of someone who is in an awkward or unenviable situation)

*tremble/shake/quake in one's shoes*: feel very nervous and apprehensive

☐ I hear there is to be an official inquiry into the affairs of that company. I bet some of the staff are trembling in their shoes.

see also **into someone's shoes**

## shoestring

*manage on a shoestring*, *run a concern on a shoestring*: on a very small or inadequate sum of money

☐ It has almost become a tradition that repertory theatres are expected to manage on a shoestring, while quite generous grants are given to orchestras.

## shoot

**1** one of several words for rapid movement

☐ He shot out (of) the room.

☐ They shot through the door.

see also **dart/dash**

**2** We also talk of shooting questions at someone and as a result of this questions are now often invited informally by saying 'Shoot!'

## shop

*shut up shop*: cease trading or (in the case of non-trading concerns) functioning

□ If we cannot recruit new members to the society, we shall soon have to shut up shop.

*shop around*: go to different shops selling similar goods to look for a bargain

for *all over the shop*, see **all over the place**

## shoplifting

theft of goods from shops by the public; also a verb: *shoplift*

## short

see **long and short of it** and **make short work of**

## short cut

see **cut** *(n)*

## short-sighted

basically myopic but much used of plans, arrangements etc. meaning 'lacking prudence and foresight'

## shortcomings

failings or inadequacies

## shot

an attempt

□ I am doubtful whether I can do it, but I don't mind having a shot.

□ Have a shot at this problem.

*Crack* is used in the same way.

see also **like a shot**

## shotgun marriage

a wedding made necessary by the bride being pregnant, the bride's father metaphorically holding a shotgun to the bridegroom's head to force him into marriage

## shoulder

see **chip on one's shoulder**, **cold shoulder**, **look over one's shoulder**, **look over someone's shoulder** and **straight from the shoulder**

## shove

see **push and shove**

## show *(n)*

**1** a theatrical performance

□ When I was living in London I reckoned to go to a show once every week.

**2** business: *to run the show*, *to boss the show*; see also **run**

**3** in a vague way, the place: *all over the show*; see **all over the place**
**4** *good show*: an exclamation of strong approval; see also **steal the show**

**show** *(v)*

used in various phrases and constructions elliptically, with the sense of teaching someone a lesson which will disillusion him
□ I'll show him.
□ That'll show you.

**show-down**

a final confrontation
□ It is to be hoped that a settlement can be negotiated, for if it comes to a show-down between the two sides, there can be no doubt which is in the stronger position.

**show a leg**

(never plural) This is shouted to urge people to get up (e.g. in the army, or camping).

**show one's paces**

demonstrate one's capacities

**shut up shop**

see **shop**

**sick**

**1** (of a business, shares etc.) not flourishing; in an ailing condition
□ I've a few Rhodesian shares that are looking pretty sick.
□ That used to be quite a flourishing business, but it's been looking rather sick for the last year or two.
**2** (of humour, jokes etc.) playing on fascination with macabre or gruesome subjects
An example of a sick joke is
□ 'What do you think is a real drag?' 'Going out for a walk with a dog with no legs.'
This is a pun on the word *drag* (pull). For the colloquial meaning see **drag 3**.

**sick of**

tired of; made miserable by
□ I'm sick of this constant rain.
□ I'm sick of listening to his complaints.
□ Things that you like in moderation, you can soon become sick of if you have them to excess.
*Sick and tired of* used to be rather stronger in meaning, but is so widely used that it is now merely a cliché.

281

**sickening**

such as makes one sick (in the sense of the word given above)

□ Rain, rain, rain, day after day: it's sickening.

**side**

*on the side* **1** confidentially

□ I'm telling you this on the side.

**2** apart or aside from the main source or subject

□ My nominal wage is fifty pounds a week, but I make a few pounds more on the side.

*on the dear/short/heavy* etc. *side*: rather dearer, shorter, heavier etc. than one requires or than one expected

□ It's good material, but it's on the dear side.

see also **get on the right/wrong side of**, **laugh on the other side of one's face** and **let the side down**

**sidetrack**

distract from the main subject or course

□ We sidetracked the physics teacher and he spent a good twenty minutes telling us about his holidays.

**sight**

**1** a spectacle (usually with a derogatory connotation, but it depends on the context)

□ You ought to have seen the tulips in bloom. They did look a sight.

□ She did look a sight in those clothes. They didn't suit her a bit.

**2** an amount (used in comparisons): *a sight more than you'd think, a sight uglier, a sight more ugly, not by a long sight*

**sight for sore eyes**

a very pleasing sight

□ The splendid way the hall was decorated was a sight for sore eyes.

**sign on the dotted line**

a jocular way of expressing the idea of signing one's name on an official form or in an official register, though in a particular case there may not be a dotted line to sign on (a facetious use of the instruction often printed on a form where such a line is provided)

□ When we arrive at the office each morning we have to sign on the dotted line.

**silly-billy***

(countable) a silly person (*Billy* is familiar for William but the phrase is not confined to males.)

**silver spoon**

see **born**

**sing another tune**

express a different opinion; speak differently; adopt a different attitude in what one says

□ At first he was most dictatorial and aggressive in what he said, but when he realised that he would get nowhere by that means, he began to sing another tune.

□ At one time he was all for 'soaking the rich', as he said, but now that he has inherited a considerable fortune he sings another tune.

the same as **change one's tune**

**sink**

see **heart**

**sit on**

keep something, thus preventing other people from being able to use it (not literally sitting on it)

□ Hey! You've been sitting on that dictionary all morning—I need it now.

**sit on someone's tail**

used of a vehicle driving too close to the car in front

**sitting duck**

an obvious easy target for attack—usually verbal, not physical

**six of one and half a dozen of the other**

very little difference between the two; very little to choose between them

□ Who was really responsible for the quarrel it is difficult to say. It seems to me it is a case of six of one and half a dozen of the other.

**sixes and sevens**

see **at sixes and sevens**

**size**

*That's about the size of it.* Those are the true facts concerning the case or the situation.

see also **cut someone down to size**

**skate (a)round a problem**

avoid discussing or tackling the real problem

**skedaddle**

escape rapidly, go away in a hurry

**skeleton in the cupboard**

a domestic secret which the family will try not to reveal to outsiders

**sketch***

a grotesque sight (applied to a person)

□ She does look a sketch in those clothes.

**skin**

I caught the train *by the skin of my teeth*. I was only just able to catch the train.

Two useful phrases are:

*thin-skinned*: sensitive, easily upset

*thick-skinned*: insensitive, stolid

see also **save one's (own) skin**

**skinny**

(of people) very thin

**skip**

miss out, omit: *skip a lesson, a meeting, a few pages of a book* etc.

**skit**

a humorous piece of writing or acting, mimicking something or someone well-known (similar to a **send-up** and a **take-off**)

**skive**

(often in school or the Forces) avoid work or duty, probably by hiding

**skive off**

disappear from work, school etc. for a while without permission

□ He skived off down to the football field as soon as the boss's back was turned.

**skunk**

as a metaphor used to denote a person whom one holds in contempt; in the literal sense, a species of North American animal that is notorious for its smell

□ Kevin's a real skunk; he's pinched all my best records and says they're his.

**skylarking**

see **lark about**

**slack**

**1** (adjective) lazy, rather careless, slow

**2** (verb) *slack off*: become slacker, especially of people working

□ In some firms, people slack off on Friday afternoons before it's time to go home.

**slam**

To *slam a door* is to shut it noisily and violently.

To *slam someone/something* is:

**1** to defeat him completely (e.g. in a game) *or*

**2** to criticise him/it strongly.

□ My tutor slammed my essay because he didn't like my style of writing.

**slanging match**

an exchange of insulting or abusive language between two or more people

□ What started as a well-conducted argument soon developed into a slanging match.

**slap-happy**

similar to **slapdash**, but with less stress on haste, more on cheerfulness; carefree, without worries (mostly applied to people)

**slap-up**

exceptionally good, usually only referring to meals

**slapdash**

(used of work or workers) careless and hasty

□ The slapdash plumber has done a slapdash job on my boiler.

**sleazy**

shabby, dirty, perhaps even shady

**sleep around**

have sex with quite a few different people

**sleep on it**

think about the matter and make a decision by tomorrow

**sleep rough**

sleep in uncomfortable conditions, probably out of doors (rather similar to **rough it**)

**sleeve**

see **have something up one's sleeve**, **heart** and **laugh up one's sleeve**

**slightest**

see **faintest**

**slip**

**1** You shouldn't let a chance like that *slip through your fingers*: You mustn't miss this chance (to do something profitable, exciting etc.)

**2** I'll *slip round* to the shop. I'll go quickly to the shop.

**3** It *slipped my mind*: I forgot about it.

**4** a *slip of the tongue*: some word(s) spoken in error

**5** Remember the noun *slip* is a woman's petticoat.

**6** *You're slipping*. Your skills are weakening.

see also **give someone the slip**

**slippery customer***

an elusive person, whom it is difficult to hold down to a promise or an undertaking

□ He's such a slippery customer that you can never trust him.

**slog**

slog *away at a job, a task, a subject* etc.: work hard and patiently at it
also used as a noun of a long tiring journey
☐ The last 500 kms was a hard/long slog.

**slope off**

go away inconspicuously

**sloppy**

As slang, *sloppy* means very sentimental (*a sloppy song*), but in serious
colloquial use, it is more likely to be used of poor quality work (similar
to **slapdash**): *a sloppy piece of workmanship*.

**slowcoach**

a slow or stupid person
☐ Come on, you slowcoach.

**slow on the uptake**

the opposite of **quick on the uptake**

**sly**

see **on the sly**

**smack in the eye**

a humiliating rebuff
☐ He felt sure he would get the post, but he was never even considered
for it. That was a smack in the eye for him.

**small beer**

something or someone of no great significance
☐ The present holder of the position is quite small beer compared with
his predecessor.

**smarmy**

fulsomely polite or ingratiating
☐ His smarmy attitude to those in authority earned him the dislike of
the other inmates of the almshouses.

**smart alec**

a person who imagines himself to be very smart or clever (a term of
disparagement)
☐ These smart alecs may get away with it for a time, but they always
come to grief sooner or later.

**smashing**

splendid, wonderful

**smattering**

I only have *a smattering of* Spanish: I know only a very little Spanish.

**smile**

see **wipe that smile off your face**

**smithereens**
small pieces
□ The vase crashed to the floor and smashed to smithereens.
This is used only in the phrase *to smithereens*. We do not say *the smithereens were scattered all over the floor*, or *we picked up the smithereens*.

**smutty**
usually *smutty jokes/stories*: having or suggesting sexual meanings

**snag**
Most dictionaries state that this is a sharp piece of wood hidden underwater which tears a hole in a boat. Most English speakers are not aware of this original meaning, as it is in frequent use for a hidden difficulty or unexpected factor which makes a job harder, more expensive, more dangerous etc. (very similar to **catch**)
□ I'd love to come to Greece with you. The snag is, I can't leave my old aunt.

**snake in the grass**
Despite the rarity of snakes in Britain, this is not uncommon for 'a hidden enemy' (who may be very near—**under one's nose**).

**snap**
**1** (noun) abbreviation of *snapshot* (a small photograph, taken on the spur of the moment); hence the verb *to snap* a person, a group or a scene
**2** (verb) *snap at someone*: make a quick unfriendly or critical remark
**3** *snap up*: buy something quickly (e.g. a bargain)
**4** *snap out of it*: (a) stop living in a fantasy world, be realistic
(b) try and come out of that (sulky, morose, angry etc.) mood

**snappy**
*make it snappy*: do (or say) it quickly; don't take long about it
□ 'Do you mind if I slip into this shop?' 'All right, but make it snappy, because we haven't much time to spare.'

**snarl-up**
a traffic-jam

**sneak**
*A sneaking feeling* is a suspicion in one's mind.
*To sneak in/out/away* etc. is to go very quietly, hoping not to be seen.

**snide**
unfair, underhand, sneering (usually of remarks, comments, criticism)

**sniffy***
contemptuous, expressing disdain

□ I put the suggestion to her, but she was very sniffy about it.
probably from the idea of sniffing the nose, as a sign of contempt or
disdain; not very common

**snoop**
pry furtively into other people's affairs or activities, with the idea of
finding something on which one can 'catch them out'
□ He was not a very popular character in the office, as he was
suspected of snooping on his colleagues.
hence *snooper*: one who snoops

**snooty**
conceitedly disdainful
□ She's a very snooty sort of person.
□ He was rather snooty about the nextdoor neighbours.

**snooze**
a short sleep (usually in the daytime)
□ I think I'll have a snooze for a while.
hence the verb *to snooze*

**snorter**
an angry letter, written in strong language
□ I've sent him a real snorter; if that doesn't have any effect, nothing
will.
also used of exceptionally hard questions, e.g. in an exam

**snow**
*be snowed under* with work: have a great deal of work to do

**snowball**
**1** (noun) *There isn't a snowball's chance in hell*. There isn't the slightest
hope (of something happening).
**2** (verb) grow, like a large snowball gathering more snow and
momentum as it is pushed down a hill
□ The whole movement is snowballing now, more new members join
every week and we are getting stacks of publicity.

**so-and-so**
an unspecified person, thing or subject
In the case of people the speaker may have no particular person in
mind, but on the other hand he may sometimes use the expression to
conceal the identity of an actual person whom he does not wish to
name.
□ 'If that's So-and-so,' he said (naming a person whom we both
knew), 'I do not wish to speak to him.'
This is not to be confused with *so-so*.

**so long!**

goodbye; used only to a person with whom one is on very familiar terms (A popular explanation is that it is a corruption of the Arabic salutation *salaam*, but it is doubtful whether this is correct)

□ So long, Charlie!

**so-so** (*adv*)

only moderately

□ 'How is your wife getting on?' 'So-so.'

(*adj used predicatively*)

moderate

□ 'What were your examination results like?' 'So-so.'

**so what?**

a question to show indifference, either humorous or unfriendly

□ 'Have you heard Mike is getting married next week?' 'So what?' (i.e. 'I'm not interested')

**sob one's heart out**

see **cry one's eyes out**

**sob-stuff**

writing or narration that seeks to move pity by exaggerated pathos (a derogatory term)

□ She is one of these writers for girls' and women's magazines who specialise in sob-stuff.

**soccer**

(pronounced -*kk*-) abbreviation for *association football*

□ Does your school play rugger or soccer?

**sock**

a hit/blow

□ He gave me a nasty sock on the jaw.

see also **put a sock in it**

**soft**

stupid or sentimental (of a person or an idea)

□ Don't be so soft.

□ She's soft enough to believe anything.

□ That's a soft idea.

**soft job**

an easy job, that requires little effort or exertion

□ I wouldn't mind having a soft job like that.

This is less slangy than **cushy job**.

**soft option**

the easiest of two or more possible choices

☐ Many examination candidates choose to take English Literature because they regard it as a soft option.

**soft-pedal**

refrain from emphasising; diminish the prominence given to

☐ It would be advisable to soft-pedal those parts of our programme which might not be popular with the electorate.

**soft soap**

(uncountable) flattery

also as a verb *soft-soap*: flatter

**soft spot**

*have a soft spot for*: be fond of

**soldier on**

carry on doggedly in the face of difficulties

☐ Several of his colleagues suggested to the Prime Minister that, with so many problems looming ahead, he should resign and leave the task to someone else, but he decided to soldier on.

**some**

Besides the several normal uses of *some*, colloquially it is used in two contradictory senses.

**1** in a depreciatory sense, when it is virtually equivalent to 'very little', 'not much', 'not any' or 'not at all'

☐ That's some help, isn't it?

☐ It's some good looking to me for assistance, when I'm having to borrow money myself.

*some hopes*: no hope at all (note the plural)

☐ 'You may become manager of the firm one day.' 'Some hopes!'

**2** in a complimentary or commendatory sense, with the meaning 'extraordinary'

☐ That's some apple. (i.e. a very big one)

Perhaps the best-known example is Sir Winston Churchill's reply to Hitler's prophecy:

☐ 'In three weeks England will have her neck wrung like a chicken.' 'Some chicken, some neck!'

**some time**

a considerable time (how long this represents depends on the circumstances or the situation)

☐ It will be some time before the work is finished.

☐ I met him once, but that was some time ago.

*some little time*: a fair time; not a long time, but rather more than might be understood by *a little time*

□ I had been waiting there some little time, when I was accosted by a stranger.

**somebody**

a person of importance

□ He thinks himself somebody now he's been left a bit of money.

**somehow**

for some inexplicable reason; for some reason that I do not understand

□ Somehow, I could never get to like him.

□ Somehow, I had a feeling that this would happen.

Used in this way, *somehow* is a sentence-adverb; i.e. it modifies not any particular word, but the whole of the sentence that follows it.

**something like**

**1** approximately

□ The book runs to something like 350 pages.

□ It takes you something like two hours to get there by a good train.

**2** to express admiration or approval (stress on *like*)

□ That's something like a rose. (i.e. a really good specimen)

The object of *like* is sometimes left unexpressed, especially when the idea of it is not something definite, but a general feeling of approval, satisfaction, envy etc.

□ Three months' holiday a year? That's something like.

**song**

see **for a song** and **make a song about**

**soppy**

silly and sentimental

**sore thumb**

see **stick out a mile**

**sort**

sort of person: *she's a good sort/a decent sort* etc.

It is generally used only with adjectives that are complimentary. We do not, as a rule, say *he's a bad sort*, or *he's a mean sort*, but *he's not a bad sort* is quite common; *not* cancels out the pejorative sense of *bad*: *He's not a bad sort, when you get to know him.*

see also **of a sort**

**sort of**

for *these sort*, *those sort*, *he sort of glared at me*, see **kind**

**sort someone out**

Colloquially, this may mean to disentangle the peculiarities of someone's temperament or character; it is sometimes used in the sense

of giving someone a severe reprimand or even hitting or fighting him.
□ Leave him to me; I'll sort him out. I don't think you will have any
trouble with him after that.
note the very common basic use of this phrasal verb:
□ I'm going to sort out all these papers/letters/documents and arrange
them in my files.

**sorts**
see **out of sorts**

**soul**
see **heart and soul**, **keep body and soul together** and **life and
soul**

**soup**
*Now you'll be in the soup*: be in trouble (and be punished)

**sow one's wild oats**
*to have sown one's wild oats*: to have had a time of wild living (and to
become now more serious)

**sozzled**
very drunk

**spade**
for *call a spade a spade*, see **call**

**spade work**
the hard, preliminary work
□ I have now done all the spade work on my thesis; it only remains to
get it into shape.

**span**
see **spick and span**

**spank**
beat across the buttocks, either with a stick or with the open hand;
hence the noun a spanking: *give someone a spanking*, *get a spanking*
etc.

**spanner**
*throw* (or *put*) *a spanner in the works*: introduce a suggestion, demand
etc. or make a move that upsets arrangements or makes things difficult
to achieve

**spare**
usually *go spare*: get upset/angry
see **nervy**

**spark**
*He's a live spark*. He's an intelligent (young) man.
*have a spark*: (of people) be bright, interesting or stimulating

**spark off a (chain) reaction**
(a phrase taken from atomic physics) initiate a succession of related events

**spec**
short for *speculation*; see **on spec**

**specimen**
a derogatory way of referring to a person
□ He's a poor specimen.
□ You're a fine specimen, aren't you? (ironic)

**specs**
abbreviation of (*a pair of*) *spectacles*
□ I've mislaid my specs.
In fact *spectacles* now sounds old-fashioned and despite all the ambiguity, most people say *glasses*.

**speed**
he was *caught for speeding* last week: prosecuted for driving too fast/exceeding the speed limit

**speed cop**
see **cop**

**spick and span**
smart, clean and tidy;
not often used attributively, though we do sometimes say *in spick-and-span condition*
□ She always keeps her house spick and span.

**spiel**
(pronounced *shpeel*) The German word has a new meaning in English: a glib, easy flow of talk.
□ We had to sit through his usual spiel about the decline of Western civilisation. (i.e. his favourite subject about which he always says the same boring lengthy things)
It is similar to **hobby-horse** and having a *bee in one's bonnet* (see **bee**) but *spiel* refers to the talk itself, not the subject talked about.

**spill the beans**
see **beans**

**spin it out**
make something last as long as possible

**spin-off**
(countable) unexpected by-product(s)

**spirits**
see **high spirits**

**spit** *(n)*
>exact likeness (occurs chiefly in the phrase *the very spit of* his father/his uncle/the vicar etc.; a variant is *the spit and image of* ... or *the spitting image of* ...)

**spit and image**
**spitting image**
>see **spit**

**spit and polish**
>a colloquial expression (originating in the army) for polishing leather, brass etc. by first spitting on it, and then rubbing it with a cloth
>□ We could well do without so much spit and polish as part of our daily routine.

**spit it out**
>say what you have to say now (perhaps near slang)

**splash**
>see **make a splash**

**split second**
>a fraction of a second; almost instantaneously
>□ It all happened in a split second, so no-one knows what really did occur.

**split the difference**
>accept a figure or amount halfway between two others
>□ He asked for £6 an hour, and I offered him five. In the end we agreed to split the difference.

**spoke in the wheel**
>*put a spoke in someone's wheel*: spoil someone's plans, upset what is being done
>□ I didn't want to put a spoke in their wheel, so I let them take my car.

**spoon***
>to kiss
>□ There were several couples sitting out spooning at the back of the dimly-lit hall.

**sport***
>a good-natured and obliging person (more often used of a man than of a woman)
>□ Be a sport, and treat me to a dinner.
>*old sport*: a familiar and jocular way of addressing someone
>□ Come on, old sport, have another drink.

**spot** *(v)*
>**1** catch sight of suddenly or for a moment only

☐ I've just spotted him amongst the crowd.

**2** pick out from amongst many, or from a number of names in a list: *spot a winner*, *spot a bargain*

**3** *spotting*: watch for, in the hope of seeing, and possibly recording: *train-spotting*

**spot** *(adj)*

*spot cash*: cash paid on the spot

☐ All our bargains are for spot cash only.

*spot-on*: marvellous; just what was needed

*spot check*: a random (chance) examination made by an inspector, the police, customs etc.

**spot** *(n)*

*in a spot*: in an awkward/embarrassing/difficult situation

Allied to this, *he put me on the spot* is often used when you were unable to answer a question.

see also **soft spot** and **bother**

**sprawl**

This is a pejorative word for 'spread (out)'. You may *sprawl* (rather indecorously) in a chair. We also talk of *urban sprawl*: cities spreading across the countryside.

**spread**

a noun to describe a large amount of food prepared as for a party.

**spree**

revelry and merrymaking, usually including drinking (The commonest constructions are *have a spree* and *go out on the spree*.)

☐ We are having a spree tonight. Do you feel inclined to join us?

☐ We always reckoned to go out on the spree at least one night a week.

**spruce oneself up**

make oneself smart; rather more used of men than of women

**spud**

a potato

**square**

*a square meal*: a good, usually large, well-balanced meal

*a square*: a person who is not up-to-date, not enjoying modern ideas, fashions, records etc. (much used in the 1960s but now rare)

*a square peg in a round hole*: a person doing a job unsuited to their talents and/or personality

**squash (a person *or* an idea)**

repress; suppress

☐ Considering he's a new member of the committee, that young fellow has far too much to say for himself; it's about time someone squashed him.

☐ It was proposed that women should be admitted to the club, but that idea was soon squashed.

**squeak**

*I couldn't get a squeak out of her*. This either means (a) she refused to speak to me, or (b) she did not answer my letters or phone calls.

see also **narrow squeak**

**squib**

see **damp squib**

**squiggle**

rather like **doodle**, but you might use it of some foreign writing system which you can't read

☐ He could only make out a few squiggles on the paper.

**squint**

*Let me have a squint*: Let me see (quickly).

**stacks of**

a great deal of (work etc.)

**stag party**

a social gathering consisting entirely of men, especially one held the night before someone's wedding

compare **hen party**

**stager**

see **old stager**

**stagger**

literally, almost lose balance when walking or standing, but used in emotional situations too

☐ He staggered into his room exhausted.

☐ I was staggered (i.e. shocked, amazed) to hear the news.

☐ The view was staggeringly beautiful.

**stand**

tolerate; bear; put up with

☐ I can't stand this cold weather.

☐ I can't stand her, with her affected ways.

It is used mainly in negative clauses, and clauses beginning with *if* (*if you can stand the noise*), but is not impossible in positive contexts:

☐ I can stand a certain amount of teasing, but too much of it annoys me.

see also **leg**

## stand-offish
(of people) rather haughtily remote in their attitude
□ She is so stand-offish that you can never really get to know her.

## stand on one's own feet
not rely on others for help or support
□ When once they are in an established position, young people should not think they can look to their parents for financial assistance: they must learn to stand on their own feet.

## stand someone a treat/a drink/a holiday *etc.*
give a person a treat, drink, holiday etc. at one's own expense
□ He offered to stand us a drink.

## standing on one's head
*do something standing on one's head*: do it quite easily
□ I could work out that problem standing on my head.

## star turn*
a person who attracts attention on account of the amusement or amazement that he or she causes

## start
*for a start*: in the first place (the first of a number of reasons or explanations)
□ 'What are your objections to the suggestion?' 'Well, for a start, it doesn't meet the real problem.'
see also **flying start**

## start off on the wrong foot
make a mistake to begin with; start a project or operation in the wrong way (sometimes *set off on the wrong foot*)
□ I'm afraid we started off on the wrong foot; if we had been a little more tactful we might have gained his co-operation.
see also **get off to a good start**

## state
*the States*: the United States of America
see also **in a state** and **nervy**

## statistics
see **vital statistics**

## stay put
stay where (it) is placed
□ I can't get this ladder to stay put.

## steady on !
exclamation urging one to stop or moderate whatever one is doing
□ Steady on with that sugar! That's all we have.

□ Steady on! You'll have us through that hedge before you've done.
Sometimes only *steady* is used with the same meaning.

## steal

several euphemistic synonyms exist

see **nab**, **nick**, **rip off**, **swipe** and **whip**

## steal the show

The little girl who sang the solo *stole the show*: was the most enjoyable
and memorable part of the whole entertainment.

## steam

*under one's own steam*: by one's own efforts (especially referring to
travel)

□ Thank you for the offer of a lift, but I think we can get home under
our own steam.

see also **full steam ahead**

## steep

*That's a bit steep*: rather disconcertingly high (of prices), unpleasant,
unreasonable, rude etc. (depending on the circumstances)

□ 'He says we've got to pay an extra £10 within a week to ensure
delivery.' 'That's a bit steep!'

□ 'That's a bit steep—John has left all this work for me to do this
weekend.'

outside this phrase, usually only applied to prices

□ There was some very attractive furniture on show, but the prices
were pretty steep.

## step

see **into someone's shoes** and **watch one's step**

## stew

see **in a stew**

## stick *(n)* *

one of the several jocular terms for a man; mainly in the
combinations *a funny old stick*, *a decent old stick* etc.

## stick *(v)*

bear, stand

□ I can't stick pop music.

## stick at nothing

go to any limits, undeterred by any scruples

□ He would stick at nothing to get his own way.

## stick in one's throat

offend one morally, so that (metaphorically) one cannot swallow it
(also *stick in one's gullet*)

□ It is his treatment of his aged mother that really sticks in my throat.

**stick-in-the-mud**

**1** (adjective) strongly attached to old ways, ideas etc.; reluctant to change

□ So far Parliament has remained just about the most inefficient, stick-in-the-mud, time-wasting of all British institutions. (*The Times*, 22 April 1966)

**2** (noun) a person of such a kind: *an old stick-in-the-mud*

**stick out a mile**

be very obvious

□ What sticks out a mile in these manoeuvres [for Church unity] is the fact that the Roman Catholics and the Anglicans are not surrendering any of their basic principles, whereas the Free Churches appear to be doing little else. (*Inquirer*, 11 June 1966)

*Stick out like a sore thumb* is also very common, and is more likely to be of something objectionable.

□ You can't miss their new house—it sticks out like a sore thumb.

**stick out for**

stand firmly and unyieldingly by a demand

□ We shall stick out for every penny to which we feel we are entitled.

see also **neck**

**stick-up**

a more slangy word for a *hold-up* in the sense of 'armed robbery'

**stick up for**

give one's support to

□ You should always stick up for the persecuted and the oppressed.

*He cannot stick up for himself.* He allows others to take advantage of him, or to treat him unfairly.

*stick up for one's principles*: stand by one's principles; remain loyal to them

**sticker**

a badge to stick on windows etc., probably having some publicity slogan

**sticky**

(of a person) inclined to make difficulties; awkward

□ Our manager can be very sticky about granting even the most reasonable request.

**sticky business**

a difficult and unpleasant business

□ Getting the affairs of the company sorted out is a sticky business, which I would rather have nothing to do with.

**sticky end**

an unpleasant end (of one's life)

□ If he goes on persecuting people and stirring up hatred of himself, one of these days he'll come to a sticky end.

**sticky patch**

a difficult and unpleasant stage or period: a period of bad luck

□ Don't worry. We've done well in the past, and we shall do well again. At the moment we've struck a sticky patch.

**sticky wicket**

a cricket term with similar meaning to **sticky patch**

**stiff**

that's *a bit stiff*: unfair, unreasonable

**stiff upper lip**

the quality of not complaining of pain or misfortune (now usually used jocularly)

□ Just keep a stiff upper lip, my lad.

**stile**

see **help a lame dog over a stile**

**sting**

charge heavily

□ It's a good hotel, and you get good service, but they sting you for it.

**stingy**

miserly, mean, not generous

**stink**

trouble, scandal

□ If this gets to be known there'll be a stink about it.

also *make a stink* or *kick up a stink* about something

**stinker**

meanings **1** and **2** coincide with **snorter**

**1** a difficult question, problem, puzzle etc.

□ One of the questions on the examination paper was a real stinker.

**2** an angry, strongly worded document, especially a letter

□ I have written him a real stinker.

□ Young Jones's school report was a proper stinker.

**3** an unpleasant person

**stint**

see **do one's stint**

**stir**

*cause a stir*: stimulate a lot of interest

## stitch

*not a stitch on*: not a single item of clothing on; completely naked
□ She saw a small child running about in the warm sunshine with not a stitch on.

## stitches

*have someone in stitches*: cause a person to laugh hysterically so that he cannot stop (The reference is not to a stitch with needle and cotton, but to the pain in the side known as a stitch.)
□ The comedian had us in stitches.

## stock

(only attributive) *a stock reply*, *a stock example*, *a stock illustration*: kept among one's stock of such, and used over and over again, when one is required (cf. a shopkeeper's *stock sizes* of his goods: the sizes that he keeps in stock)
see also **lock, stock and barrel** and **on the stocks**

## stodgy

heavy, dull, too solid (used of people, books, lectures, food etc.)

## stomach

not only used of food; I can't *stomach* his ideas: can't tolerate them
I have *no stomach for that*. It upsets me emotionally.

## stooge

a person used by another to carry out his wishes, or who willingly lends himself to his master's designs (originally a term for the theatre or music-hall, where a stooge is the willing butt of a comedian, and plays up to him in order that he may bring off his jokes)

## stops

see **pull out all the stops**

## storm in a teacup

a great fuss about something unimportant

## stools

see **fall between two stools**

## story

lie, untruth; used especially to and by young children, more particularly in Victorian times, when *lie* was felt to be an impolite word for the young to use
□ You shouldn't tell stories.
hence *story-teller*: liar
see also **tall story**

## straight and narrow

(an allusion to 'the straight and narrow way' of the Bible) A strict and rigid way of life, allowing of no deviation into vices or irregularities

□ When he was younger he lived a rather wild life, but nowadays his wife keeps him on the straight and narrow.

## straight from the horse's mouth

direct from an authoritative source; direct from the person who is most likely to know

□ Here is the reply, straight from the horse's mouth.

(Sometimes the word *straight* is omitted.)

## straight from the shoulder

(words) expressed quite frankly

## straight-laced

old-fashioned, especially in the matter of morals; similar to *narrow-minded*

## strangely enough

see **enough**

## stranger

*You are a stranger* (stressing *are*) is part of the welcome on meeting a friend whom you haven't seen for a very long time.

## strap-hanger

a person who travels to work daily on such crowded trains that (s)he has to stand and hang on to a strap as there aren't enough seats; also, *to strap-hang*

## straw

see **last straw**

## street

*not in the same street as*: far inferior to

□ As a scholar, he is not in the same street as his predecessor in the post.

*streets ahead of*: very far ahead of (in attainments, progress, amenities etc., but not in distance)

□ As far as modernisation is concerned, there are several other towns that are streets ahead of us.

*up one's street*: within one's sphere of interest or knowledge

□ See what you can make of this problem; it's just up your street.

□ It's no good asking my opinion on anything to do with psychology; that's not up my street.

## stretch

**1** a term of imprisonment

□ He's doing a stretch at the moment, so we shall see nothing more of him for a little while.

**2** *at a stretch*: continuously; without a break (*work for hours at a stretch*)

## stride

*get into one's stride*: get accustomed to an activity one is engaged in, and settle down to a steady and regular pace of working

□ I find that I am taking rather a long time about things at present, but no doubt it will be better when I get into my stride.

*take something in one's stride*: do it without the need for any special practice, training or exertion

□ A person of your capabilities and experience should be able to take a simple task like that in his stride.

## strike

*it strikes me*: it seems to me; I think

□ It strikes me he'll never be satisfied, whatever job he has.

*strike while the iron is hot*: act now while it is favourable/opportune

## strings

conditions; chiefly in the phrase (*no*) *strings attached*

□ What makes the grant even more acceptable is that there are no strings attached to it.

see also **pull strings**

## stroke

In the last week, he *hasn't done a stroke* (*of work*): absolutely no work (*A scrap of work* is also sometimes used.)

## strong as a horse

very strong (used of human beings, but the reference is usually not to muscular strength)

□ She works long hours, yet seems to feel no ill effects from it. She must be as strong as a horse.

see also **going strong**

## struck on

having a strong liking for

□ He's had various girls in his time. Jenny Brown is the latest one that he's struck on.

more often used in the negative: *I'm not too struck on that idea*. I don't care for it.

## stuck

The past participle of *to stick* is in very frequent use, meaning 'unable to advance' (in work, traffic etc.)

□ We got stuck in a traffic jam.

□ I'm stuck in the exercise.

*stuck on* (near slang): infatuated with

## stuck up

(of a person or a group of persons) haughty; conceited

☐ She is so stuck up that she refuses to talk to her neighbours.

☐ They're a stuck-up set.

## stuff

a general colloquial term for material of one sort or another—a fabric, food, drink, the contents of a book etc.

Usually the word has a derogatory connotation ('I don't want that stuff') and is often found in company with derogatory adjectives: *poor stuff*, *weak stuff*, *dreadful stuff*, but not always:

☐ There's been some good stuff on television lately.

☐ This whisky's not bad stuff.

*do one's stuff*: do the task that is expected of one

☐ I shan't speak for long; I shall just do my stuff, and then sit down.

## stuffed dummy

literally a 'dummy' figure on which clothes are exhibited in a shop; in colloquial use, mainly in the simile *like a stuffed dummy* (of a person who shows few signs of animation)

☐ He never uttered a word, and showed no interest in what was going on around him, but just stood there like a stuffed dummy.

This is less used today than a generation ago, possibly because the actual stuffed dummy has been largely superseded by one made of plastic.

## stuffy

very conventional, formal and prudish

☐ I felt oppressed by the stuffy atmosphere in that household.

☐ Old Mr Thompson was a very good-natured person, but young people always complained that they could not get on with him, as he was so stuffy.

## stump

defeat (by a question or a request that is too difficult)

☐ That question stumped him.

☐ I was stumped for words in which to reply.

☐ You've got me stumped there.

The figure of speech is probably from the game of cricket.

## stunning

super, marvellous

## style

a term of approval, especially in

*that's the style*: that's the way

□ That's the style! Give it to him hot.

□ 'Is this the right way to do it?' 'That's the style.'

**stymied**

*Stymie* is a golf expression. *Stymied* means in a difficult position; thwarted

**sub**

(noun) abbreviation of *subscription*

□ Have you paid your sub yet?

also short for *submarine*

**success**

see **howling success**

**such**

*suchlike*: other things of that kind

□ We bought a lot of pears, apples, bananas and suchlike.

*no such*, in phrases like *I said no such thing*: nothing like that

*such and such*: a given amount, depending on the circumstances

□ When I buy such and such a quantity of fabric in a shop I expect the assistant to be able to say the cost immediately.

**suck eggs**

see **teach one's grandmother to suck eggs**

**suffer fools gladly**

(perhaps more a cliché than an idiom but used in a colloquial way) tolerate anyone stupid, used with a negative

□ She's the kind of woman who won't suffer fools gladly.

**suggestive**

Increasingly this has come to be 'suggestive of sex': *a suggestive joke/remark/glance*.

**suit**

see **down to the ground**

**sums**

see **do one's sums**

**Sundays**

see **month of Sundays**

**sunk**

(of persons, organisations etc.) ruined

□ If the bank won't come to our aid with a loan, we're sunk.

**suppose**

*I don't suppose . . .?* a negative way of making a request to which one hopes for a positive answer, felt to be more courteous than making the request direct

□ I don't suppose you could lend me a quid, could you?

**sure**

certainly

□ 'Might I borrow that newspaper for a few minutes, please?' 'Sure.' (actually American usage, but has now found its way into colloquial British English, though to older British speakers it does not sound natural)

*I don't know, I'm sure*: (a well-established British idiom) apparently, though not really, a contradiction, since it means 'I am sure I don't know'

*as sure as* we arrange a cricket match, it rains: every time, without fail that (probably an exaggeration)

*as sure as fate*: no doubt about it; certain to happen

□ As sure as fate he'll have an accident with that motor bike.

*for sure*: for certain

□ I think I shall be able to come, though I don't know for sure.

see also **not so sure**

**sure enough**

see **enough**

**surprise surprise!**

spoken sarcastically when your fears of something poor or unsatisfactory are confirmed (similar to *I thought as much*, see **think**)

**suss (out)**

get to know about, discover about, as in *you've sussed me out*: discovered exactly what I wanted to do; *I'll suss the scene*: investigate and find out about it

**swallow hook, line and sinker**

see **hook, line and sinker**

**swallow the dictionary**

said of someone using lots of long words

□ He's swallowed the dictionary.

**swap**

(also sometimes written *swop*; rhymes with *top*)

exchange: *swap places, swap a watch for a camera*

*do a swap*: effect such an exchange

*a swap-shop*: a shop where one article is taken in exchange for another

**sweat**

work hard

□ I have been sweating all day at this job, and am not much farther on than when I began.

□ I don't see the sense of sweating here for a few pounds a week, when I could get a better-paid post elsewhere.

hence the use as a noun, *it's a sweat*: it's hard work (The reference is not always to physical work; indeed *he was all in a sweat* is likely to be used of tension or agitation.)

**sweep**
see **make a clean sweep**

**sweeping statement**
a(n absurd) generalisation

**sweet on***
very fond of; in love with
□ That young fellow seems to be sweet on your sister.

**sweet tooth**
a taste for food, drink etc. that is sweet: *have a sweet tooth, be sweet-toothed*

**swim**
see **in the swim**

**swine***
(applied to people) a term of abuse, not used in polite speech or conversation, expressing intense dislike on account of objectionable habits or traits of character (often expressing no more in fact than a personal dislike or prejudice)
□ What swine has scratched my car?
□ You swine!

**swing**
be hanged
□ If he's found guilty, he'll have to swing for it.
also, not literally:
□ Whoever took my money will swing for it. (i.e. suffer for it)

**swing the lead**
(*lead* rhymes with *red*) attempt to evade doing something by malingering or by false excuses
□ Don't believe his tale; he's just swinging the lead.
This is of naval origin, and is probably connected with the idea of taking soundings by literally swinging the lead weight.
for *not room to swing a cat* (*in*), see **cat**

**swipe**
**1** hit
**2** one of the slightly slangy words for **steal**
□ Who swiped my books?

**swizz**

something like **con**

□ What a swizz!

*What a swizzle* is sometimes used.

**swop**

alternative spelling of **swap**

**swot**

study hard and intensively

The constructions are (a) swot a subject (*swot mathematics*), (b) swot at a subject (*spend the whole evening swotting at mathematics*), (c) swot up a subject (*I shall have to swot it up before I can teach it*), and (d) swot for an examination (*I'm swotting for my finals*).

*A swot* is a person who swots or studies hard. In schoolboy vocabulary the word has a derogatory meaning, since among schoolboys intense study is not a popular activity. If one schoolboy describes another as *a swot*, he is certainly not paying him a compliment.

# t

**T**

(pronounced *tee*) to a T (or *t*): exactly; to a nicety (mainly in the expressions *done to a T* and *cooked to a T*) possibly an abbreviation of *to a turn*, or the *T* may represent a clipping of the last syllable of *nicety*

**ta**

a nursery word for 'thank you'; when used by adults, regarded by some speakers as uneducated

It cannot be treated as a verb and given a subject (we cannot say *I ta*), nor is it often used with *no* or *yes* (*no, ta* and *yes, ta*).

**tab**

*keep a tab* (or *tabs*) *on someone or something*: watch; keep an account of; note what happens; observe

**tackle**

**1** (noun, uncountable) formal English, equipment needed for some particular task (especially *fishing tackle*); colloquial, a miscellaneous collection of articles

□ What's all that tackle lying in the corner?

**2** (verb) set about, begin on; cope with

□ I don't know how to tackle the job.

□ I have just had one good helping of meat, I couldn't tackle another.

**tag along with**
**tag oneself on to**
   attach oneself to another person, or group of people, without their invitation or consent
   □ There were five of us in the party to begin with, but before we had gone very far two or three strangers had tagged themselves on to us.

**tail**
   *the tail wagging the dog*: a small, and often unrepresentative, part of an organisation, controlling the whole body
   □ That the few left-wingers should exert such an influence on the policy of the party is a case of the tail wagging the dog.
   *with one's tail between one's legs*: frightened; dejected (from the habit of a dog)
   □ He went in to the interview in a defiant mood, but came out with his tail between his legs.
   see also **head(s)** and **sit on someone's tail**

**tail end**
   the very last part
   □ All the good weather came at the tail end of our holiday.

**take a back seat**
   assume a subordinate or inconspicuous position
   □ After being Chairman of the company for so long, it was not a pleasant thought that he would now have to take a back seat.

**take a dim view**
   regard pessimistically; not regard with favour
   □ The doctors take a dim view of his chances of recovery.
   □ Your proposal seems quite a sensible one, but I am afraid the manager will take a dim view of it, if he does not get anything out of it himself.

**take a hand in**
   see **hand**

**take a knock**
   suffer a setback or a misfortune
   □ The economy of the country has certainly taken a knock this year.
   □ What with one illness after another, there's no denying that he's taken a knock just recently.

**take a leaf out of someone's book**
   copy (whoever is named) in a certain respect or certain respects (It is usually implied that the thing to be copied is a good point.)

☐ Why can't you get here on time? You want to take a leaf out of your father's book. In all his working life he was never late.

**take a lot of**
**take much**

(+gerund) be difficult to

☐ His story takes a lot of believing.

☐ That doesn't take much doing.

☐ That won't take a lot of doing.

**take French leave**

see **French leave**

**take heart**

see **heart**

**take it in one's stride**

see **stride**

**take it out of someone**

**1** exhaust: take the energy out of

☐ This hot weather takes it out of you.

**2** work off one's ill temper, displeasure, annoyance etc. on someone who has done nothing to deserve it

☐ If he has been annoyed by anything at the office, he takes it out of his wife and children.

You also often hear *take it out on* in this second sense.

**take it with a pinch of salt**

You must not really believe all of it—some or all of it may not be truthful.

**take 'no' for an answer**

see **no**

**take on**

give expression to grief, excitement or some other emotion

☐ We all sympathise with your loss, but don't take on so; that won't help matters.

As you see, it is usually followed by *so*.

**take one all one's time**

be only just possible for one (The reference is not necessarily to time in the literal sense of the word.)

☐ I am feeling so unwell that it takes me all my time to keep going.

☐ It takes me all my time to pay the rent.

☐ It took him all his time to keep his temper.

**take oneself off**

leave; go away

☐ You'd better take yourself off these premises, or I'll call the police.

☐ With this final remark, he took himself off in a fit of temper.
The idiom implies or suggests displeasure or anger.

**take some**

( +gerund) *It'll take some doing* : be difficult to do

see **take a lot of**

☐ That record will take some beating.

☐ This document takes some understanding.

☐ I got him to agree at last, but he took some persuading.

Especially common is the phrase *it takes some getting used to*
(referring to new experiences, such as a new taste, life in a foreign
country, marriage).

see **used to** for gerund use

**take someone down a peg (or two)**

disillusion him of his idea of his own superiority, importance etc.

☐ She has got far too great an idea of her own importance; it is time
she was taken down a peg or two.

The reference is to the pegs by which a ship's colours were at one time
raised and lowered. The height at which the colours were flown was an
indication of the status of the ship; thus to take the colours down a
peg was to lower the status of the vessel.

**take something lying down**

accept something unpleasant submissively or without protest

☐ You don't expect me to take an insult lying down, do you?

**take something to heart**

see **heart**

**take the bull by the horns**

see **bull**

**take the good with the bad**

accept both the good and the bad, and not complain

☐ Some years we have a plentiful harvest, others a very poor one, but
you have to take the good with the bad.

**take the micky (out of someone)**

tease or make fun (of a person)

☐ Don't listen to Kate; she's just taking the micky.

**take the rough with the smooth**

accept the difficult or the unpleasant along with the easier and the
more pleasant

☐ You can't expect things always to go in your favour. There are
bound to be setbacks and difficult times, but you must take the rough
with the smooth.

## take the wind out of someone's sails

make it impossible for a person to say what he intended, either (a) by anticipating him, or (b) by cutting the ground from under his feet by revealing something that changes the circumstances, so that the intended remark would be inappropriate

□ I had made up my mind what I was going to say, but the news quite took the wind out of my sails.

## take the words out of someone's mouth

say exactly what someone else was about to say

□ I was about to protest when he took the words out of my mouth.

## take to doing

**1** quickly acquire a skill

□ He took to skiing in no time.

A familiar way of finishing the sentence is to say *he took to it like a duck to water*.

**2** become in the habit of

□ She took to sitting in the garden every afternoon.

## takes

see **what it takes**

## tales

see **tell on someone** and **old wives' tales**

## talk

see **Dutch** and **man-to-man talk**

## talk about

used colloquially in an exclamatory sense to express amazement or to give emphasis: *Talk about rain!* It rained very hard. *Talk about eat!* They (he) ate ravenously.

## talk nineteen to the dozen

talk very fast indeed

## talk of the devil, and he's sure to appear

a proverbial phrase sometimes used when the very person who is under discussion, or whose name has just been mentioned, unexpectedly appears (Usually only the first four words are spoken.)

## talk out of/through one's hat

talk nonsense; talk on a subject about which one really knows nothing

□ Don't take any notice of what he says; he's just talking out of his hat.

## talk someone into doing something

persuade someone to do something against their initial wishes

□ He talked her into selling her pictures.

## talk someone out of doing something
the opposite of the previous entry: dissuade
□ I talked him out of making the trip.
## talk the hind leg off a donkey
go on talking for a very long time (used disparagingly)
□ She would talk the hind leg off a donkey if you gave her the chance.
Perhaps the reference is to the belief that donkeys live a very long time.
In place of *talk*, *argue* is often used.
## talking-to
(noun) reproof; rebuke; reprimand
□ Give Joe a good talking-to.
the same as **ticking-off** and **telling-off**
## tall order
an order which is unreasonable, or would be difficult to execute
□ To expect me to get all that work completed in less than a month is rather a tall order.
## tall story
a story that is exaggerated
□ His account of how he tackled that robber and saved the money sounds to me rather a tall story.
## taped
summed up as regards character, motives etc.
□ When I first got to know him, I did not know what to make of him, but I've got him taped now.
Also when you know your job well, you may say *I've got the job taped*.
## tarred with the same brush
having the same failings or the same unpleasant characteristics (as someone else)
□ I wouldn't trust either of the two brothers; they are tarred with the same brush.
□ I think Christine is arrogant and spiteful; and her friend Janet is tarred with the same brush.
## tart
At one time this meant 'sweetheart' (of which word it is a corrupt abbreviation, by a humorous mis-division into *sweet tart*). Now it is applied to a woman of loose sexual morals. Hence the adjective *tarty*:
□ She is a rather tarty bit of goods.
□ How can you go out got up in that tarty fashion?
see also **tarted up**

**tartar**

a bad-tempered, ferocious person

□ None of the servants like her. She's a real tartar.

*catch a tartar\** : find oneself involved with someone of this kind

□ He hadn't been married long, when he realised that he had caught a tartar.

equally used of men

**tarted up**

(of something previously rather old or shabby) painted or decorated rather tastelessly (but in an effort to be smart)

□ Their local pub had been tarted up with orange carpets and red tables.

see **tart** above

**tatty**

**1** of inferior quality

**2** bedraggled and untidy

**taxed (up) to the hilt**

having to pay a maximum amount of taxes

**tea**

see **cup of tea**

**teach**

*that'll teach you* : that will teach you not to do that kind of thing again

□ So you were ill after eating those green apples, were you? That'll teach you.

sometimes humorously corrupted to *that'll larn* (learn) *you*

**teach one's grandmother to suck eggs**

attempt to teach, or give advice to, one's elders or those more experienced than oneself

□ One of the things that you young people have to learn is that you can't teach your grandmother to suck eggs.

**teacup**

see **storm in a teacup**

**tear out**, **in** *etc*.

(rhyming with *chair*) one of the group of verbs showing rapid movement

see under **dart/dash** ; see also **torn**

**tear someone off a strip**

the same as **dress down**

**tears**

(rhyming with *clears*) see **crocodile tears**

**teaser**

a problem or a puzzle to which it is difficult to find the solution

□ The problem looks simple enough, but when you come to try and solve it you'll find it's a real teaser.

**tech**

(rhyming with *deck*) abbreviation of *technical college* or *technical school*

□ My brother Jack is attending evening classes at the tech.

**teeth**

really something you can *get your teeth into*: a task/book/subject etc. which is a real challenge (but which is welcomed)

(a noise that) *sets one's teeth on edge*: irritates one intensely (also *puts one's teeth on edge*)

*armed to the teeth*: carrying as many weapons as possible

see also **fed up**, **fight tooth and nail**, **grit one's teeth**, **lie in one's teeth**, **long in the tooth**, **skin** and **sweet tooth**

**telephone**

usually shortened to *phone*

It seems useful to gather here all the phrases used. The least informal is 'I'll telephone you'. (Note 'I'll (tele)phone *to* you' is not correct.)

I'll phone you.  I'll call you.

I'll ring you.  I'll call you up.

I'll ring you up.  I'll give you a call.

I'll give you a ring.  I'll give you a tinkle.

I'll give you a phone call.

NOTE *He's on the (tele)phone* can mean:

**1** He is using the phone now.

**2** He has a phone in his house/lodging/flat.

see also **blower**

**tell**

*I'll tell you what*: used to introduce a suggestion

*I can tell you*: appended to a statement to emphasise it and to suggest that the speaker really means what he says

□ I am not going to be treated in that way, I can tell you.

□ It's pretty hard work, I can tell you.

*You're telling me*. You're telling me something I know already.

(a reply which amounts to an agreement with the statement that has just been made)

□ 'By Jove! It's hot today, isn't it?' 'You're telling me.'

In speech, the stress falls on *me*.

*I'm telling you*: a speaker's reinforcement of a previous statement he has made, and on which doubt has been cast, or which his interlocutor seems reluctant to take seriously

□ 'But surely he wouldn't dismiss old-established members of the staff at a moment's notice, like that?' 'I'm telling you. You wait and see.'
In speech, the stress is on *telling*.

for *tell someone where he gets off*, see **get off**

for *there's no telling*, see **there's no** ( + gerund)

see also **hear tell**

## tell it/that to the marines

This is a sarcastic reply indicating that the speaker does not believe what has just been said. At one time the Marines were looked down upon by the regular sailors as incompetent and ignorant, and therefore likely to believe anything that was told them.

## tell on someone

give him away by telling of something he has done which will get him into trouble or earn him disfavour (nearer to slang, though it may perhaps just qualify as a colloquialism)

□ You had better keep quiet about it, or someone is sure to tell on you.
The phrase *to tell tales* was formerly used for this meaning and the noun *a tell-tale* is still used for a person who reports on others' misdeeds.

## tell someone flat

see **flat**

## tell someone straight

tell someone candidly, without modification or without beating about the bush

□ I tell you straight, I'm not going to be a party to such a dishonest scheme as that.

## telling-off

(the same as **talking-to** and **ticking-off**)

If he catches you doing that he'll *give you a good telling-off*: rebuke/reprimand you

## telly

abbreviation of *television*

## ten to one

almost certainly (a term taken from betting)

□ Ten to one they will not be punctual.

## tenner

a ten-pound note

see also **fiver**

**terrible**

very bad: *a terrible cough*, *the pain is terrible*

**terrific**

marvellous, wonderful

**terror***

*a terror for work*: one who is inordinately addicted to work (similarly *a terror for correctness*, *speed* etc.)

*a young terror*: a troublesome child; one who is always getting into mischief

☐ As a boy, Robert Clive is said to have been a young terror.

**tether**

*at the end of one's tether*: at the end of one's resources/patience/energy (like the goat which has eaten all it can reach in the circle round its post, to which it is attached with a *tether*)

**thank one's lucky stars**

consider oneself very lucky or fortunate

☐ It was foolish of you to dash across the road like that without looking first. Thank your lucky stars you weren't knocked down.

usually used in the second person, but other persons are possible: *he can thank his lucky stars*, *she can thank her lucky stars*; a reference to astrology

**that**

sometimes used in a depreciatory or derogatory sense: *that Hitler*; and occasionally in a commendatory one, but for the latter *this* is more usual

☐ This penicillin is wonderful stuff.

*This* can also mean 'which is now in the news' or 'which we hear so much of nowadays'.

*that's a good boy/girl/fellow*: a complimentary observation on the action of the person to whom it is addressed

☐ 'I gave grandma one of my sweets.' 'That's a good boy.'

It may anticipate the performance of an act in compliance with a request.

☐ Pass me the newspaper, will you, please, that's a good fellow.

(It is equally common to say *there's a good fellow* here.)

*it is/was that*: used to confirm and emphasise a previous remark by another person; the verb is stressed

☐ 'It is cold out tonight, isn't it?' 'It is that.'

*how's that?* equivalent in sense to *why?* or *for what reason?*

☐ 'I don't think I shall be able to get to see him after all.' 'How's that?'

sometimes also used to ask one's opinion of something considered outstanding

□ How's that for an apple?

*that's what you think/say*: suggestive of unlikelihood or of doubt on the part of the speaker: a reminder that other opinions or points of view are possible

□ That's what you think/say, but there are many people who would disagree with you.

*that cold, that scared, that eager* etc.: here, *that* is used colloquially as an adverb of degree, where in more literary English *so* would be used

□ My hands were that cold, I had scarcely any feeling in them.

This is often condemned as unidiomatic, but we may allow it as a colloquialism; similarly with *all that*, in such sentences as *I'm not all that old*.

## that was

(*That* is a relative pronoun.) used in referring to a married woman by her maiden name: *Mrs Jameson* (*Miss Cook that was*); also of a place that has changed its name: *Oslo* (*Christiania that was*)

## that's all

(appended to a statement) there is no alternative; that is all that can be done

□ If all the seats are booked, we shall have to stay at home, that's all.

This is sometimes extended to *that's all there is to it*.

## that's it

**1** an observation expressing approval

□ That's it; keep straight ahead until you come to the traffic lights, and then turn to the left.

**2** sometimes used ironically

□ That's it! Fall over and break your leg!

## that's that

that concludes the matter

□ I had hoped that we should be able to stay with Jim and Alice for the week-end, but now I learn that they will not be at home; so that's that.

## then

see **every now and then**

## there you are

said triumphantly, to point out that what one said would happen has happened

□ There you are! Didn't I say this would happen?

**there's**

($+$ a complimentary adjective or noun) used in a commendatory observation

□ Be quiet, there's a good boy.

□ Just pour my tea, there's a love!

(equally, *That's a . . .*)

**there's no**

($+$ gerund) means more or less the same as *it's impossible* $+$ infinitive

□ There's no saying what may happen.

□ When once she starts talking, there's no stopping her.

**these**

see **that** and **this**

**thick**

**1** dull of understanding (thick-headed)

**2** very friendly with

□ I see Vernon is thick with several of the Aldermen nowadays.

**3** unfair; inconsiderate

□ It's a bit thick, his asking for a second loan of money, when he's not paid the last one back yet.

see also **in the thick of**, **lay it on thick**, **skin** and **through thick and thin**

**thin end of the wedge**

see **wedge**

**thin time**

a time characterised by lack of money, pleasures etc.

□ We've had a pretty thin time of it lately.

**thing**

*just the thing*: just the thing that is needed

*not quite the thing*: not quite the kind of thing that is considered socially correct

□ It's not quite the thing to wear an open-necked shirt to a formal evening dinner.

*little thing*: an affectionate way of referring to a small child or, jocularly, to someone behaving like a child (*dear little thing*, *poor little thing*)

With a derogatory adjective *thing* can be used of adults: *you stupid thing*, *you silly thing*, *you nasty thing*.

*just one of those things*: see **one of those things**

*your things*: your clothes (and any other belongings, depending on the circumstances)

for *it's one thing to . . . another to . . .* , see under **sell**

*the thing is*: often used to emphasise an important remark which follows

*have a thing about*: an older phrase for a **hang-up**

for *old thing*, see **old man 4**

**thingammy *or* thingummy**

This is a very useful word when you just can't remember the correct name for something. By definition, this and the following words are rarely written so the spelling is not really established; any of these may be used: *thingammybob, thingammyjig, what d'you call it, what's it, what-not*

**think**

*What do you think?* asked as a preliminary to imparting a piece of news that is likely to be a surprise

□ What do you think? Dorothy is getting married.

*I thought I told you/I thought I said*: something in the nature of a reprimand, for an instruction or a promise that has not been carried out

□ I thought I told you to lock the door behind you.

*come to think of it*: an ellipsis of *When I come to think of it* or *Now I come to think of it*

□ Come to think of it, I did once have dinner at the Savoy.

*I should think so*: an indication by the speaker that what has just been said is no more than he would have expected

□ 'I refused to pay so exorbitant a price.' 'I should think so.'

*Hot! I should think it was hot.* (The stress is on *was*.) This use of *I should think* endorses the previous assertion.

*I don't think\**. Spoken with the emphasis on *don't*, this was, until a few years ago, used sarcastically to contradict an ironic statement. It is not heard much nowadays.

□ 'That was a very enjoyable tune.' 'I don't think.'

*I thought as much.* That is what I feared; you have confirmed my doubts.

*You've/he's* etc. *got another think coming.* You etc. will find you have made a great mistake.

see also **make someone think** and **way of thinking**

**this/these**

A curious use prevails in telling stories:

□ There was this bloke in the street you see . . .

where *a bloke* would be expected.

see also **that**

**this once**

this occasion only

□ I'll allow you to stay up late for this once, provided you go to bed when you're told.

**this, that and the other**

all kinds of things

□ We sat up very late into the night, talking about this, that and the other.

**thorn**

*a real thorn in my side* (or *flesh*): a constant irritation to me

**those were the days**

those were the most enjoyable days of our lives

□ You ought to have lived in the Edwardian times. Those were the days!

**though**

see **although**

**thoughts**

see **second thoughts**; for *a penny for your thoughts*, see **penny**

**thousand and one things**

a great many things (not literally 1001)

□ I've a thousand and one things to do before we set out for our holiday.

**three R's**

the three basic subjects of the junior school curriculum—reading, writing and 'rithmetic (arithmetic)

□ It is important that every child should get a good grounding in the three r's.

**thrilled to bits/death**

very pleased/excited

□ I was thrilled to bits to be invited.

**throat**

see **frog in one's throat** and **stick in one's throat**

**through thick and thin**

through good and bad times; often *to stick with someone through thick and thin*

**through with someone (*or* something)**

unable to endure any longer; having the patience exhausted

□ I've put up with him as long as I can, but now I'm through with him.

**throw a spanner in the works**
  see **spanner**
**throw one's hand in**
  stop working/helping
  see also **chuck**
**throw out the baby with the bath water**
  see **baby**
**throw someone in at the deep end**
  fail to give a person (sufficient) preparation for a job but let him learn
  as time and experience permit (The phrase comes from swimming in a
  pool.)
**thumb**
  *have a person under one's thumb*: have him entirely at one's command
**thumb a lift**
  see **lift**
**thumbs**
  see **finger** and **twiddle one's thumbs**
**thumbs up**
  the gesture meaning that all is well
  (The less common opposite is of course *thumbs down*.)
  □ The director gave us the thumbs-up on our new design. (i.e. he
  agreed to it)
**thumping\***
  big, large; usually followed by an adjective denoting size, *great*, *big*,
  *large*, etc.: *a thumping big meal*, *a thumping great pie*; or by one which,
  within its context, suggests size (*a thumping good meal*)
**thunderstorm**
  see **dying duck in a thunderstorm**
**tick**
  **1** a brief moment of time (probably from the ticking of the clock)
  □ I'll be there in a tick. It won't take me a tick to do it.
  **2** *What makes him tick?* What makes him behave/think/act as he
  does?
  see also **on tick**
**ticking-off**
  a reprimand; same as **telling-off** and **talking-to**
**tickle**
  amuse
  □ Uncle Herbert's stories never failed to tickle the children.
  also in the passive:

They were tickled by his stories.
To intensify this phrase, *tickled pink* is often used.

**ticklish**

*ticklish job*, *ticklish business* etc.: difficult, delicate, needing great care

□ Repairing a small radio like this is a ticklish job.

□ To put the suggestion to him without offending him is going to be a ticklish business.

**tiddly**

see **drunk**

**tidy**

fairly large (in amount, size etc.): *a tidy while*, *a tidy distance*, *a tidy sum of money*, *a tidy amount*, *a tidy-sized house*

**tied to someone's apron-strings**

This is usually used of a young person who is no longer a child, but is still treated as such by his (or her) mother, and accepts this position. We say that such a person is *tied to his mother's apron strings*.

**tied up**

**1** confused, unable to progress

□ He's all tied up.

**2** *get it* (*all*) *tied up*: get it arranged/fixed/settled

**3** *get tied up in*: get involved in (e.g. in an organisation, so that one has little free time)

**tight**

**1** We may say that a person is *tight for money* (has insufficient of it) or is *tight with money* (mean) or that *money is tight* (difficult to get).

**2** drunk: see **drunk**

**tight corner**

*in a tight corner*: in a difficult or dangerous position or situation

□ I'm in a tight corner just at present; I've several large bills to pay, and I've already an overdraft at the bank, so I can hardly borrow more from there.

**tight-fisted**

reluctant to part with money

**tighten one's belt**

primarily means 'eat less food' (by necessity) and by extension, 'spend less money by living a simpler life'

**tighten the screws**

apply pressure (to get people to work harder etc.), ultimately a phrase coming from torture

□ We must tighten the screws if we are to meet that deadline.

**tiles**

*a night (spent out) on the tiles*: a night spent on living it up; usually drinking too much

**till the cows come home**

for a very long time

□ You can call till the cows come home, and you will not attract the attention of those children while they are playing with the kittens.

**tilt***

attack; (a word which has survived from medieval jousting), found as a noun in the phrases *have a tilt at*, *take a tilt at*

**tilt the scales**

Different from *tilt* above, this refers to the factor that determines someone's decision, after hesitation.

□ 'What made you live in a flat in town? I thought you wanted to live in the country.' 'It was the children's schools that tilted the scales. There seems more choice in town.'

**time**

*What time do you make it?* is probably more common than *What time is it?* or *What is the time?*

*by the time (that)*: often means no more than *when* or *after*

□ By the time income tax and other charges are deducted, your salary amounts to little more than half the nominal amount.

*half one's time*: see **half**

*how's the time?* What is the time? (The question usually takes this form only when we are thinking of the present time in relation to some specific time that lies ahead, and which therefore we are interested in. It therefore means more or less, 'How much time have we left?')

□ How's the time? We shall have to leave here by three o'clock.

*It's (high) time we went home, to work, away* etc.: an important construction meaning 'It's time for us to go' (As shown here, it involves using a tense further back than seems necessary.)

see also **have a time of it**, **have no time for**, note in **hell**, **in no time**, **in one's time**, **kill (the) time**, **lean time**, **next to no time**, **nick** *(n)*, **no use for**, **some time**, **take one all one's time**, **thin time** and **while away the time**

**time of one's life**

the best time one has had during the whole of one's life; a very enjoyable time

□ We are having the time of our life, here in the student quarter of Paris.

□ 'How are you liking your job?' 'Very much. I'm having the time of my life.'

**tinker**

**1** (verb) vaguely means to (try to) repair something, probably rather unsuccessfully

□ Daddy's tinkering with the car again.

**2** (noun) a mild word for 'rascal, naughty child'*

**tinker's cuss** (*or* **curse**)*

see **cuss**

**tinkle**

see **telephone**

**tip**

**1** (noun only) a little information given (fairly confidentially) from which you may benefit

□ My brother-in-law gave me a few tips on what shares I should buy.

**2** (noun and verb) money given for services above the price asked; scarcely colloquial, but *gratuity* is certainly more formal

□ When I'd paid the bill and the waiter came back with the change, I left him a tip.

**3** *It's (just) the tip of the iceberg. Tip* is the 'top' which we can see, knowing far more exists out of sight under the water—to our peril. This is used of anything unpleasant/worrying/threatening, which may get far worse.

**4** *tip someone a wink*: warn someone secretly, as if by winking

**5** *a tip-off*: an indirect hint, especially to the police

**6** *tip-top*\*: excellent (in fact not used as much now in Britain as in some Continental countries)

see also **on the tip of one's tongue**

**tipsy**

slightly drunk; see **drunk**

**tit for tat**

a retaliatory blow for a blow, but often used for verbal exchanges

**titivate**

the female equivalent of **spruce up**: make oneself elegant/attractive

**tittle-tattle**

(uncountable) idle chatter, gossip

**tizzy**

*get in(to) a tizzy*: get agitated

see also **nervy**

**to**

Among the many uses of this preposition, the following should be noted.

**1** in comparison with

□ This weather is certainly unpleasant, but it is nothing to what we may get yet.

**2** restricted within the limits of

□ As a price, I had about fifty pounds in mind, but I am not bound to a pound or two.

**3** for *to + ing*, see **used to**

**to a T**

see **T** at the start of this section

**to-do**

a fuss; a confused or rowdy scene

(Notice this is quite different from a **do**)

□ It's nothing serious: there's no need to make such a to-do about it.

□ You ought to have seen them trying to get those cows off the road and back into the field; there *was* a to-do.

**to my mind**

in my opinion

□ To my mind that's not a fair way of doing things.

**to the good**

see **good**

**toes**

*tread on someone's toes*: offend his feelings by what one says or does; run counter to his wishes or his policy

□ I am wholly in sympathy with the idea, but if you persist in it you are likely to tread on the toes of several of the city fathers.

see also **keep someone on his toes** and **on one's toes**

**together**

similar to **with it**

□ I'm not together today.

**Tom, Dick and Harry**

the ordinary man (usually used in a derogatory sense in the phrase *every Tom, Dick and Harry*)

□ We can't admit every Tom, Dick and Harry to membership of the club.

**tomfoolery**

(uncountable) senseless talk or action (from *Tom Fool*, a one-time nickname for a madman)

☐ Most of the so-called comic incidents were just a lot of tomfoolery.

**tommy**

the ordinary private British soldier; from *Tommy Atkins*, the name for many years bestowed on this rank

**tommyrot**

(uncountable) foolish, rubbishy talk

☐ So much of what he says is just tommyrot, that you never know when to take him seriously.

**ton**

The motor-cyclist slang/jargon *ton-up* (meaning reaching a speed of 100 miles an hour) has come into use in journalism. A *ton* is now used for 100 in other contexts, e.g. for a *century* in cricket, or for an age of 100 years.

see also **come down on someone like a ton of bricks**

**tongs**

see **hammer and tongs**

**tongue**

*have a tongue in one's head*: be able to speak (used as a rebuke or reproach to a person who does not speak when he should)

☐ If you didn't know the way, you should have asked. You have got a tongue in your head, haven't you?

(*have*) *one's tongue in one's cheek*: pretend to speak seriously, when all the time one is hiding or suppressing a humorous intention

☐ When she said that she was waiting for a handsome prince to carry her off on a white horse, she was speaking with her tongue in her cheek.

see also **on the tip of one's tongue**, **hold one's tongue** and **slip**

**tongue twister**

a word or phrase that is difficult to pronounce

Here are some well-known examples:

Red leather, yellow leather.

She sells seashells on the sea-shore.

Bug's black blood.

**too**

**1** very (only in negative sentences, and then usually as an understatement)

☐ It's not too warm today.

☐ I'm not feeling too well this morning.

☐ Your father's not too pleased with you about this affair of yours.

**2** to express a modified or qualified satisfaction (also in negative sentences)

□ We've not had too bad a winter.

□ The holiday was not too expensive.

**3** *It's too bad* may also deplore the fact in question.

□ It's too bad of you to tease the child like that.

**4** (*It's*) (*just*) *too bad*: the phrase which dictionaries usually fail to give as the opposite of *so much the better* (*So much the worse* is scarcely ever heard.)

□ 'I'm afraid we shall arrive rather late for the party.' 'That's just too bad.'

□ 'You've missed the first ten minutes of the lesson. I shan't repeat any of it for you.' 'Too bad.'

People usually shrug their shoulders as they say it and it can sometimes sound quite impolite.

**too big for one's boots**
  see **boots**

**too clever by half**
  see **by half**

**too much of a good thing**
  see **good thing**

**tooth**
  see **teeth**

**tootle off/away***
  a vaguely humorous word for 'go'

**top dog**
  the person who is in the position of power; the one who emerges victor from a conflict (The opposite idea is expressed, not by *bottom dog*, but by *under dog*.)

  □ In every struggle for power in which he has engaged, he has so far come out top dog.

**top up**
  all you really need to say if you want your car petrol tank to be filled at a garage; also *fill up* but this is less colloquial

  see also **blow one's top**, **off the top**, and **out of the top drawer**

**topsy-turvy**
  (adjective or adverb) confused, in disorder

**torn**
  usually *that's torn it*: that is bad, we'll have to start again; that's ruined his/our etc. chances

**toss-up**

a matter of luck or chance, with the odds on the whole against the thing in question

□ At ten o'clock this morning it was still a toss-up whether we should be able to get here.

The origin is from *tossing* or throwing up a coin for 'heads or tails'; see **heads**

**tot up**

add up (a bill)

**touch wood**

This is a formula sometimes added to, or interpolated in, a statement regarding one's good fortune, that might seem rather boastful or in some way 'tempting fate'. Touching wood in such circumstances is supposed to be a charm against a perverse fate bringing the boast to nothing.

□ I've gone all through the winter so far without catching a cold— touch wood.

**touchy**

easily irritated

see also **nervy** and note that *touched* in older slang meant 'crazy'

**tough luck**

bad/hard luck

**tough on**

cruel, unjust, unfair towards someone (like **rough on**)

□ 'I really had to do two people's jobs.' 'That was tough on you.'

see also **get tough**

**town**

see **go to town**

**track**

**1** *be on the right track*: be tackling some work in the right way; also note the opposite: *be on the wrong track*

see also **make tracks** and **on one's tracks**

**2** On long-playing records, separate items are referred to as separate *tracks*.

**trades**

see **jack of all trades**

**trail (about)**

walk wearily (about a town etc.), probably also *trailing in* and *out of* shops

The word *traipse* is used in the same way.

**trashy**

of very poor quality: *trashy goods*

**treat**

**1** (noun) a pleasant experience

☐ It's a treat to have a fine spell of weather like this.

**2** (verb) to pay for (someone else)

☐ He treated us to a splendid dinner at the hotel.

☐ I see you've ordered your drinks—let me treat you!

NOTE You can be *treated* (medically) *for* a disease etc. at a hospital or a clinic.

**trek**

Both noun and verb are used: (to go on) a long tiring walk or journey. It is also used of long trips by horse (*pony-trekking*) or on foot, which are increasingly popular ways of spending a holiday. It is originally a Dutch word.

**trendy**

fashionable, establishing a new *trend* in fashion (similar to **groovy**)

**trick**

see **bag of tricks**, **dirty trick**, **do the trick** and **monkey tricks**

**trig**

abbreviation of *trigonometry*

**trigger off**

cause, precipitate

☐ My migraine attacks are usually triggered off by bright light or loud noise

☐ What triggered off the strike? (*or* What triggered the strike off?)

**trot**

see **on the trot**

**trouble-shooter**

a person whose job it is to get rid of trouble by finding a solution to the problems which caused it, or to track down mechanical faults in a piece of machinery

see also **in** (*or* **into**) **trouble**

**trousers**

see **wear the trousers**

**truck**

(uncountable) dealings

☐ I shouldn't have any truck with a fellow like that.

**truly**

see **yours truly**

**trump**

*play one's trump card*: use one's most valuable means of gaining success (especially after other methods were no good)

*turn up trumps*: (of people) succeed or provide something beyond one's expectations

□ I thought I would never be able to visit Africa, but now David's turned up trumps and invited me to Nairobi.

*trump up an excuse/a charge/evidence* etc.: invent a (totally false) excuse/charge etc.

**trumpet**

see **blow 3**

**trundle**

(jocular) to walk

**trust**

*Trust someone to do* (*something*), or *you can trust someone to do* (*something*) is sometimes used colloquially with the meaning 'You may be sure he will do (the thing specified)'.

□ Trust Martin to look after himself.

The word is also used sarcastically:

□ You can trust him to do something foolish.

□ Trust Ken to make a mess of things! (which is exactly what he has done!)

**truth**

*to tell you the truth*: a kind of formal confession and apology sometimes used to preface a statement which the speaker feels needs an apology

□ 'What did you think of his letter?' 'To tell you the truth, I've not looked at it yet.'

**try**

attempt (like **go** *(n)* **2**)

□ If you can't do it, let me have a try.

□ It's your try now.

□ He passed his driving test at the second try.

for *try one's hand at*, see **hand**

**try and do something**

'Try *to* do something' (meaning effort is needed) is usual, especially when the main verb is *tried* and *trying* but the imperative is almost always *try and do*.

**try something on**

do something in the hope that one will succeed in 'getting away with it'

□ Don't take any notice of him. He's not really ill; he's just trying it on.

also a noun: *try-on*

**TT**

teetotal: teetotaller (The use as an adjective is more frequent than as a noun.)

□ It's no good offering him wine; he's TT (*or* a TT).

**tub-thumper**

an orator who uses exaggeration

□ We spent Sunday afternoon in Hyde Park, listening to the diversion provided by those addressing the crowds at Speakers' Corner. Some really were speakers, but others were just tub-thumpers.

**tube**

the colloquial word, in common use, for the London underground railway (from the shape of the tunnels, which resemble large tubes into which the trains fit very neatly; similarly *a tube train*, *a tube station*)

**tuck in**

eat a good, hearty meal

□ After that long walk we did not need any encouragement to tuck in.

also *tuck into*, followed by the name of the food or the meal: *tuck into a good breakfast*, *tuck into the mutton*

also as a noun: *a good tuck-in*

**tummy**

a children's word for 'stomach' but used by adults in *tummy bug* to refer vaguely to an upset in the digestive system

□ I couldn't come last week, I had a tummy bug.

**tune**

*to the tune of*: to the extent or amount of (of sums of money)

□ He owes debts to the tune of eight hundred pounds.

□ I was presented with a bill to the tune of twenty-two pounds.

see also **change one's tune** and **sing another tune**

**turf out**

eject, remove, throw out

□ The police turfed out several hecklers.

**turn** (*n*)

see **give someone a turn**, **good turn** and **star turn**

**turn** (*v*)

*There are so many odd jobs to be done, that I don't know which way to turn.* I don't know which to do first, or what order to do them in. (The expression suggests a state of mental confusion.)

**turn a hair**
used mainly in negative sentences or contexts (*didn't turn a hair*, *without turning a hair*), where it means 'without showing any sign of fear, terror, horror or similar emotional reaction'
□ He listened to the whole of that horrible story without turning a hair.
□ I watched him closely throughout the interrogation, but he didn't turn a hair.

**turn down**
reject
□ After very careful consideration, they decided to turn the offer down.

**turn over a new leaf**
make a fresh start and mend one's ways (The reference is to the leaf of a book.)
□ The boy confessed that he had behaved irresponsibly, and promised his father that he would turn over a new leaf.

**turn someone off**
(the opposite of the following entry) cause someone to lose interest, sometimes even cause disgust

**turn someone on**
stimulate someone's interest, especially in fashion, the pop scene, sex or drugs

**turn the heat on**
intensify the investigation, or the treatment used to elicit the information required
□ We are getting nowhere by this method; it's about time we turned the heat on.

**turn someone's blood cold**
horrify
□ That gruesome story about the murder was enough to turn your blood cold.

**turn up one's nose**
show or express disdain
□ I made him what I thought was a fair offer, but he turned up his nose at it.

**turn up trumps**
see **trump**

**turps**
an abbreviation of *turpentine*

**TV**

an abbreviation of *television*; in spoken English pronounced as the names of the two letters (*tee vee*)

☐ I see your son is appearing on TV tonight.

**twerp**

a stupid person (also written *twirp*)

**twiddle one's thumbs**

sit idly doing nothing, for want of any definite occupation

☐ For the next half hour I was twiddling my thumbs, waiting for my friends to arrive.

**twig***

understand; see; get the meaning of

☐ For a moment I did not twig what he meant.

☐ Do you twig what I'm getting at?

**twist someone's arm**

persuade someone

☐ He won't want to do it but I think I can twist his arm.

also with the same meaning: *I can twist him round my little finger*.

**twit**

a stupid person

**two-faced**

insincere; hypocritical

**two left feet**

said of someone who walks or dances clumsily

☐ I feel as if I've got two left feet this morning.

**two pins**

see **for two pins**

**type**

In most contexts, *a type of* can be used indifferently for *a kind of* and *a sort of* but there are a few limitations given under **kind**.

**typical**

often used sarcastically

☐ How typical! (that there should be no coffee available on the train, that it rains when you want to go out, that your friend is an hour late for dinner etc.)

☐ Isn't that just typical! (i.e. typically bad)

# u

**umpteen(th)**

a facetious word on analogy with the *-teen* numbers, but meaning any comparatively large number

□ That's the umpteenth time the phone has rung this evening.

**Uncle Sam**

This is a personification of the United States of America, and current since the early years of the nineteenth century. The origin is uncertain, but it may be a humorous alternative for the initials U.S.

see also **Dutch uncle**

**under dog**

see **top dog**

**under one's nose**

directly before one

□ I spent three or four minutes looking for my pen, and there it was under my nose all the time.

**under one's own steam**

see **steam**

**under the influence**

an abbreviation of *under the influence of drink*

□ He was charged with driving while under the influence.

**under the weather**

not very well in health

□ I am afraid I am heading for influenza. I've been feeling under the weather the last day or two.

**undergrad***

abbreviation of *undergraduate*; used mainly in the informal speech of those who are, or have been, connected with a university

**underhand**

secret(ly) and probably dishonest or shady

**undies**

women's underclothing

**unearthly**

used with a derogatory sense with no very clear meaning except to express the idea that the speaker dislikes the thing so referred to

□ What is that unearthly noise?

□ Why do you get up at that unearthly hour?

□ I am not having you staying out till this unearthly time of night.

**unholy**

used before certain nouns to convey disapproval; *an unholy row*, *an unholy mess*

**union**

short for *Trade(s) Union*.

NOTE The word *syndicate* has no connexion with a Trades Union.

**unisex**

equally suited to or used by both sexes; used of clothes, hairdressers etc.

**unless**

used to introduce a clause added as an afterthought to a statement or a question and partially retracting it

□ There's a train at 3.30—unless you prefer to go by bus.

□ How much did that cost you? Unless you prefer not to say.

□ There's a good film on at the Forum tonight—unless you would rather spend the evening at home.

The idea is that the initial statement or question makes a certain assumption; but that assumption may be wrong, in which case the information given, or the question asked, is irrelevant.

see also **if** and **because**, both of which may be used in similar contexts

**unstuck**

see **come unstuck**

**up**

*What's up?* What's the matter?

Often followed by *with*: *What's up with you? What's up with this engine? It won't start.*

see also **up to**

**up a gumtree**

see **gumtree**

**up against**

opposed by; in conflict with

□ We've won the last three matches we have played, but I don't think we shall be so lucky tomorrow: we're up against a much stronger team.

□ It's difficult to get new ideas over to people when you're up against prejudice and vested interests.

**up against it**

in difficulties; faced by seemingly insuperable obstacles

□ When you're up against it, you're thankful for a friend's help.

**up and coming**

(attributive) promising; likely to succeed

□ He's one of the up and coming young men of the party.

□ They are representatives of an up and coming company.

**up in arms**

protesting furiously

□ The trade unions are up in arms about the proposed legislation on wage increases.

(a metaphorical use of *arms* in the sense of weapons)

**up one's sleeve**

see **have something up one's sleeve**

**up one's street**

see **street**

**up the creek**

in an awkward position

*You're right up the creek!* You have it all wrong, you're in a mess!

**up to**

**1** capable of

□ He's not up to the work.

In this phrase, *to* is a preposition and a verb following must have an *-ing*.

□ I don't feel up to walking much farther.

*Be/feel equal to* (*+ing*) are also used.

**2** doing (often implying it is something naughty)

□ What are those children up to?

□ Don't get up to mischief.

□ Be careful what you are up to with that knife.

The chief idiomatic expressions are *be up to* and *get up to*.

**3** the duty, obligation, privilege, right etc. of whoever is named

□ It is up to you to make the most of the opportunities provided for you.

□ Whether or not you accept the offer is up to you.

**up to much**

usually found in negative sentences like *not up to much*: not very good, or, in the case of one's health, not very well

□ The accommodation was quite comfortable, but the food wasn't up to much.

□ 'How is your mother today?' 'Not up to much.'

**up to no good**

having evil intentions (an example of litotes)

□ I'm rather suspicious of that fellow hanging about at the street corner. I'm afraid he's up to no good.

**up to scratch**
see **scratch**

**up to the (or one's) eyes in work**
having almost more work to do than one can cope with; almost submerged in it
□ For the next few weeks I shall be up to the eyes in marking examination papers.

**up to the mark**
see **mark**

**up to the nines**
see **dressed up to the nines**

**update**
from the important phrase *up-to-date*, this verb has been coined:
□ We must update our brochure very soon.

**upgrade**
put someone into a higher level or grade in employment (Sometimes the position itself is *upgraded*, i.e. with more pay and responsibility.)
see also **on the upgrade**

**uphill work**
hard and strenuous work, that gets more strenuous as one goes on, as walking uphill does

**upon my word!**
an exclamation of pleasant surprise
NOTE *Upon* has in almost all contexts been replaced by *on*. The traditional 'Once upon a time' remains; *depend upon* and *rely upon* just survive but *on* is more usual.

**upper crust**
the upper class of society
□ In those days you did not count unless you belonged to the upper crust.
see also **stiff upper lip**

**uppish**
inclined to be conceited; behaving as though one were superior to those around one or to one's circumstances
□ Some working-class parents did not like the idea of their children receiving an education beyond what they themselves had received, as they feared they would get uppish.
*Uppity* is also used.

**ups and downs**

vicissitudes: times of prosperity and times of misfortune

☐ We all have our ups and downs in life.

**upset the** (*or* **someone's**) **applecart**

upset someone's plans or intentions

☐ I wish you had consulted me before you took that step; you've upset my applecart now.

**upstage** *(adj)*

haughty, snobbish

**uptake**

see **quick on the uptake**

**uptight**

hostile; irritated; tense

see **nervy**

**U/S** *or* **U.S.\***

(pronounced *you ess*) useless, used of equipment and also people

**use your loaf**

This means 'use your head'; it comes from Cockney rhyming slang: *head* becomes *loaf of bread*, and this in its turn is shortened to *loaf*.

(**brass tacks** and **not on your nelly** are other examples of rhyming slang.)

**used to**

Two important uses must be distinguished:

**1** *He used to live in London.* At some time in the past he lived in London, and he no longer lives there. (This implied contrast is to be noted: there is no present tense form.)

**2** In the following expressions, *to* is a preposition, and a verb following will have to be a gerund:

☐ I'll never get used to living in this climate.

☐ I'm quite used to working here now.

☐ We'll never get used to (eating) English food.

So the phrases in question are *be used to* and *get used to* and can be used in other tenses at will:

☐ People were used to walking long distances in those days.

*Be/get accustomed to* are less common ways of saying the same thing.

# V

**vac**

abbreviation of *vacation* (at a university)

normally used only by university students, those who have been
university students, and those who are in close contact with them and
are speaking to them in their own jargon

**vamoose\***

(stressed on the second syllable) means 'get out—I don't want you here.'

**varsity**

a colloquialism for *university* (but not *the Varsity of Oxford* or
*Cambridge Varsity*, as part of a name of a particular university)

Confined mostly to university personnel, and those closely identified
with university life and affairs, it is sometimes found also in newspaper
headlines, where it is probably used partly for brevity, and partly to
suggest familiarity.

**V.D.**

venereal disease; frequently used in conversation in place of the actual
words, as a euphemism

**veg**

(rhyming with *ledge*) short for *vegetable*

**very well**

an introductory formula expressing acceptance of what has just been
said

□ Very well, if you'd rather do that, do it.

□ Very well, if you refuse to follow my advice, you must take the
consequences.

see also **all very well**

**vet**

abbreviation, in common conversational use, of *veterinary surgeon*

□ Brutus, our dog, was so ill that we had to fetch a vet to him.

To use the full words *veterinary surgeon* in such sentences as the above
would be considered very formal and stilted.

The word is increasingly used as a verb, meaning to investigate, to
ensure that things are in good order, or being run honestly. This is no
doubt from journalists who value such concise words for headlines.

□ Could you vet this car before I buy it?

**view**

see **take a dim view**

**V.I.P.**

the initials of *Very Important Person*; plural—*V.I.P.s* (now often written without the stops: VIPs)

□ We were warned that we were being inspected by a party of VIPs that afternoon.

□ I understand that he is a V.I.P. in the steel industry.

□ They went to the V.I.P. lounge at the airport.

**vital statistics**

the measurements of a woman's/girl's bust, waist and hips

**vocab**

short for *vocabulary*

**vote**

express an opinion

**1** followed by an accusative + an objective complement

□ They voted the idea a good one.

In the passive voice this becomes

□ The idea was voted a good one.

**2** followed by a noun clause used as an object

□ I vote we have a dinner to celebrate the occasion.

Here *vote* approximates to *suggest*.

# W

**waffle**

talk or write at some length, but with very little meaning

□ I haven't the patience to listen to some of these local politicians: they just waffle.

also *waffle on*

□ He waffled on for twenty minutes, and at the end of it had said very little of any importance.

There is also noun *waffle*: lengthy meaningless talk or writing.

**wag**

see **tail 1**

**wake**

see **enough to wake the dead**

**walk someone off his feet**

tire someone out by walking

□ Our guide was so anxious for us to see everything of interest that he walked us off our feet.

**walk out on someone**

suddenly leave someone's society, employment etc. so leaving him without one's companionship or services

□ As he would not grant her request for an increase in salary, his secretary walked out on him.

□ After a domestic quarrel, Joe Thomas's wife walked out on him.

**walk-over**

an easy victory

□ The match against Redcoats was a walk-over for us.

**wall**

see **drive someone up the wall** and **back**

**wallflower\***

a woman at a dance who is left sitting out (against the wall) because no-one asks her to dance with him

(The term usually connotes a certain degree of disparagement.)

**wallop**

(near slang)

**1** (verb and noun) hit

**2** (uncountable) beer

**3** *walloping*: used to intensify an adjective of large size (*a walloping great mouthful*)

**wangle**

**1** achieve a desired result by dubious means, or by exploiting one's influence with others

□ Officially the booking-list is closed now, but I think I can wangle you a place.

*wangle something out of someone*: get it by means of wangling also used as a noun: *I managed it by a wangle.*

**2** arrive at (a correct answer or solution) by dishonest means

□ He wangled his accounts so it looked as if he was making a profit.

**want**

*What does someone want with . . . ?* Why does someone need . . . ?

□ What does he want with a house that size?

□ What do you want with two cars? You can't drive both at once.

**want to**

should; ought to (used mainly in the second person)

□ You may be proud of your garden, but you want to see my neighbour's.

□ To see Kent at its best, you want to go when the fruit trees are in blossom.

Sometimes a warning or a rebuke is implied.
□ You want to look where you are going.
□ You want to be more careful.
□ You want to mind what you're saying.
The negative is expressed by *don't want to*.
□ You don't want to drink strong coffee just before going to bed; it may keep you awake.

**warmed up**
see **feel like 4**

**wars**
*You have been in the wars!* a jocular remark when you see someone has been hurt/wounded etc. (stress on *have*)

**wash** *(n)*
*come out in the wash*: come to light, or be revealed, in the course of investigation
□ There are still a number of things unexplained in connexion with this affair, but they will probably all come out in the wash.
The reference is probably to stains on linen coming out when the linen is washed.

**wash** *(v)*
(of a story, excuse etc.) pass for true; be accepted or believed
□ It's no good giving that excuse, because it won't wash.

**wash one's dirty linen in public**
make public, either by narration or discussion, one's private or family affairs that are discreditable
□ I would rather we settled this affair privately, between ourselves, instead of through the law courts. For the sake of our families I have no desire that we should wash our dirty linen in public.

**wash-out**
a failure; something or someone that falls far short of expectations
□ The competition in public speaking was a wash-out.
□ As a teacher he is a wash-out.

**watch one's step**
be circumspect: be very careful what one does or says
□ There are two or three people who would like to build up a case to deprive you of your position, so you had better watch your step.
*Mind one's step* is also used, with the same meaning.

**water**
see **fish out of water**, **hold water** and **hot water**

## way

*in a big way*: on a big scale (*in a big way of business*, *a fruit-grower in a big way*)

*There are no two ways about it.* There is no alternative.

□ There are no two ways about it: we shall have to comply.

*put one in the way of something*: **1** show one how to do something

□ You shouldn't find the process difficult, when once I've put you in the way of it.

**2** tell one where to find or obtain something: *put one in the way of a good bargain.*

You can't always *have* (or *get*) *your own way.* You must consider other people's wishes.

*it was* (or *is*) *this way*: see **like this**

see also **go one's own way**, **go out of one's way to**, **in a bad way**, **in a way** and **in the way of**

## way of thinking

chiefly in the phrase *to my way of thinking*: in my opinion; as I regard it

□ To my way of thinking, to do that would be dishonest.

## way-out

marvellous, wonderful (chiefly used in the 1960s and early 1970s)

## we

in colloquial English sometimes used for the singular *I*, as *us* is for *me*, but only in conversation of a very informal kind

□ 'Could I have leave of absence next Friday?' 'We'll have to think about that.' (i.e. I shall)

□ Could you tell us the time? (i.e. me)

*Let's* for *Let me*, in a request, is especially common:

□ Let's have a look at your birthday present.

## wear

see also **heart**

## wear the trousers

exercise the authority in a family or a household (usually applied to a woman who assumes this position, to the exclusion of her husband)

□ There is no doubt who wears the trousers in that household.

## weather

see **keep one's weather eye open** and **under the weather**

NOTE the phrase *in all weathers* which is the only case where weather is used as a countable noun

## weaving

see **get weaving**

**wedge**

*the thin end of the wedge*: merely the beginning of a process which later will be carried farther (Usually the reference is to a process or a development which one considers undesirable.)

□ We must think twice before we accede to the union's request for representation on the board of directors of the company; we may find that is the thin end of the wedge.

**weedy**

of poor quality; weak; insufficient

**weep one's heart out**

see **cry one's eyes out**

**weight off someone's mind**

a relief

*To take a weight off someone's mind* is to relieve him of a burden of worry, anxiety or responsibility.

□ It's a great weight off my mind to know that my children are well looked after at school.

**well**

**1** to introduce a statement by relating it to something that has been mentioned just before

□ You know old Brown, the grocer who has that shop in the High Street? Well, he's just won a thousand pounds in a lottery.

**2** to express surprise

□ Well! Who would have thought it?

□ Well, I declare!

for *Well, I never*, see **never**

**3** to signify expectancy

□ Well, what have you got to say now?

□ 'Why did you do that?' (No reply) 'Well . . .?'

**4** appended to certain adjectives or past participles to make a combination that has the force of an adverb: *pretty well*, *jolly well*, *damned well*

□ The job is pretty well finished.

□ If you don't like my advice, you can jolly well fend for yourself in future.

see also **as well**, **in with**

**well done**

a formula used to convey congratulation

□ 'I came out top of the pass-list in the final examination.' 'Well done!'

**well-heeled**
see **heel**

**well off**
having a large amount (of something stated, or, if nothing is stated, of money)

□ Although she is well off, she lives quite simply.

*Comfortably off* also has this meaning.

□ John seems to be quite well off for girl-friends.

□ How well off are we for beer?

**well rid of**
fortunate to be rid of whoever or whatever is in question

□ I don't regret his leaving us. In fact, I think we are well rid of that man.

see also **rid**

**well up in**
well informed on (a subject): *well up in local history, well up in nineteenth-century literature*

**west**
see **go west**

**wet blanket**
a person who damps our enthusiasm; just as a wet blanket will dampen down (and put out) a fire

□ With his gloomy countenance and doleful manner, George was a wet blanket in any company or assembly in which he appeared.

**whacking (big/great)**
emphatic, similar to **walloping**

(Both words are near slang.)

see also **do one's whack**

**whale**
*a whale of a time*: a magnificent time (at a party, on holiday etc.)

**what**
**1** used to express an interest or surprise, and usually followed by an interrogative

□ What! He doesn't expect me to do that, does he?

□ What, are you going to the concert?

□ 'I shall not be at home all next week.' 'What, are you going on holiday?'

**2** *I'll tell you what*: used to make a suggestion (see **tell**)

**3** *or what*: an ellipsis of *or what the fact/cause/position* etc. *is*

□ She seems to avoid me as much as she can nowadays; I don't know whether I've offended her, or what.

☐ I can't make up mind whether I ought to see him personally, or what (i.e. or what I ought to do).

**what about . . . ?**

What do you think about (something)? What is your opinion concerning? (This is an indirect way of making a suggestion; it is an alternative to *how about?* and both are also used to invite someone to contribute to a conversation.)

☐ It's nearly one o'clock now. What about a bit of lunch?

☐ What about going to Spain for our holiday this year?

☐ What about asking the Bensons to dinner on Friday evening?

The same idioms may also be used for voicing an objection in the form of a query.

☐ 'I have just been thinking that you and I might go to London for the weekend.' 'But what about the children?' (i.e. What is to happen to the children while we are away?)

**what cheer** *or* **whatcher**

see **wotcher**

**what for**

see **give someone what for**

**what have you**

the same as **whatever** and **what-not**

**what it is**

the reason, or the explanation

☐ 'That porter didn't look too pleased.' 'You didn't give him a big enough tip; that's what it is (was).'

**what it takes**

*Takes* here rather means *needs*.

*He's got what it takes.* He has the qualities needed for the job/situation in question.

**what next?**

a half query and half explanation expressing surprise, amazement, disgust etc.; an abbreviated form of *What will be the next thing?* or *What will happen next?*

☐ You say they are asking us to pay for the goods before we have received them? What next?

☐ You certainly can't have my new typewriter to play with. What next? also *whatever next?*

**what-not**

other unspecified things

☐ They loaded the suitcases, parcels, boxes and what-not into the boot of the car.

see also **thingammy**

**what price\***

What do you think of (someone or something)? What is your opinion of?

☐ 'We have been to Blackpool for our holiday for the last few years: I should like to go somewhere else for a change this time.' 'Well, what price Torquay?'

☐ What price Sheffield Wednesday, now that they are in the semi-final for the Cup?

The expression presumably means: 'What price would you be willing to give were you to buy or bet on the thing in question?'

**what with**

an introductory phrase to link together two or more reasons for one assertion

☐ What with rain, wind, snow and frosts, we have had a wretched month for weather.

*What with*, together with the words that it governs, usually comes before the general assertion, but it may come after.

☐ We have had a wretched month for weather, what with rain, wind, snow and frosts.

**whatcher**

see **wotcher**

**whatever**

other things of a similar nature that are unspecified

☐ If you have prawns or crab or whatever, you might get an upset stomach.

**what's-his/her-name**

used in place of a name that for the moment has slipped one's memory

☐ I gave your message to Mrs What's-her-name.

☐ I met old What's-his-name in town this morning.

**what's up?**

What is the matter? What is wrong?

often followed by *with* to indicate the thing or the person to whom it is intended to apply

☐ They are making a great fuss about something or other. What's up?

☐ What's up with Alastair? He seems very short-tempered this morning.

☐ Why do you need a new gas-cooker? What's up with this one?

**where do we go from here/there ?**
see **go** *(v)*

**while away the time**
pass the time, usually pleasantly; *away* may be used at the end here
(Surprisingly, *while* can readily replace *time* in phrases such as *a little
while/time*, *a short while/time* etc.)
see also **good while**

**whip**
steal; but used of small things, like **nick**
□ Who's whipped my biro?

**whip out**
pull (something) out (of the pocket etc.) quickly

**whip round**
(countable) a collection made to give someone a present, by
friends/colleagues
□ Mary Carter's getting married next month. Let's have a whip-round.

**whisk away**
remove (something) quickly

**whiskers**
see **cat's whiskers**

**whitewash**
basically, to cover house walls with a cheap form of whitening; by
extension, to try to hide someone's weaknesses or mistakes to make
him look blameless

**whiz(z)**
move very quickly
see **dart/dash**

**whiz-kid**
a young bright person who will go far
□ That new executive manager is a real whiz-kid.

**whodunit**
(formed from *who has done it ?*) a colloquial word for a detective novel

**whoever**
a person or people unspecified
□ Somebody will be here to help you with your cases—Hugh or Mr
Carter or whoever.

**whoopee**
see **make whoopee**

**whopping**
another spelling of **wopping**

**wide in the beam**
  having broad hips
**wide of the mark**
  (probably derived from shooting and badly missing the target)
  nowhere near correct
  □ I'm afraid your answer was wide of the mark.
**widow**
  see **grass widow**
**wild oats**
  see **sow one's wild oats**
**wildcat** (strike)
  sudden and unofficial
**wildfire**
  see **like wildfire**
**wind**
  *There's something in the wind.* There are signs that something is going
  to happen.
  see also **get the wind up**, **get wind of** and **take the wind out
  of someone's sails**
**windfall**
  an unexpected piece of good luck, especially in the form of money (so-
  called because a strong wind may blow fruit off the trees, so they will
  not have to be picked)
**winking**
  see **easy**
**wink**
  see **forty winks** and **tip 4**
**winner**
  see **back a winner**
**wipe that smile off your face**
  a sharp reprimand from a superior if an offender smiles inappropriately
  at remarks being made to him
**wire**
  see **live wire**
**wisecrack**
  a quick humorous answer
**wishful thinking**
  belief that something is true because you want it to be
  □ To say that everything gets better all the time is just wishful
  thinking.

**wit**

*at one's wit's end*: unable to decide what to do next, used of serious/desperate situations

**with it**

*To be with it* was originally to be fashionable, similar to **in**, but its most common meaning now is 'to be fully alert and bright'. (often in negative sentences)

□ I forgot to stamp the letters I posted and now I've lost my keys—I'm really not with it this morning.

**with someone**

*Are you with me?* Can you follow what I say? (not infrequently used sarcastically if you think someone is daydreaming)

see also **what with** and **in with**

**without so much as a 'by your leave'**

see **by your leave**

**without saying**

see **go without saying**

**witter** (on)

talk ineffectively

□ What are you wittering (on) about?

**wobbly**

When you first ride a bicycle, your balance is *wobbly*.

The word is often jocularly used of other things: *My maths has got a bit wobbly since I left school. Rusty* could also be used here.

**womaniser**

a man persistently pursuing the opposite sex

**wonky**

not stable—used of things that should not move (rather like **rickety**); also sometimes used to mean 'not straight'

**wood**

see **out of the wood** and **touch wood**

**woollies**

woollen clothing

□ I prefer to wash woollies by hand.

**woolly ideas/thinking**

unclear or unreasoned thought

**woman**

see **old woman**

**wopping**

very similar to **whacking**

**word(s)**

The two following similar expressions have totally different meanings. Both are very common.

**1** *To have a word with someone* is merely to talk to someone— supposedly serious but not emotional.

**2** *To have words with someone* is to have an unpleasant argument or quarrel. (This is now often also called a *contre-temps* though its true French meaning is adhered to by some people.)

see also **cross words, get a word in edgeways, good, last word, loss for words, mark, mince (one's) words, mum's the word, my word, take the words out of someone's mouth** and **upon my word**

**work**

for *have one's work cut out*, see **cut out 2**; see also **donkey work, gum up the works** and **uphill work**

**work off one's anger/frustration**

get rid of these feelings by doing hard physical work or exercise

**world**

see **dead to the world, end, for all the world, on top of the world, out of this world** and **set the world on fire**

**worse things happen at sea**

a consoling remark to someone who has suffered a misfortune; similar to *it isn't the end of the world*, see **end**

**worth one's salt**

*Salt* here surprisingly is 'salary' (originally 'salt ration'). Consequently, if he's *not worth his salt*, he's not worthy of his pay, because he is not working properly. It is now used outside this narrow meaning: '(he's not) serious or earnest in his activities'.

see also **for all one is worth**

**wotcher**

a familiar greeting among people who know each other; it was originally *what cheer?* meaning 'what state or frame of mind (are you in)?'

**would**

*You would* (*do that*) (stressing *would*): spoken to show impatience

□ You *would* walk in with dirty boots just after I've cleaned the floor.

**write**

see also **nothing to write home about**

**write-off**

originally a commercial/insurance term, now used widely by the

general public when something has been damaged too badly to be
mended

□ His car's a write-off.

**wrong**

for *put a foot wrong* and *set off on the wrong foot*, see **foot**; see also
**get on the right/wrong side of someone**

# X

**Xerox**

used as noun and verb for 'photocopy'
(from a trademark)

# y

**yarn***

story

□ That was a good yarn you told last night.

**year dot**

see **dot**

**year in, year out**

see **day**

**years**

see **donkey's years**

**yellow**

cowardly

□ We can't afford to have anyone in this enterprise who is likely to
turn yellow when the testing-time comes.

**yen**

a longing; a yearning

□ Just recently Jack has developed a yen for a cine camera.

**yes and no**

a rather ambiguous answer to a question, indicating that from some
aspects the answer is in the affirmative, and from others in the negative

□ 'Would you like to emigrate to Australia?' 'Yes and no. I should like
the weather, and I believe there are plenty of opportunities there, but I
should find it difficult to start a new way of life at my age.'

**yes-man**
  one who will readily agree with his superior, and comply with his
  wishes without protest or question
  □ The only way to retain the favour of the Director is to be a yes-man.
**yet awhile**
  for some time yet (used in negative sentences)
  □ The bus is not due yet awhile.
**yob(bo)**
  an uncouth young man of irresponsible behaviour; apparently the
  word 'boy' backwards (with a vowel sometimes added)
**you know**
  see **know 3**
**you see**
  (used in an explanation) see **see**
**you see if**
  (+negative) a formula suggesting that a statement by the speaker will
  be proved by events to be true
  □ He'll back out of his promise at the last minute, you see if he
  doesn't.
**yours truly**
  facetiously used for 'I/me'
  □ Well, I can tell you that yours truly isn't going to have anything to
  do with it.

# Z

**zany**
  (originally a noun, meaning a clown) now only used as an adjective
  meaning 'absurd' or 'crazy': *zany ideas*, *zany clothes*
**zombie**
  a person in a dazed or apathetic state, as if in a trance or even raised
  from the dead (taken from a Kongo word meaning 'fetish')

# Addenda

Given the chance to make an addenda, I have mainly concentrated on phrases rather than individual words. To avoid the need for cross references, they are listed where possible under their noun; phrases without nouns are listed under the verb if they have one.                                                February 1983

**after**

*to be after something*: to want something, often heard in

☐ It's your money they're after.

**badly**

surprisingly used to emphasise the verbs *want* and *need*

☐ I badly need a cup of coffee.

**ball**

*get/start the ball rolling*: start the conversation/activity; similarly, *keep the ball rolling* means don't let things stop

**biscuit**

see **cake**

**blink**

*on the blink*: not working properly

☐ The telly is on the blink – what's wrong with it?

**bore**

a person or a thing may be described as *a bore* but you will also often hear: *I was bored stiff/to tears/to death*

**breather**

a pause or rest in activity: *let's have/take a breather*

**bud**

*nip something in the bud*: stop it from developing right at the beginning

**bush**

*Stop beating about the bush*: say what you mean and stop being irrelevant

**business**

**1** *he means business*: he is very serious

**2** *we're in business (at last)*: we are (finally) able to function as we hoped

**3** *mind your own business*: don't interfere in things that don't concern you

**cake**

*that takes the cake* or *biscuit*: that is the most surprising thing that could have

355

happened. (From an American dance where the couple who performed the most elegant dance in a competition were given a cake as a prize. A dance called the *cake-walk* came from this, but now we commonly say *the biscuit.*)

**cap**

*If the cap fits (wear it)*: if you think a remark or comment was intended for you, take note of it

**cat**

*That'll put the cat among the pigeons*: it will cause consternation/trouble, will make everyone talk (sometimes *set* replaces *put*)

**clockwork**

*it's all going like clockwork*: everything is working smoothly, as it should

**clued up**

*to be clued up*: to be well informed

□ I hope you're more clued up than I am. (Detectives look for clues in trying to solve crimes.)

**cock-up**

said of anything badly or wrongly done

**flying colours**

usually to *pass (an exam/test) with flying colours*: to be very successful; (the colours here are presumably flags waving in the wind)

**come-uppance**

*He'll get his come-uppance*: he'll get what he deserves i.e. punishment

**cop**

*It wasn't much cop*: an extension of the use of *cop* meaning something caught. Here what is "caught" is of little value, so the phrase means it was mediocre/poor

**Coventry**

*to send somebody to Coventry*: to show disapproval by ostracising a person i.e. not speaking; (the origin of the phrase is disputed)

**cry**

*a far cry from*: very different from

□ £5 for a paperback – a far cry from the days when you could buy 4 or 5 for only £1 (*a long cry* is also occasionally used)

*for crying out loud*: used at moments of exasperation or anger

**day**

*It's early days*: it is too soon for us to expect changes/developments yet

**death**

*sick to death of*: one of a number of phrases used in great impatience

□ I'm sick to death of hearing you say that.

**dog**

*let sleeping dogs lie*: don't disturb things which give trouble

*in the dog house*: in disgrace

☐ When they heard what I'd done, I was in the dog house for days.

(Curiously a small house for a dog is called a *kennel*.)

**drop-out**

a person who stops taking part in ordinary life, or who does not continue a
course in school or college. University authorities can be heard talking of
their *drop-out rate* i.e. how many students fail a course; also used as a verb.

**ear**

*play it by ear*: decide what to do (next) from the situation as it is. From
playing an instrument without music to read from.

**elephant**

*a white elephant*: a possession which is of no use, may even be expensive to
keep but is difficult to get rid of. It is said the Siamese King used to make such
a gift to courtiers he wanted to ruin.

☐ That house he inherited has become something of a white elephant.

**eye**

**1** *more than meets the eye*: other unpleasant things hidden

☐ We must be careful, there's more in/to this than meets the eye.

**2** *see eye to eye with someone*: agree

☐ I'm afraid I don't really see eye to eye with you about this.

**finger**

*get/pull your finger out*: begin working hard(er)

**fort**

*to leave someone holding the fort*: (i.e. fortress or castle) to leave someone
alone in charge of the situation

☐ Do you mind if we leave you holding the fort while we go out for lunch?

(The phrase dates back to the American Civil War.)

**frazzle**

the state of being mentally or physically exhausted; to be *in a frazzle* and
*worn to a frazzle* are both in common use

**game**

*Don't give the game away*: don't reveal the secret (and spoil the joke)

**get on**

*She's getting on a bit*: she is becoming older, often said as a comment that a
person is less agile than before

(*knocking on a bit* has the same meaning but closer to slang)

**go easy on**

*please go easy on the butter*: don't use a lot of butter

## going

*That's good/fast going*: a comment made about a fast journey or about a job completed in less than the usual time (*fast* is less common)

## goose

**1** *cook one's goose*: to make a very serious mistake for which one is not forgiven

**2** *a wild goose chase*: a long search for something, taking much time and probably in vain

## grain

*It goes against the grain (to have to do something)*: it is against one's wishes, inclinations, or one's sense of what seems right

## grey matter

(uncountable) brain, intelligence

□ The poor chap hasn't got much grey matter.

## grip

*get a grip on yourself*: don't panic, calm down

## grow

*This sort of music grows on you*: you find gradually that you like it, though on first hearing, you disliked it

## gun

*stick to your guns*: an encouragement to persist with your point of view in an argument and not give in

## hair

*he didn't turn a hair*: he showed no emotion

## hand

Several more important idioms:

**1** *to get the upper hand*: to begin to win in the course of a struggle

**2** *can we have a show of hands?*: can we have a quick open vote on this?

**3** *all hands on deck*: everybody's help is needed (from sailing ships in an emergency when all the crew must help)

**4** *a hand-out*: papers distributed during a lecture, often having notes about it

**5** *you've got to hand it to him*: you must admit he's very clever

**6** *to win hands down*: to have an easy victory (apparently derived from horse-racing)

## hat

*Now I'm wearing another hat/putting on a different hat, etc.*: these phrases have become something of a cliché at meetings to avoid the longer: now I'm speaking in another capacity/from a different point of view

## haul

*it will be a long haul*: it will take a long time (some work or a journey)

## have

**1** *he'll have it in for you*: he will be (deliberately) unkind/unpleasant to you

**2** *he's having you on*: he's teasing you

**3** *the haves and the have-nots*: the rich and the poor

## head

*on your head be it*: you must take the responsibility for the action which you have recommended me/us to follow (implying I am not convinced it is right)

## heart

*he's set his heart on a new bike*: he is determined to have a new bicycle

## heel

*to dig one's heels in*: to refuse stubbornly to do something (from a tug of war)

## hog

*to go the whole hog*: to do something entirely; having started it, finish it (This *hog* was not a pig, but a coin so the phrase meant: spend all the money.)

## hone down

to get rid of unnecessary details so as to concentrate on essentials (*honing a knife* – on a stone – is now rarely heard but shows the original use)

## house

*We're getting on like a house on fire*: everything is going very well

## inch

*he's every inch a snob*: he is a total snob

## joke

**1** *to crack a joke*: to make a joke, especially a quick spontaneous one

**2** *a standing joke*: someone or something that has been the object of the same joke for a long time

**3** *it's beyond a joke/no joke*: it is becoming very serious/unpleasant

## key

**1** *low key*: subdued

□ The party was rather low-key as her father had just died. (*low key* on a musical instrument is the use of deep notes)

**2** *keyed-up*: tense (almost another word for **nervy**)

## kingdom come

*We shall be waiting/standing here till kingdom come*: i.e. for ever

## knock-down

*knock-down prices*: absurdly low prices

## knock-off

*let's knock off (work) now* i.e. stop work

## level

truthful, honest, genuine in the phrases *on the level* and *do your level best*

**live it down**
to be forgiven, often used in the negative jokingly, when referring to
something causing shame or embarrassment
☐ I'll never live that down.

**lump**
*like it or lump it*: to resign oneself to unpleasant conditions
☐ Those builders are likely to go on making that noise for days, so we'll have
to like it or lump it. (Sometimes *like it or* is omitted.)

**mean well**
to have good intentions, often used jokingly of someone whose plans go
wrong
☐ Poor chap, he means well anyway.

**mill**
*to put someone through the mill*: to test someone very severely e.g. in a
driving test or in a job interview

**mind**
*have a good mind to*: to be strongly inclined to do something (a threat)
☐ I have a good mind to write to your parents about this, young man.

**nerves**
*It gets on my nerves*: it irritates me

**once-over**
*Would you give this tape-recorder a once-over please?* i.e. examine it, see if
anything is wrong with it

**one-off**
usually an adj., describing something which has not been done before and
will probably not be done again (not necessarily anything important)

**pain in the neck**
an irritation, something unpleasant but unavoidable; a boring person

**parting shot**
*to have the parting shot* is to say a final word before leaving in an argument, or
to make some action similarly. (The phrase was orginally not *parting* but
*Parthian*, whose soldiers used to shoot arrows backwards as
they retreated).

**pieces**
*to go to pieces*: to lose all self-control

**plain-sailing**
*From now on, it's all plain-sailing*: we should have no more problems

**plough**
*to plough money into something*: to invest a lot of capital into it
(*to plough money back into something*: to reinvest profits or surplus)

**press-gang**

to force (people) to do something against their wishes

☐ I don't want to press-gang the staff to help, I hope they'll volunteer.

(Originally used of gangs who went round the country in the 18th century pressing young men to join the navy.)

**put past**

*I wouldn't put it past him*: I can imagine him doing such a silly thing

**rhyme or reason**

used with negatives: *to act without rhyme or reason*, *ideas with no rhyme or reason* i.e. with no sense or logic

**rolling in it**

having plenty of money

**serve right**

*After the way you treated her, it serves you right if she doesn't talk to you* i.e. you merit nothing better, that is what you should expect

**shot in the dark**

a guess, an answer not based on reasoning

**sins**

*for my sins* expresses the idea that one is doing something disagreeable as a kind of penance, though without any real religious feeling

**sniff**

*It's not to be sniffed at*: this (offer) looks promising and we must consider it seriously. (From an animal sniffing at something to see if it can be eaten.)

**stead**

*This will stand you in good stead*: it will be useful to you later

**steady on there**

don't be in such a hurry; sometimes used after *whoa* (pronounced *wo*). The whole phrase was often used to make horses go more slowly.

**stick**

*to get hold of the wrong end of the stick*: to misunderstand something entirely

**story**

*a likely story*: a sarcastic comment said when you doubt if something is true or even probable

**time**

**1** *take your time*: don't hurry

**2** *behind the times*: having old-fashioned ideas, not up to date

**3** *have no time for*: be hostile to

☐ I've no time for gossip.

(*have little time for* almost the same)

**4** *about time too* (compare with **time** and the phrase *it's (high) time*): this

---

phrase is spoken when something awaited has happened but people were very impatient about it

**top**

*to be/go over the top* (about something): to over-react, to respond too strongly

**track**

*You've got a one-track mind*: you only think about one thing (spoken critically)

**turkey**

*to talk turkey*: to talk seriously, especially about business

**turn-out**

the number of people who attend an event: *We had a very poor turn-out.*

**warts and all**

*In the end, she found she loved him, warts and all*: i.e. despite the bad side of his nature. The phrase goes back to Oliver Cromwell and his warts.

**way**

**1** *to pave the way for*: to make it easier to introduce something else new later
☐ His plans will pave the way for further changes later on.
**2** *both ways*: *You can't have it both ways*: It is impossible for you to take advantage of two alternatives – you must choose one or the other.

**weather**

*to make heavy weather of*: to find something difficult or to make it unnecessarily difficult for oneself

**while**

☐ I'll make it worth your while: you can be sure I shan't forget you. (Usually said when suggesting or promising a bribe or present for favours given.)

**word**

**1** *Don't go back on your word*: don't break your promise
**2** *put in a good word for*: speak favourably about, recommend (someone)